THE PATH OF SERENITY AND INSIGHT

THE PATH OF SERENITY AND INSIGHT

An Explanation of the Buddhist Jhānas

HENEPOLA GUNARATANA

MOTILAL BANARSIDASS PUBLISHERS
PRIVATE LIMITED • DELHI

First Edition : Delhi, 1985
Reprint : Delhi, 1992, 1994, 1996, 2002

ISBN: 81-208-0871-1 (Cloth)
ISBN: 81-208-1236-0 (Paper)

Also available at:
MOTILAL BANARSIDASS
41 U.A. Bungalow Road, Jawahar Nagar, Delhi 110 007
8 Mahalaxmi Chamber, 22 Bhulabhai Desai Road, Mumbai 400 026
236, 9th Main III Block, Jayanagar, Bangalore 560 011
120 Royapettah High Road, Mylapore, Chennai 600 004
Sanas Plaza, 1302 Baji Rao Road, Pune 411 002
8 Camac Street, Kolkata 700 017
Ashok Rajpath, Patna 800 004
Chowk, Varanasi 221 001

Printed in India
BY JAINENDRA PRAKASH JAIN AT SHRI JAINENDRA PRESS,
A-45 NARAINA, PHASE-I, NEW DELHI 110 028
AND PUBLISHED BY NARENDRA PRAKASH JAIN FOR
MOTILAL BANARSIDASS PUBLISHERS PRIVATE LIMITED,
BUNGALOW ROAD, DELHI 110 007

TO

MY PARENTS

AND

TEACHERS

CONTENTS

PREFACE

The teaching of the Buddha is essentially a path leading to the cessation of suffering. Central to this path is the practice of meditation. Meditation may be considered the heart of applied Buddhism, to which all the preliminary stages of the path lead and out of which the higher stages flow. One of the most important aspects of Buddhist meditation encountered repeatedly in the scriptural texts of early Buddhism is a set of attainments called, in Pali, the *Jhānas*. The *jhānas* were instrumental in the Buddha's own achievement of enlightenment and recurrently enter into the course of training he formulated for his disciples. They appear in the stage of the path preparatory to the higher insights, again in immediate association with the liberating wisdom, and still again in the end as a spiritual endowment of the fully liberated man.

It is the purpose of the present work to examine the *jhānas* in order to determine their role in the Buddhist spiritual discipline. The perspective from which they are viewed is that of Theravāda Buddhism, the Buddhist school to which the author belongs as a fully ordained monk. Theravāda Buddhism is probably the oldest continuous Buddhist tradition, maintaining the most accurate record of what the Buddha himself actually taught. Theravāda Buddhist meditation, inclusive of the *jhānas*, has been reliably treated by several contemporary writers of scholarly stature. The present work, however, approaches the *jhānas* from a different angle. Whereas most scholars deal principally with the topics of meditation and only incidentally with the *jhānas* themselves, in this work we focus primarily upon the *jhānas* as they are in their own nature, treating the topics of meditation only in a summary way. Our approach is psychological and analytical, our intent to look into the inner constitution of the *jhānas*, lay bare their inner dynamics, and see how they contribute to the purification and liberation of mind which is the goal of the Buddhist discipline.

Our work draws principally upon the scriptures and exegetical literature of Theravāda Buddhism. These sources, composed almost entirely in the Pali language, fall into three primary layers of differing degrees of authoritative weight. The first and most authoritative is the Pali Canon. This is the Tipiṭaka—the three "baskets" or collections of scripture: the Vinayapiṭaka, the collection of monastic discipline; the Suttapiṭaka, the collection of the Buddha's discourses; and the Abhidhammapiṭaka, the collection of psycho-philosophical treatises. The texts in these collections belong to different chronological strata, but a good portion, particularly of the Vinaya and suttas, can be reasonably ascribed to the Buddha himself.

The Suttapiṭaka was the most useful of the three for our purposes. This collection is divided into five sections: the Dīgha Nikāya (long discourses), the Majjhima Nikāya (middle length discourses), the Saṃyutta Nikāya (topically related discourses), the Aṅguttara Nikāya (numerically arranged discourses), and the Khuddaka Nikāya (miscellaneous discourses). We have relied most heavily on the first four and parts of the fifth as containing the most ancient parts of the Pali Canon.

The Abhidhammapiṭaka gives the appearance of being a somewhat later scholastic attempt at systematization, but its teachings are fully consistent with the suttas and help shed light on many points requiring precise analysis and fine definition. The difference between the suttas and the Abhidhamma is that between a practical pedagogical approach and a philosophically rigorous one, but the two standpoints harmonize and repeatedly illuminate each other. The first two books of the Abhidhamma, the Dhammasaṅgani and the Vibhaṅga read in conjunction with their commentaries, are especially helpful in clarifying a number of knotty points concerning the *jhānas*.

The second layer of Pali literature is the commentaries (*aṭṭhakathā*). The commentaries were composed for the purpose of elucidating the words of the Tipiṭaka and for drawing out their implications. Their origins go back to very ancient times but they were edited and cast into final standardized versions in the 5th century A.C. by the great Buddhist commentator Bhadantācariya Buddhaghosa, who came from India to Sri Lanka expressly for that purpose. Fundamental to the entire commentarial collection is Bhadantācariya Buddhaghosa's own original work, the *Visuddhimagga* (*Path of Purification*), a massive masterpiece which orders the complex field of Buddhist meditation into an organic comprehensive whole.

The third class of Pali texts we drew upon is the *Ṭikās*. The *Ṭikās* are subcommentaries, composed with three principal purposes in view: to elucidate difficult points in the commentaries, to explore important side issues, and to systematize still further the material of the Tipiṭaka. The most useful of these has been the great *Ṭikā* to the *Visuddhimagga*, called *Mahāṭikā* and the *Paramatthamañjūsā*, composed by Ācariya Dhammapāla who lived in South India in the 6th century A.C. This same teacher is also the author of the *Ṭikās* to the Dīgha Nikāya, the Majjhima Nikāya, and the Saṃyutta Nikāya.

For passages from the Suttapiṭaka we have principally relied upon the editions of the Pali Text Society. For the commentaries and subcommentaries we have used the editions of the Burmese Buddha Sāsana Samiti, which started its work in connection with the Sixth Buddhist Council held in Burma in 1956. Sinhalese and Devanāgarī editions were also consulted when available. For the sake of easy cross-reference we generally refer to commentaries and subscommentaries by their full scriptural titles rather than by their individual names; e.g. we refer to the commentary to the Majjhima Nikāya as *Majjhima Nikāya Aṭṭhakathā* rather than as *Papañcasūdani*. But in two cases where the individual name is best known we use that : the *Aṭṭhasālini* which is the commentary to the Dhammasaṅgani and the *Paramatthamañjūsā*, the commentary to the *Visuddhimagga*. Both names for commentarial works can be found in the list of abbreviations of works used.

For passages cited from the Pali Canon we have preferred to give our own translations rather than rely on existing ones as a way to maintain consistency in renditions. A few exceptions to this have been noted. Fortunately we could draw confidently from the excellent translation of the *Visuddhimagga* by the Venerable Bhikkhu Nanamoli, published under the title *The Path of Purification*. For the convenience of the reader a Pali-English Glossary is provided in the back giving our usual preferred renderings of technical terms connected with Buddhist meditation appearing in the text.

Footnote and bibliographical references to books published in Sri Lanka use "Ceylon" or "Sri Lanka," as indicated on the title page; the latter is used when no country is mentioned. The systems of transliteration used in citations of Pali texts in the

Sinhalese and Burmese scripts are based upon those used by the Pali Text Society.

Our sincere thanks are due to Professor David F. T. Rodier, Chairman, Department of Philosophy and Religion, The American University, and to Professor Charles S. J. White of the American University and Professor Cornelia Dimmitt of Georgetown University, for reading the entire manuscript and for making valuable suggestions. We are very sincerely grateful to the Venerable Dr. Bhikkhu Bodhi who made many very valuable suggestions and helped polish the style and structure of the work. Also we are thankful to Mr. S. A. D. Subasinghe for designing the cover, to Mr. Will Pozzi for indexing and to Mr. Leonard Price for his valuable suggestions. Last but not least we must sincerely thank Dr. Hazel Marie Griffin for her kind hospitality and valuable suggestions in arranging the footnotes and bibliography.

Washington Buddhist Vihara
Washington, D. C. 20011
U. S. A.

HENEPOLA GUNARATANA

CHAPTER I

INTRODUCTION

The Doctrinal Context of Jhāna

In the discourses the Buddha says that just as in the great ocean there is but one taste, the taste of salt, so in his doctrine and discipline there is but one taste, the taste of freedom (*vimutti-rasa*).[1] The taste of freedom that flavors the Buddha's doctrine and discipline is the taste of spiritual freedom, and it is to the full experience of this taste that the entire teaching of the Buddha is directed. Spiritual freedom, from the Buddhist perspective, means freedom from suffering. The problem of suffering is the wellspring out of which the whole current of Buddhist teaching arises; freedom from suffering is the end towards which it moves. Thus the Buddha could say throughout his ministry: "Previously, monks, as also now I make known only suffering and the cessation of suffering."[2]

This focal concern with the issue of suffering is evident from the formula of the Four Noble Truths in which the Buddha summed up his doctrine. The formula of the Four Noble Truths deals entirely with the problem of suffering, looked at from four different angles. The first truth exposes the forms and the range of suffering. It shows suffering to be an inextricable ingredient of life itself, tied on the physical side to the vital processes of birth, aging, sickness and death, cropping up on the psychological side as sorrow, grief, dejection, and despair. Even more, in the Buddha's picture of the world the mass of suffering becomes multiplied to infinite proportions due to the fact of rebirth. The cycle of pain and sorrow does not turn only once; for all but the enlightened it turns over and over through beginningless time in the form of *saṁsāra*, the round of repeated becoming.

Having exposed the range and modes of suffering in the first Noble Truth, in the remaining three the Buddha points out the cause of suffering, its cessation, and the way to its cessation. The

1. AN. 4:203.
2. MN. 1-140.

cause is craving, the insatiable drive for enjoyment and existence that keeps the wheel of rebirths in constant motion. The cessation of suffering is the reversal of this genetic relation, the complete abandoning and destruction of craving. The way to the end of suffering is the middle way of ethical and mental training that avoids all extremes of conduct and views—the Noble Eightfold Path made up of right view, right intention, right speech, right action, right livelihood, right effort, right mindfulness, and right concentration.

Whereas the first three truths provide the doctrinal perspective of the Buddha's teaching, the fourth truth, the truth of the path, prescribes its practical regimen. This regimen focusses upon personal experience. The Buddha does not come into our midst as a savior descended from on high. He comes as an enlightened teacher, a man who has found the way to the end of suffering and who points the way out to others. The path itself every man must follow for himself. It is each man's own delusions and defilements that chain him to the cycle of suffering, and again each man's own efforts at inner purification that pave the road to his deliverance. Since bondage ultimately springs from ignorance (*avijjā*) the key to liberation, the Buddha declares, is found in wisdom (*paññā*), a wisdom which must be generated inwardly as an immediate personal understanding of the basic truths of existence. The Dhamma is *paccattaṁ veditabbo vinnūhi* "to be realized by the wise within themselves."

It is because personal realization of truth is needed to reach the end of suffering that meditation assumes a position of such crucial importance in the Buddhist formulation of the liberating path. Meditation, for Buddhism, is the means of generating the inner understanding required for deliverance from suffering. Its diversity of techniques stems from the differences in the people to be taught, but its purpose and procedure is the same for all: to produce that purity of mind and clarity of vision needed for the liberating wisdom to arise.

The methods of meditation taught in the Pali Buddhist tradition are based on the Buddha's own experience, forged by him in the course of his own quest for enlightenment. They are designed to re-create in the disciple who practices them the same essential discovery the Buddha himself made when he sat beneath the Bodhi tree, the discovery of the Four Noble Truths.

The various subjects and methods of meditation expounded in the Pali scriptures divide into two inter-related systems. One is called the development of serenity (*samathabhāvanā*), the other the development of insight (*vipassanābhāvanā*). The former also goes under the name of the development of concentration (*samādhibhāvanā*), the latter under the name of the development of wisdom (*paññābhāvanā*). The practice of serenity-meditation aims at developing a calm, concentrated, unified state of consciousness as a means of experiencing inner peace and generating wisdom. The practice of insight-meditation aims at gaining direct understanding of the real nature of phenomena. Of the two, the development of insight is regarded by Buddhism as the essential key to liberation, the direct antidote to the ignorance underlying bondage and suffering. Whereas serenity-meditation is recognized as common to both Buddhist and non-Buddhist contemplative disciplines, insight-meditation is held to be the unique discovery of the Buddha and an unparallelled feature of his path. However, because the growth of insight presupposes a certain degree of concentration (*samādhi*), and serenity-meditation serves to secure this concentration, the development of serenity claims an incontestable place in the Buddhist meditative process. Together the two types of meditation work to make the mind a fit instrument for enlightenment. With his mind unified by means of the development of serenity, made sharp and bright by the development of insight, the meditator can proceed unobstructed to reach the end of suffering.

Focal to both systems of meditation, though belonging inherently to the side of serenity, is a set of meditative attainments called the four *jhānas*. The Pali word *jhāna* has been rendered by translators into English in various ways—as "meditation," which to us seems too general; "rapture" and "ecstasy," which suggest a degree of elation and exuberance inappropriate to the higher *jhānas*; as "musing," which is too weak and archaic; and as "trance," which misleadingly implies a sub-normal state, quite the opposite of *jhāna*. The word "absorption," used by some translators, is the most suitable of the lot, but that is needed for the Pali *appāna*, which includes the *jhānas* and corresponds closely to "absorption" in literal meaning. For obvious reasons, therefore, we prefer to leave the Pali *jhāna* untranslated.

The *jhānas* themselves are states of deep mental unification characterized by a total immersion of the mind in its object. They result from the centering of the mind upon a single object with such a degree of attention that the discursive activity of thought is slowed down and eventually stopped. The members of the fourfold set of *jhānas* are named simply after their numerical position in the series: the first *jhāna*, the second *jhāna*, the third *jhāna*, and the fourth *jhāna*. The four appear repeatedly in the suttas described by a stock formula showing their process of attainment:

> Herein, monks, a monk, quite secluded from sense pleasures, secluded from unwholesome states of mind, enters and dwells in the first *jhāna*, which is accompanied by applied thought and sustained thought with rapture and happiness born of seclusion.
>
> With the subsiding of applied thought and sustained thought he enters and dwells in the second *jhāna*, which has internal confidence and unification of mind, is without applied thought and sustained thought, and is filled with rapture and happiness born of concentration.
>
> With the fading away of rapture, he dwells in equanimity, mindful and discerning ; and he experiences in his own person that happiness of which the noble ones say: 'Happily lives he who is equanimous and mindful'—thus he enters and dwells in the third *jhāna*.
>
> With the abandoning of pleasure and pain, and with the previous disappearance of joy and grief, he enters and dwells in the fourth *jhāna*, which has neither-pain-nor-pleasure and has purity of mindfulness due to equanimity.[1]

To attain the *jhānas*, as the passage shows, the meditator must begin by eliminating the unwholesome mental states obstructing inner collectedness. These are generally grouped together as the five hindrances (*pañcanīvaraṇā*) : sensual desire, ill will, sloth and torpor, restlessness and worry, and doubt.[2] The mind's absorption on its object is brought about by five opposing mental states —applied thought, sustained thought, rapture, happiness and

1. DN. 2:314-15. MN. 1-182.
2. In Pali: *Kāmacchanda, byāpāda, thīnamiddha, uddhaccakukkucca, vicikicchā.*

one-pointedness[1] called the *jhāna* factors (*jhānaṅgāni*) because they lift the mind to the level of the first *jhāna* and remain there as its defining components.

After reaching the first *jhāna* the ardent meditator can go on to reach the higher *jhānas*. This is done by eliminating the coarser factors in each *jhāna*, those that remain being in each case the defining factors of the successive *jhānas*. In this way the meditator can move from the first *jhāna* up to the fourth. Beyond the four *jhānas* lies another fourfold set of higher meditative states which deepen the element of serenity developed in the *jhānas*. These attainments, known as the immaterial states (*āruppā*) because they correspond ontologically to the immaterial realms of existence, are the base of boundless space, the base of boundless consciousness, the base of nothingness, and the base of neither perception nor non-perception.[2] In the Pali commentaries this set comes to be called the four immaterial *jhānas* (*arūpajjhāna*), the four preceding stages being renamed, for the sake of clarity, the four fine material *jhānas* (*rūpajjhāna*). Often the two sets are joined together under the collective titles of the eight *jhānas* or the eight attainments (*aṭṭhasamāpattiyo*). These will all be explored in detail in the body of this work.

The four *jhānas* and four *āruppās* appear initially as mundane states of deep serenity pertaining to the preliminary stage of the Buddhist path. On this level they help provide the base of concentration needed for wisdom to arise. But the four *jhānas* again re-appear in a later stage in the development of the path, arising in direct association with wisdom. They are then designated the supramundane (*lokuttara*) *jhānas*. These supramundane *jhānas* are the levels of concentration pertaining to the four degrees of enlightenment-experience called the supramundane paths (*lokuttaramagga*) and the stages of deliverance resulting from them, the four fruits (*phala*). Finally, even after full liberation is achieved, the mundane *jhānas* can still remain as attainments available to the liberated person, part of his untrammeled contemplative experience.

1. In Pali : *Vitakka, vicāra, pīti, sukha, ekaggatā.*
2. In Pali: *Ākāsānañcāyatana, viññāṇañcāyatana, ākiñcaññāyatana' nevasaññānāsaññāyatana.*

The Importance of Jhāna

The importance of the *jhānas* in the Buddhist path to deliverance can readily be gauged from the frequency with which they are mentioned throughout the suttas. The *jhānas* figure prominently both in the Buddha's own experience and in his exhortation to disciples. In his childhood, while attending an annual ploughing festival, the future Buddha spontaneously entered the first *jhāna*. It was the memory of this childhood incident, many years later after his futile pursuit of austerities, that revealed to him the way to enlightenment during his period of deepest despondency.[1] After taking his seat on the banks of the Nerañjarā, the Buddha entered the four *jhānas* immediately before directing his mind to the threefold knowledge that issued in his enlightenment.[2] Throughout his active career the four *jhānas* remained "his heavenly dwelling" (*dibbavihāra*) to which he resorted in order to live happily here and now.[3] His understanding of the corruption, purification and emergence in the *jhānas* and other meditative attainments is one of his ten powers which enable him to turn the matchless wheel of the Dhamma.[4] Just before his passing away the Buddha entered the eight attainments in direct and reverse order; the passing away itself took place directly from the fourth *jhāna*.[5]

The Buddha is constantly seen in the suttas encouraging his disciples to develop *jhāna*. The four *jhānas* are invariably included in the complete course of training laid down for disciples.[6] They figure in the training as the discipline of higher consciousness (*adhicittasikkhā*), right concentration (*sammā samādhi*) of the Noble Eightfold Path, and the faculty and power of concentration (*samādhindriya*, *samādhibala*). Though a vehicle of dry insight can be found, indications are that this path is not an easy one, lacking the aid of the powerful serenity available to the practitioner of *jhāna*. The way of the *jhāna* attainer seems by comparison smoother and more pleasurable.[7]

1. MN. 1:246-47
2. *Ibid.*
3. DN. 3-220.
4. MN. 1:68-83.
5. DN. 2:156.
6. DN. 1:47-87. Mn. 1:175-84, 256-80.
7. AN. 2:150-52.

The Buddha points to the bliss of the *jhānas* as his alternative to sense pleasures. He says:

> There are, Cunda, four pursuits of pleasure which lead to ultimate disenchantment, dispassion, cessation, peace, direct knowledge, enlightenment, and *nibbāna*. Which four ? Here, Cunda, secluded from sense pleasures, a monk enters and dwells in the first *jhāna*...the second *jhāna*...the third *jhāna*...the fourth *jhāna*.[1]

His own disciples live devoted to these four pursuits of pleasure, and for them four fruits and benefits are to be expected, namely, attainment of the four stages of deliverance—stream-entry, once-returning, non-returning, and arahatship.[2] Just as the river Ganges slopes, inclines, and flows to the east, a bhikkhu who develops and cultivates the four *jhānas* slopes, flows, and inclines to *nibbāna*.[3] The Buddha even refers to the four *jhānas* figuratively (*pariyāyena*) as a kind of *nibbāna*; he calls them immediately visible *nibbāna*, final *nibbāna*, a factor of *nibbāna*, and *nibbāna* here and now.[4]

Etymology of Jhāna

The great Buddhist commentator Bhadantācariya Buddhaghosa traces the Pali word *jhāna* (Skt. *dhyāna*) to two verbal forms. One, the etymologically correct derivation, is the verb *jhāyati*, meaning to think or to meditate. Buddhaghosa explains: "By means of this yogins mediate, thus it is called *jhānata*. The meaning is that they cognize a given object."[5] The commentator offers in addition a more playful derivation of *jhāna*, intended to illuminate its function rather than its verbal source. This derivation traces the word *jhāna* to the verb *jhāpeti* meaning "to burn up", the reason being: "It burns up opposing states, thus it is called *jhāna*."[6] The purport of this second account is that *jhāna* "burns up" or destroys the mental defilements preventing the development of serenity and insight.

1. DN. 2:131-32.
2. *Ibid.*
3. SN. 5:308.
4. *Sandiṭṭhikanibbāna, parinibbāna, tadaṅganibbāna, diṭṭhadhamma nibbāna*. AN. 4:453-54.
5. Vin. A. 1:116.
6. *Ibid.*

Buddhaghosa says that *jhāna* has the characteristic mark of contemplation (*upanijjhāna*). Contemplation, he states, is twofold; the contemplation of the object (*ārammaṇūpanijjhāna*) and the contemplation of the characteristics of phenomena (*lakkhaṇūpanijjhāna*). The former type of contemplation is exercised by the eight attainments of serenity together with their access, since these contemplate the object taken as the basis for developing concentration. For this reason these attainments, particularly the first four, are given the name "*jhāna*" in the mainstream of Pali meditative exposition. However, Buddhaghosa also allows that the term "*jhāna*" can be extended loosely to insight (*vipassanā*), the path (*magga*), and fruits (*phala*), on the ground that these perform the work of contemplating the characteristics:

> Here, insight contemplates the characteristics of impermanence, [suffering and selflessness]. Insight's task of contemplation is perfected by the path, thus the path is called the contemplation of characteristics. The fruit contemplates the actual characteristic of cessation, thus it is called the contemplation of characteristics.[1]

In brief the twofold meaning of *jhāna* as "contemplation" and "burning up" can be brought into connection with the meditative process as follows. By fixing his mind on the object the meditator reduces and eliminates the lower mental qualities such as the five hindrances and promotes the growth of the higher qualities such as the *jhāna* factors. These, as they emerge, fix upon the object with increasing force, leading the mind to complete absorption in the object. Then, by contemplating the characteristics of phenomena with insight, the meditator eventually reaches the supramundane *jhāna* of the four paths. With this *jhāna* he burns up the defilements and attains the liberating experience of the fruits.

Jhāna and Samādhi

In the vocabulary of Buddhist meditation the word *jhāna* is closely connected with another word, *samādhi*, generally rendered by "concentration." *Samādhi* derives from the prefixed verbal root *saṁ-ā-dhā*, meaning to collect or to bring together, thus

1. *Ibid.*

suggesting the concentration or unification of the mind. The word *samādhi* is almost interchangeable with the word *samatha*, "serenity", though the latter comes from a different root, *sam* (Skt. *śaṁ*), meaning "to become calm."

In the suttas *samādhi* is defined as mental one-pointedness, *cittass' ekaggatā*,[1] and this definition is followed through with technically psychological rigor in the Abhidhamma. The Abhidhamma treats one-pointedness as a distinct mental factor (*cetasika*) present in every state of consciousness. It is a universal mental concomitant with the function of unifying the mind upon its object, ensuring that each state of consciousness takes one and only one object. Those occasions of one-pointedness which go beyond the bare stabilizing of the mind on an object to give the mind some degree of steadiness and non-distraction are subsumed under the name *samādhi*. Thus the Dhammasaṅgani equates these more prominent types of one-pointedness with a string of synonyms inclusive of serenity (*samatha*), the faculty of concentration (*samādhindriya*), and the power of concentration (*samādhibala*). From this strict psychological standpoint *samādhi* can be present in unwholesome states of consciousness as well as in wholesome and neutral states. In its unwholesome forms it is called "wrong concentration" (*micchā-samādhi*), in its wholesome forms "right concentration" (*sammāsamādhi*).

As a technical term in expositions on the practice of meditation, however, *samādhi* is limited to one-pointedness of the wholesome kind. Bhadantācariya Buddhaghosa, in the *Visuddhimagga*, defines *samādhi* as wholesome one-pointedness of mind (*kusalacittass'ekaggatā*), and even here we can understand from the context that it is only the wholesome one-pointedness involved in the deliberate transmutation of the mind to a heightened level of calm that is intended by the word *samādhi*.[2] Buddhaghosa explains *samādhi* etymologically as "the centering of consciousness and consciousness concomitants evenly and rightly on a single object."[3] He calls it "the state in virtue of which consciousness and its concomitants remain evenly and rightly on a single object, undistracted and unscattered."[4]

1. MN. 1:301.
2. PP., p. 84. Vism., p. 68.
3. PP., p. 85. Vism., p. 68.
4. PP., p. 68. Vism., p. 68.

Despite the preciseness of this definition, the word *samādhi* is used in the Pali literature on meditation with varying degrees of specificity of meaning. In the narrowest sense, as defined by Buddhaghosa, it denotes the particular mental factor responsible for the concentrating of the mind, namely, one-pointedness. In a wider sense it can signify the states of unified consciousness that result from the strengthening of concentration, i.e. the meditative attainments of serenity and the stages leading up to them. And in a still wider sense the word *samādhi* can be applied to the method of practice used to produce and cultivate those refined states of concentration, here being equivalent to the development of serenity (*samathabhāvanā*).

It is in the second sense that *samādhi* and *jhāna* come closest in meaning, sharing to a large extent the same reference. The Buddha equates right concentration with the four *jhānas*, and in doing so allows concentration to encompass the meditative attainments signified by the *jhānas*. However, even though *jhāna* and *samādhi* can overlap in denotation, certain differences in their suggested and contextual meanings prevent unqualified identification of the two terms. Firstly, behind the Buddha's use of the *jhāna* formula to explain right concentration lies a more technical understanding of the terms. According to this understanding *samādhi* can be narrowed down in range to signify only one factor, the most prominent in the *jhāna*, namely one-pointedness, while the *jhāna* itself must be seen as encompassing the state of consciousness in its entirety, or at least the whole group of mental factors individuating that meditative state as a *jhāna*.

In the second place, when *samādhi* is considered in its broader meaning it involves a wider range of reference than *jhāna*. The Pali exegetical tradition recognizes three levels of *samādhi*.[1] The first is preliminary concentration (*parikammasamādhi*), which is produced as a result of the novice meditator's initial efforts to focus his mind on his meditation subject. The second is access concentration (*upacāra-samādhi*), marked by the suppression of the five hindrances, the manifestation of the *jhāna* factors, and the appearance of a luminous mental replica of the meditation object called the "counterpart sign" (*paṭibhāganimitta*). The third is absorption concentration (*appanāsamādhi*), the complete immer-

1. Narada, *Manual*, pp. 389, 395-96.

sion of the mind in its object effected by the full maturation of the *jhāna* factors. Absorption concentration is equivalent to the eight attainments, the four *jhānas* and the four *āruppas*, and to this extent *jhāna* and *samādhi* coincide. However *samādhi* still has a broader scope than *jhāna*, since it includes not only the *jhānas* themselves but also the two preparatory degrees of concentration leading up to them. Further, *samādhi* also covers a still different type of concentration called "momentary concentration" (*khaṇikasamādhi*), the mobile mental stabilization produced in the course of insight-contemplation on the passing flow of phenomena.

Jhāna and the Constituents of Enlightenment

The principles of meditative training expounded by the Buddha during his teaching career were organized by him into seven basic categories comprising altogether thirty-seven *bodhipakkhiyā dhammā*, "states pertaining to enlightenment" or "constituents of enlightenment." The seven categories among which they are distributed are: the four foundations of mindfulness, the four right endeavors, the four bases of success, the five spiritual faculties, the five spiritual powers, the seven enlightenment factors, and the Noble Eightfold Path.[1] The four *jhānas* enter either directly or implicitly into all these sets of training principles, and to appreciate their significance in the Buddhist discipline it will be of value to see how they do so. We will consider first the place of the *jhānas* in the Noble Eightfold Path, the most important and inclusive of the seven groups; then we will go on to note briefly their relation to the other sets.

The eight factors of the Noble Eightfold Path are right view, right intention, right speech, right action, right livelihood, right effort, right mindfulness, and right concentration. These eight are frequently divided into three broader categories: the group of moral discipline (*silakkhandha*), the group of concentration (*samādhikkhandha*), and the group of wisdom (*paññākkhandha*).[2] The group of moral discipline comprises the factors of right speech, right action, and right livelihood; the group of concentration

1. Note : the original Pali names for these categories and their members can be found in Appendix 1.

2. MN. 1:301. DN. 2:291-315. MN. 3:71-78.

the factors of right effort, right mindfulness, and right concentration; the group of wisdom the factors of right view and right intention. Though wisdom is seen as emerging fully only after concentration has been established its two factors are placed at the beginning of the path because a certain modicum of right understanding and right intentions are needed to embark upon the three-fold discipline of morality, concentration and wisdom.

Of the three factors in the morality group, right speech is abstinence from false speech, slander, harsh speech, and idle talk; right action is abstinence from killing, stealing, and sexual misconduct; and right livelihood is avoiding a wrong means of earning one's living and following a righteous occupation. The Eightfold Path operates at the two levels previously referred to, at the mundane level in the preliminary stages of self-cultivation and at the supramundane level with the attainment of the four supramundane paths. This twofold modality of the path applies to each of its eight factors. The morality factors, considered in the Abhidhamma as three distinct mental concomitants, arise at the mundane level whenever a person deliberately abstains from some case of moral transgression. At the supramundane level the three factors occur simultaneously in the states of supramundane path-consciousness, performing the function of cutting off the tendencies towards their opposites.

The three factors of the concentration group also receive an analytical breakdown in the suttas. Right effort is explained as four right endeavors : the endeavor to prevent the arising of unarisen unwholesome mental state, to eliminate unwholesome states already arisen, to cultivate unarisen wholesome mental states, and to increase wholesome states already arisen. Right mindfulness consists in mindful contemplation of the four "foundations of mindfulness" (*satipaṭṭhāna*)namely, the body, feelings, states of mind, and mental objects. Right concentration is the unification of the mind into one-pointedness through the four *jhānas*. At the supramundane level right effort becomes the energy factor in the paths and fruits, right mindfulness the factor of attention, and right concentration the factor of mental unification. As we will see, according to the Theravāda commentators concentration in the mundane portion of practice need not be developed to the degree of the four *jhānas*. However, because the stronger the degree of concentration the stabler the basis for insight, the *jhānas* are still commended as guaranteeing the most reliable groundwork of mental calm. And when the supramundane paths and fruits are attained, consciousness occurs with a force of absorption tantamount to the four (or five) *jhānas*. Thence the *jhānas* are included as components of the Noble Eightfold Path, entering via the group of concentration.

Concentration functions as a basis for wisdom. As the Buddha says: "Develop concentration: for one who has concentration understands things as they really are."[1] The wisdom group comprises the two factors of right view and right intention, the former being an equivalent term for wisdom proper, the latter its accompaniment. Right view is explained as the undistorted comprehension of the basic laws and truths structuring actuality. At the mundane level it consists in an understanding of the law of *kamma*, indicating the moral efficacy of action, as well as of the doctrinal contents of the Dhamma—the three characteristics, dependent arising, and the Four Noble Truths. At the supramundane level right view is the wisdom which directly penetrates the Four Noble Truths by "seeing" *nibbāna*, the unconditioned element. Right intention, its companion in this group, consists in thoughts of renunciation, of benevolence, and of non-injury. At the supramundane level right intention becomes the purified mental function free from lust, ill will, and cruelty, which fixes the mind upon *nibbāna*.

The three groups of path factors lock together as interrelated stages of training which work in harmony to accomplish the goal aspired to by the discipline, full liberation from suffering. From this angle the groups are designated the three trainings (*tisso sikkhā*). The morality group makes up the training in the higher morality (*adhisīla-sikkhā*), the concentration group the training in the higher consciousness (*adhicittasikkhā*), and the wisdom group the training in the higher wisdom (*adhipaññāsikkhā*).[2] Each of these trainings arises in dependence on its predecessor and provides the support for its successor. Moral training provides the foundation for concentration, since mental composure can only be established when the coarser impulses towards ethical transgressions are controlled and res-

1. SN. 3:13.
2. AN. 1:235-36.

trained. Concentration provides the foundation for wisdom, since clear perception of the true nature of phenomena requires the purification and unification of the mind. Wisdom reaches its climax in the four paths and fruits, which uproot the subtlest strata of defilements and issue in final liberation from suffering.

From the Noble Eightfold Path we can now turn briefly to the other groups to see how *jhāna* fits in with their constituents of enlightenment. The four foundations of mindfulness and the four right endeavors are identical, respectively, with right mindfulness and right effort of the Eightfold Path. Insofar as these are called the bases (*nimitta*) and requisites (*parikkhāra*) for concentration, and concentration includes the four *jhānas*, *jhāna* can be seen to arise from the training in these two groups of principles. The four bases of success are the base of success consisting in zeal, the base consisting in energy, the base consisting in consciousness, and the base consisting in inquiry.[1] Since these four constituents of enlightenment are said to be supports for obtaining concentration, and to be directed towards the *abhiññās* and the supramundane attainments, their connection with the *jhānas* is evident.[2] The five faculties and powers comprise the five identical factors—faith,[3] energy, mindfulness, concentration, and wisdom—each classified as a faculty (*indriya*) in that they exercise dominance in a particular sphere of spiritual endeavor and as a power (*bala*) in that they cannot be shaken in confrontation with their opposites.[4] The faculty and power of concentration are said to be found in the four *jhānas*.[5] The seven enlightenment factors are mindfulness, investigation of phenomena, energy, rapture, tranquility, concentration, and equanimity.[6] *Jhāna* can be fitted into this group explicitly as the enlightenment factor of concentration; it is also closely associated with the factors of rapture, tranquility, and equanimity, which each rise to prominence in the course of developing the *jhānas*.

1. SN. 5:249-93.
2. *Ibid.*, 268.
3. *Ibid.*, 193-252.
4. Dhs., pp. 162-67.
5. SN. 5:196.
6. *Ibid.*, 63-140.

Chapter II

THE PRELIMINARIES TO PRACTICE

The *jhānas* do not arise out of a void but in dependence on the right conditions. They are states of mind which can come to growth only when provided with the nutriments conducive to their development. Therefore, prior to beginning meditation, the aspirant to the *jhānas* must prepare a groundwork for his practice by fulfilling certain preliminary requirements. He first has to purify his moral virtue, since virtue forms the irreplaceable support for concentration. Then he must sever the outer impediments to practice and place himself under a qualified teacher. The teacher will assign him a suitable subject for developing *jhāna* and explain to him the methods of contemplation. After learning the methods the disciple must then seek out a congenial dwelling and diligently strive for success. In this chapter we will examine in order each of the preliminary steps which have to be fulfilled before commencing to develop *jhāna*.

The Moral Foundation for Jhāna

A disciple aspiring to the *jhānas* first has to lay a solid foundation of moral discipline. Moral purity is indispensable to meditative progress for several deeply psychological reasons. It is needed firstly, in order to safeguard against the danger of remorse, the nagging sense of guilt that crops up when the basic principles of morality are ignored or deliberately violated. Scrupulous conformity to virtuous rules of conduct protects the meditator from this danger, disruptive to innner calm. Therefore the Buddha states that wholesome moral pıinciples have non-remorse as their benefit and reward, non-remorse has joy and rapture as its benefit and reward, and joy and rapture lead to a succession of purifying states culminating in concentration.[1]

A second reason a moral foundation is needed for meditation follows from an understanding of the purpose of concentration. Concentration, in the Buddhist discipline, aims at providing a

1. AN. 5:1-7.

base for wisdom by cleansing the mind of the dispersive influence of the defilements. But in order for the concentration exercises to effectively combat the defilements, the coarser expressions of the latter through the instruments of bodily and verbal action have to first be checked. Moral transgressions being invariably motivated by defilements—by greed, hatred, and delusion—when a person acts in violation of the precepts of morality he excites and reinforces the very same mental factors his practice of meditation is intended to eliminate. This involves him in a crossfire of incompatible aims which renders his attempts at mental purification ineffective. The only way he can avoid frustrating his endeavor to purify the mind of its subtler defilements is to prevent the unwholesome inner impulses from breaking out in the coarser form of unwholesome bodily and verbal deeds. Only when he establishes control over the outer expression of the defilements can he turn to deal with them inwardly as mental obsessions that appear in the process of meditation.

The practice of moral discipline consists, negatively, in abstinence from immoral actions of body and speech and, positively, in the observance of ethical principles of promoting peace within oneself and harmony in one's relations with others. The basic code of moral discipline taught by the Buddha for the guidance of his lay followers is the five precepts (*pañcasīla*): abstinence from taking life, from stealing, from sexual misconduct, from false speech, and from intoxicating drugs and drinks. These principles are binding as minimal ethical obligations for all practitioners of the Buddhist path, and within their bounds considerable progress in meditation can be made. However, those aspiring to reach the higher levels of the *jhānas*, and to pursue the path further to the stages of liberation, are encouraged to take up the more complete moral discipline pertaining to the life of renunciation. Pali Buddhism is unambiguous in its emphasis on the limitations of household life for following the path in its fullness and perfection. Householders can achieve proficiency in serenity and insight, and even reach the supramundane path and fruits. But by way of providing the conditions for leading the holy life the inadequacy of household existence as compared to the life of renunciation is clearly recognized. Time and again the texts tell that the household life is confining, a "path for the dust of passion," while the life of homelessness is like open space.

For those inclined to the homeless life of renunciation, Buddhism offers a supporting communal structure in the form of the Bhikkhu-sangha, the order of monks. After leaving the household life, therefore, the aspiring meditator, if he is free from impediments, will generally seek admission into the order, taking first the lower ordination of "going forth" (*pabbajjā*) which makes him a novice, then the higher ordination (*upasampadā*) which makes him a bhikkhu, a fully ordained monk. The monastic life, with its emphasis on purity, simplicity, and seclusion, was especially designed by the Buddha to establish the optimal outward conditions for inner progress in the practice of his teaching. The foundation for this practice is the training in the higher moral discipline. The moral training for monks has been shaped into a scheme called the fourfold purification of morality (*catupārisuddhisīla*), made up of four components: [1] the moral discipline of restraint according to the Pātimokkha; [2] the moral discipline of sense restraint; [3] the moral discipline of purity of livelihood; and [4] the moral discipline concerning the use of the requisites.[1]

[1] The moral discipline of restraint according to the Pāti-mokkha (*pātimokkhasaṁvarasīla*) consists in scrupulous observance of the rules of the Pātimokkha, the code of 227 training precepts promulgated by the Buddha to regulate the conduct of the monks. The rules provide the backbone of monastic discipline, aiding the purification of conduct needed to ensure success in contemplation.[2]

[2] The moral discipline of sense restraint (*indriyasaṁvarasīla*) means exercising restraint over the sense faculties in the engagement with their objective fields. The canonical text reads:

> On seeing a visible object with the eye, he apprehends neither the signs nor the particulars through which, if he left the eye faculty unguarded, evil and unprofitable states of covetousness and grief might invade him; he enters upon the way of its restraint, he guards the eye faculty, undertakes the restraint of the eye faculty.[3]

1. For a detailed treatment of the fourfold purification of morality see Vism., pp. 13-37; PP., pp. 16-46.
2. For the full code, see Ñāṇamoli, transl., *The Pātimokkha: 227 Fundamental Rules of a Bhikkhu*, (Bangkok : Mahamakutarajavidyalaya, 1969).
3. MN. 1:180.

The same is repeated for the remaining sense faculties and their objects. The purpose of this training is to prevent sense experience from occasioning the rise of the defilements. The untrained mind apprehends sense objects through the "signs" or false notions that they are intrinsically attractive and repulsive; thence agreeable objects tend to arouse craving, disagreeable ones aversion. To conquer this dualistic pattern of emotional involvement, so detrimental to the nascent pool of calm forming within his mind, the aspiring meditator has to keep watch over his senses when they encounter diverse sense data. By means of vigilant mindfulness he must ward off the spontaneous impulses to cling to the pleasant and reject the unpleasant, replacing them with a detached equanimity which looks upon all sense objects equally.

[3] The moral discipline of purified livelihood (*ājīvapārisuddhisīla*) requires that the meditator avoid a wrong means of livelihood. For a monk this stricture has an even more exacting application than the right livelihood binding on the laity. A monk must obtain his basic requisites—robes, food, lodgings, and medicines—only in ways consistent with the principles of the monastic life, that is, either as alms offerings freely given by the laity or by making requests on invitation from faithful supporters. He is forbidden to make false claims to spiritual achievement as a way of bolstering his prestige in the eyes of the laity, and must also avoid resorting to such methods as scheming, persuasion, hinting, and belittling to gain his means of subsistence.

[4] The moral discipline concerning the use of the requisites (*paccayasannissitasīla*) follows naturally upon purified livelihood. After obtaining his requisites by righteous means, the monk is enjoined to use them mindfully, cognizant of the real purpose they serve in the framework of the holy life. He must reflect that he uses his robes only to protect his body from cold and heat and to cover up nakedness, his food only to sustain his body and keep it in good health, his dwelling only to ward off the inclemencies of the weather, and medicines only to recover from illness and gain maximum well-being.[1] By using the requisites after making these reflections, the meditator can avoid the lure of craving for comfort and enjoyment. Recognizing the material

1. MN. 1:10.

supports of life to be subordinate in value to a spiritual goal, he is able to develop the virtues of contentment, frugality, and simplicity with regard to his physical requirements.

Cutting off Impediments

After establishing a basis of purified morality, the aspirant is advised to sever any outer impediments (*palibodha*) he may have that can hinder his efforts to lead a contemplative life. The *Visuddhimagga* enumerates these impediments as ten: a dwelling, family, gain, a class, building, travel, kin, affliction, books, and supernormal powers.[1]

[1] A dwelling, which can be a single room, a hut, or a whole monastery, becomes an impediment for those who allow their mind to become excessively pre-occupied with work and business connected with it or with the belongings they have stored there. Meditation requires the abandonment of concern with the comforts and conveniences of residential life. Thus a meditator who finds his progress impeded by attachment to his dwelling is urged to relinquish it and seek a simple secluded place of shelter where he can pursue his practice.

[2] A family means either relatives or supporters. Since a disciple who lives in close association with lay devotees becomes emotionally involved with them, he is advised to develop detachment or to shift to a location where intimate involvements are unlikely to arise.

[3] Gains are the four requisites. A monk who achieves fame and distinction may be frequently sought after by lay people to receive offerings of the requisites. To thank them he must recite blessings and preach the doctrine, thus finding no chance to practice meditation. In such a case he should cut off this impediment by leaving his group and wandering to a place where he is unknown.

[4] A class is a group of students. A monk constantly engaged in instructing students has no time to undertake the work of contemplation. If he is intent on full time meditation he should turn his students over to another teacher and go off by himself.

[5] Building means new building work. This is always an

1. PP., p. 91. "*Āvāso, kulaṁ, lābho, gaṇo, kammaṁ, addhānaṁ, ñāti, ābādho, gantho, iddhi.*" Vism., p. 73.

impediment, since it demands time and mental consideration. To sever this impediment the building work should be completed as soon as possible or handed over to the community of monks.

[6] Travel is going on journeys. This should be relinquished in favor of a stable residence conducive to meditation.

[7] Kin means specifically close fellows in the Order, such as teachers and pupils, and close relations such as mother and father, who are afflicted with illness. They should be nursed back to health as quickly as possible, or their care turned over to responsible persons.

[8] Affliction is any kind of illness, which should be dealt with by taking the appropriate medicines or, if these fail, by persisting in the practice despite the illness.

[9] Books means the study of scriptures. This is an impediment for those who find the intellectual work of study obstructive to their meditation. It should be severed by leaving off study and recitation during the period of intensified practice.

[10] Supernormal powers are an impediment to insight, not concentration, since they are the products of concentration. As an impediment they can be cut off simply by neglecting to exercise them and by abandoning concern for their success.

Approaching the Good Friend

The path of practice leading to the *jhānas* is an arduous course involving specific subjects of contemplation, precise techniques, and skillfulness in dealing with the pitfalls that lie along the way. The knowledge of how to attain the *jhānas* has been transmitted through a lineage of teachers going back to the time of the Buddha himself. Each teacher passes his store of accumulated knowledge and experience on to his successor pupils, thus ensuring the continuity of the tradition. A prospective meditator is advised to avail himself of the living heritage of practice by placing himself under the care of a qualified teacher. The teacher will assign him a subject of meditation appropriate for his temperament, instruct him in the methods of developing it, and guide his steps along the path.

Unlike those Indian traditions which focus upon the guru figure as an embodiment of divinity or a link between the disciple and the divine, Theravāda Buddhism has always stressed the pedagogic role of the teacher. This much is indicated by the term selected in the Pali texts to designate the teacher of meditation, *kalyāṇamitta*, meaning "good (or noble) friend." The teacher is not a god or an incarnation of the divine, equipped with the means to deliverance in his own person. He is essentially an elder friend and guide. The guidance he gives along the path to be travelled stems entirely from his superior wisdom gained through personal experience. Even the Buddhas themselves can do no more than indicate the path ; the rest depends on the efforts of the aspirant.

Nevertheless, the importance of relying on a *kalyāṇamitta* is strongly emphasized in the Theravāda Buddhist tradition. When the Venerable Ānanda approached the Buddha and declared that it seemed to him that reliance on good friends is half of the holy life, the Buddha corrected him with the words that reliance on good friends is the whole of the holy life, for it is reliance on good friends that leads to the practice of the Noble Eightfold Path.[1] On another occasion, when his attendant Meghiya prematurely sought permission to go off into solitary retreat, the Buddha explained that while the mind is not yet ripe for liberation one thing that leads to its ripening is association with good friends and companions.[2] The Buddha in fact describes himself as the good friend par excellence who leads living beings to freedom from birth, aging, suffering, and death.[3]

The good friend has the task of assigning the pupil a meditation subject. The *Visuddhimagga* points out that to do so the good friend must possess the proper qualifications, such as being worthy of reverence and esteem, uttering profound speech, and having solicitude for the welfare and progress of his disciples. It says that since the Buddha himself is the ideal good friend, while he is alive a meditation subject should be sought directly from him. But after the Buddha's passing the qualified meditation teachers that remain may be ranked in the following descending series: the great disciples that survive him, an arahat who attains *jhānas*, a non-returner, a once-returner, a stream-enterer, an ordinary man who obtains *jhānas*, and various masters of the scriptures. After learning of a qualified teacher, the prospective meditator

1. SN. 1:88.
2. AN. 4:354-58.
3. SN. 1:88.

should approach him and take up residence in his monastery. He should not ask for a meditation subject immediately upon arriving, but should first perform the duties of a pupil towards the teacher, doing them with respect and humility. He should pay homage to the teacher in the evening and leave when dismissed. Then after ten days or two weeks have passed, he should create an opportunity to see the teacher. When all conditions are favorable, he can explain the reason for his coming. He should dedicate himself to the Buddha and to the teacher, then with a sincere inclination and resolution ask for a subject of meditation.[1]

The teacher assigns a meditation subject that is suitable for the disciple's temperament. The ancient teachers of the Theravāda tradition recognize six principal character types (*carita*) into which prospective meditators can be classified: These are: the greedy temperament, the hating temperament, the deluded temperament, the faithful temperament, the intelligent temperament, and the speculative temperament.[2] Which temperament prevails in a particular person is determined by previously accumulated *kamma*. On the basis either of the power of penetrating others' minds, or by personal observation, or by questioning, the teacher will size up the temperament of his new pupil; then he will select a meditation subject for him appropriate to his temperament.

The Subjects of Serenity-meditation

The various meditation subjects that the Buddha prescribed on different occasions for the development of serenity have been systematized in the commentaries into a set called the forty *kammaṭṭhānas*. The word *kammaṭṭhāna* means literally a place of work. It is applied to the subjects of meditation since these are the places where the meditator undertakes the work pertaining to his calling, the work of meditation. An equivalent term occurring in the texts is *ārammaṇa*, meaning "object" in general, but in this context the object focussed on is developing concentration.

The forty meditation subjects are distributed into seven cate-

1. PP., p. 100. Vism., p. 80.

2. PP., p. 102. "*Rāgacarito, dosacarito, mohacarito, saddhācarito, buddhicarito, vitakkacarito*" Vism., p. 82.

gories. They are enumerated in the *Visuddhimagga* as follows: ten *kasiṇas*, ten kinds of foulness, ten recollections, four divine abidings, four immaterial states, one perception, and one defining[1].

A *kasiṇa* is a device representing a particular quality used as a support for concentration. The ten *kasiṇas* are the earth *kasiṇa*, water *kasiṇa*, fire *kasiṇa*, wind *kasiṇa*, blue *kasiṇa*, yellow *ksiṇa*, red *kasiṇa*, white *kasiṇa*, light *kasiṇa*, and limited space *kasiṇa*. The word *kasiṇa* has the meaning of "entirety' (*sakalaṭṭhena*). It is extended to these ten objects of meditation in that each represents the entire quality appropriate to itself. The *kasiṇa* can be either a naturally occuring form of the element or color chosen, or an artificially produced device such as a colored or elemental disk that the meditator can use at his convenience in his meditation quarters.

The ten kinds of foulness are ten stages in the decomposition of a corpse. These are: the bloated, the livid, the festering, the cut-up, the gnawed, the scattered, the hacked and scattered, the bleeding, the worm-infested, and a skeleton. The primary purpose behind these meditations is to reduce sensual lust by gaining a clear perception of the repulsiveness of the body. In order to gain the "sign" of the corpses, actual dead bodies have to be seen. Thence these subjects are also known as the cemetery meditations.

The ten recollections are: the recollections of the Buddha, the Dhamma, the Sangha, morality, generosity, and the deities, mindfulness of death, mindfulness of the body, mindfulness of breathing, and the recollection of peace. The first three are devotional contemplations on the sublime qualities of the "three jewels", the primary objects of Buddhist veneration. The second three are reflections on two cardinal Buddhist virtues and on the devas inhabiting the heavenly worlds, intended principally for those still intent on a higher rebirth. Mindfulness of death is reflection on the inevitability of death, a constant spur to spiritual exertion. Mindfulness of the body involves the mental dissection of the body into thirty-two parts, undertaken with a view to perceiving its unattractiveness. Mindfulness of breathing is awareness of the in-and-out movement of the breath, perhaps the most fundamental of all Buddhist meditation subjects. And the recollection of peace is reflection on the qualities of *nibbāna*.

1. PP., p 112. Vism , p. 89. The Pali names for the forty *kammaṭṭhānas* are given in the Appendix 2.

The four divine abidings are the development of boundless loving-kindness, compassion, sympathetic joy, and equanimity. These meditations are also called the "immeasurables" (*appamaññā*) because they are to be developed towards all sentient beings without qualification or exclusiveness.

The four immaterial states are the base of boundless space, the base of boundless consciousness, the base of nothingness, and the base of neither perception nor non-perception. These are the objects leading to the four corresponding meditative attainments called the *āruppas* or immaterial *jhānas* (*arūpajjhāna*).

The one perception is the perception of the repulsiveness of food. The one defining of the defining is the four elements, that is, the analysis of the physical body into the elemental modes of solidity, fluidity, heat, and oscillation.

The forty *kammaṭṭhānas* are treated in the Pali commentarial texts from two important angles—one their ability to induce different levels of concentration, the other their suitability for different temperaments.

Not all meditation subjects are equally effective in inducing the deeper levels of concentration. As we explained above, beyond the preliminary stage, concentration can occur either at the level of access concentration (*upacārasamādhi*) or at the level of absorption concentration (*appanāsamādhi*), depending upon the strength of the *jhāna* factors in the meditative state. Absorption too, consisting in the eight attainments—the four lower *jhānas* and the four *āruppas*—can occur at any of these eight levels. Therefore the forty *kammaṭṭhānas* are first distinguished on the basis of their capacity for inducing only access or for inducing full absorption as well; then those able to induce absorption are distinguished further according to their ability to induce the different levels *of jhāna.*

Of the forty subjects, ten are capable of leading only to access concentration. These are eight recollections—i.e. all except mindfulness of the body and mindfulness of breathing—plus the perception of repulsiveness in nutriment and the defining of the four elements. Cultivation of these subjects can cause the hindrances to subside and the *jhāna* factors to become manifest, but because they are occupied with a diversity of qualities and involve an active application of discursive thought, cannot lead beyond access. The other thirty subjects can all lead to absorption.

Of these latter, the ten *kasiṇas* and mindfulness of breathing bring all four *jhānas*, their efficiency in this regard due to their simplicity and freedom from thought construction. The ten kinds of foulness and mindfulness of the body bring only the first *jhāna*, being limited because consciousness can only hold on to them with the aid of applied thought (*vitakka*), which is absent in the second and higher *jhānas*. The first three divine abidings can induce the lower three *jhānas* but not the fourth, since they arise in association with pleasant feeling (*sukha*), present in the first three *jhānas* but replaced by neutral feeling in the fourth. Conversely, because it requires the company of neutral feeling and cannot coexist with pleasant feeling, the divine abiding equanimity occurs only at the level of the fourth *jhāna*, where neutral feeling gains ascendency. The four immaterial states conduce to the respective immaterial *jhāna* corresponding to their names; but because these latter are identical in factorial constitution with the fourth *jhāna*, differing only in their objects, the four immaterial states are said to lead to the fourth *jhāna*.

Since in the main section of the present work we wish to follow the progress of meditation through all four *jhānas*, we will presume the case of a meditator who has taken as his meditation-subject either a *kasiṇa* or mindfulness of breathing.

The forty *kammaṭṭhānas* are also differentiated according to their appropriateness for different character types. The principal temperaments recognized for this purpose are, as we said, six—the greedy, the hating, the deluded, the faithful, the intelligent, and the speculative. The danger of oversimplification involved in this scheme has been acknowledged by ancient teachers and the possibility of complex combinations of traits finds ready affirmation. But the sixfold typology is taken to be sufficient as a pragmatic guideline for the purpose it is intended to serve, the assignment of a suitable subject to a meditator.

The *Visuddhimagga* divides the forty *kammaṭṭhānas* among the different temperaments as follows. The ten kinds of foulness and mindfulness of the body, clearly intended to attenuate sensual desire, are eleven subjects suitable for those of greedy temperament. Eight subjects, the four divine abidings and four color *kasiṇas*, are appropriate for the hating temperament.[1] Mindful-

1. Exactly why the color *kasiṇas* are offered as an antidote to hatred is

ness of breathing is one recollection suitable for those of the deluded and the speculative temperaments. The first six recollections are appropriate for the faithful temperament. Four subjects—mindfulness of death, the recollection of peace, the defining of the four elements, and the perception of repulsiveness in nutriment—are especially effective for those of intelligent temperament. The remaining six *kasiṇas* and the immaterial states are suitable for all kinds of temperaments. But the *kasiṇas* should be limited in size for one of speculative temperament and large in size for one of deluded temperament.[1]

Immediately after giving this breakdown Buddhaghosa adds a proviso to prevent misunderstanding. He states that this division by way of temperament is made on the basis of direct opposition and complete suitability, but actually there is no wholesome form of meditation that does not suppress the defilements, and cultivate virtuous mental factors. He then cites a passage from the Meghiya Sutta advising a single meditator to meditate on foulness to abandon lust, on loving-kindness to abandon hatred, on breathing to cut off discursive thought, and on impermanence to eliminate the conceit "I am."[2]

Choosing a Suitable Dwelling

The teacher assigns a meditation subject to his pupil appropriate to his character, and then explains the methods of developing it. He can teach it gradually to a pupil who is going to remain in close proximity to him, or in detail to one who will go to practice it elsewhere. If the disciple is not going to stay with his teacher he must be careful to select a suitable place for meditation. The texts mention eighteen kinds of monasteries unfavorable to the development of *jhāna*: a large monastery, a new one, a dilapidated one, one near a road, one with a pond, leaves, flowers, or fruits, one sought after by many people, one in cities, among timber or fields, where people quarrel, in a port, in border lands, on a frontier, a haunted place, and one without access to

---

not explained. Perhaps the contemplation of color has a subtle psychological effect of reducing anger and aversion.

1. PP., pp. 117-18. Vism., p. 92-93.
2. PP., p. 118. AN. 4:358.

a spiritual teacher.[1] Unless he is already highly developed a novice meditator should avoid a dwelling with these faults.

The factors which make a dwelling favorable to meditation are mentioned by the Buddha himself. These are five in number: [1] it should be not too far from or too near a village that can be relied on as an alms resort, and should have a clear path; [2] it should be quiet and secluded; [3] it should be free from inclemencies of weather and from harmful insects and animals; [4] it should be easy to obtain the four requisites while dwelling there; and [5] the dwelling should provide ready access to learned elders and spiritual friends who can be consulted when problems arise in meditation.[2] The types of dwelling places commended by the Buddha most frequently in the suttas as conducive to the *jhānas* are a secluded dwelling in the forest, at the foot of a tree, on a mountain, in a cleft, in a cave, in a cemetery, on a wooded flatland, in the open air, or on a heap of straw.[3] Having found a suitable dwelling and settled there, the disciple should maintain scrupulous observance of the rules of discipline. He should be content with his simple requisites, exercise control over his sense faculties, be mindful and discerning in all activities, and practice meditation diligently as he was instructed. It is at this point that he meets the first great challenge of his contemplative life, the battle with the five hindrances.

1. PP., p. 125. Vism., p. 99.
2. AN. 5:15.
3. MN. 1:181, 269, 274.

Chapter III

THE CONQUEST OF THE HINDRANCES

The *jhānas* are attained sequentially, mastery over each lower one being a prerequisite to the practice issuing in the next higher one. The attainment of any *jhāna* comes about through a two-sided process of development—on one side is the elimination of the states obstructive to it, on the other the acquisition of the states composing it. The former set is called its factors of abandonment (*pahānaṅgāni*), the latter its factors of possession (*samannāgataṅgāni*). In the case of the first *jhāna* the factors of abandonment are the five hindrances, its factors of possession the basic five *jhāna* factors. Both are alluded to in the standard formula for the first *jhāna*:

> Quite secluded from sense pleasures, secluded from unwholesome states of mind, he enters and dwells in the first *jhāna*, which is accompanied by applied thought and sustained thought with rapture and happiness born of seclusion.[1]

In this formula the first part, the phrase "quite secluded from sense pleasures, secluded from unwholesome states of mind," refers to the elimination of the hindrances. The second part, mentioning the states found in the *jhāna*, enumerates the factors of possession. In the present chapter we will deal at length with the abandoning of the hindrances, then in the next chapter we will consider the *jhāna* factors themselves.

The Five Hindrances

The five hindrances (*pañcanīvaraṇā*) are sensual desire, ill will, sloth and torpor, restlessness and worry, and doubt. This group merits special attention because it is the principal classification the Buddha uses for the obstacles to meditation. The defilements included in this set obstruct not only the first *jhāna*, but the entire

1. "Vivicc'eva kāmehi vivicca akusalehi dhammehi savitakkaṁ savicāraṁ vivekajaṁ pitisukhaṁ paṭhamaṁ jhānaṁ upasampajja viharati." MN. 1:89. Vibh., p. 245.

thrust of man's aspiration for liberation and enlightenment. They receive the name "hindrances" because they hinder and envelop the mind, preventing meditative development in the two spheres of serenity and insight. Hence the Buddha calls the five hindrances "obstructions, hindrances, corruptions of the mind, weakeners of wisdom."[1] Again he says: "These five hindrances, monks, are causes of blindness, causes of loss of vision, causes of unknowing, opposed to wisdom, aligned with vexation, leading away from *nibbāna*,"[2]

The hindrance of sensual desire (*kāmacchanda*) is explained as desire for the "five strands of sense pleasure," that is, for visible forms, sounds, smells, tastes, and tangibles which are "desirable, lovely, agreeable, pleasing, sensuous, stimulating lust."[3] It is a form of the root defilement of greed (*lobha*) and a mode of craving (*taṇhā*), which the Buddha identifies as the cause of suffering. The hindrance of ill will (*byāpāda*) signifies aversion directed towards disagreeable persons or things, varying in range all the way from mild annoyance to overpowering hatred.[4] It is a form of the root defilement of hate (*dosa*). Thus the first two hindrances correspond to the first two root defilements. The third root defilement, delusion (*moha*), is not enumerated separately among the five hindrances, but can be found underlying all the others.

Sloth and torpor (*thīnamiddha*) the Buddha states to be a compound hindrance which can be regarded as twofold in terms of its components: "Sloth, monks, is a hindrance; torpor is a hindrance. Thus the hindrance of sloth and torpor that comes down in the summary by this method becomes twofold."[5] The Abhidhamma books pick up on this method and define the two terms separately. Thus the Dhammasaṅgani explains sloth (*thīna*) by a string of synonyms suggestive of dullness and mental inertia, torpor (*middha*) by synonyms suggestive of indolence.[6]

Restlessness and worry (*uddaccakukkucca*) is again treated as a double hindrance to be defined by breaking it down into its members before recombining them. Restlessness (*uddhacca*) is

1. SN. 5:94.
2. *Ibid.*, 97.
3. MN. 1:85.
4. See Dhs., p. 232.
5. SN. 5:110.
6. See Dhs., p. 233.

equated with excitement, agitation, and disquietude, worry (*kukkucca*) with the sense of guilt aroused by moral transgressions.[1] Finally the hindrance of doubt (*vicikicchā*) is explained principally as uncertainty with regard to four items : the Buddha, the Dhamma, the Sangha, and the training.[2] The commentaries state that doubt in regard to the Buddha is doubt as to whether or not any person has existed endowed with the physical and spiritual qualities of a Buddha. Doubt regarding the Dhamma is doubt about the existence of the supramundane paths, fruits, and *nibbāna*. Doubt regarding the Sangha is skepticism with respect to the existence of holy persons or the fruitfulness of gifts to the Order. Doubt regarding the discipline questions the effectiveness of morality, concentration, and wisdom in leading to the end of suffering.[3]

The Buddha offers two sets of similes to illustrate the detrimental effect of the hindrances. The first compares the five hindrances unabandoned in oneself to five types of calamity: sensual desire is like a debt, ill will like a disease, sloth and torpor like imprisonment, restlessness and worry like slavery, and doubt like being lost on a desert road. Release from the hindrances is to be seen as freedom from debt, good health, release from prison, emancipation from slavery, and arriving at a place of safety.[4] The second set of similes compares the hindrances to five kinds of impurities affecting a bowl of water, preventing a keen-sighted man from seeing his own reflection as it really is. The five impurities are appropriately paired off with the hind rances: sensual desire is like a bowl of water mixed with brightly colored paints, ill will like a bowl of boiling water, sloth and torpor like water covered by mossy plants, restlessness and worry like water blown into ripples by the wind, and doubt like muddy water. Just as the keen-eyed man would not be able to see his reflection in these five kinds of water, so one whose mind is obsessed by the five hindrances does not know and see as it is his own good, the good of others, or the good of both.[5]

1. *Ibid.*
2. MN. 1:101.
3. Dhs. A., pp. 388-89.
4. DN. 1:71-73.
5. SN. 5:121-24.

Although there are numerous defilements opposed to the first *jhāna*, the five hindrances alone are called its factors of abandoning. One reason, according to the *Visuddhimagga*, is that the hindrances are specifically obstructive to *jhāna*. Each hindrance obstructs attainment of *jhāna* by impeding in its own way the mind's capacity for concentration.

> The mind affected through lust by greed for varied objective fields does not become concentrated on an object consisting in unity, or being overwhelmed by lust, it does not enter on the way to abandoning the sense-desire element. When pestered by ill will towards an object, it does not occur uninterruptedly. When overcome by stiffness and torpor, it is unwieldy. When seized by agitation and worry, it is unquiet and buzzes about. When stricken by uncertainty, it fails to mount the way to accomplish the attainment of jhana. So it is these only that are called factors of abandoning because they are specifically obstructive to *jhāna*.[1]

A second reason for confining the first *jhāna's* factors of abandoning to the five hindrances is to permit a direct alignment to be made between the hindrances and the *jhāna* factors, the five mental concomitants—applied thought, sustained thought, rapture, happiness, and one-pointedness—responsible for lifting the mind to the level of absorption. Buddhaghosa states that the abandonment of the five hindrances alone is mentioned in connection with *jhāna* because the hindrances are the direct enemies of the five *jhāna* factors, which the latter must overcome: "For the hindrances are the contrary opposites of the *jhāna* factors: what is meant is that the *jhāna* factors are incompatible with them, eliminate them, abolish them."[2] To support his contention the commentator cites a passage demonstrating a one-to-one correspondence between the *jhāna* factors and hindrances:

> Concentration is incompatible with lust, happiness [rapture] with ill will, applied thought with stiffness and torpor, bliss [happiness] with agitation and worry, and sustained thought with uncertainty [doubt].[3]

1. PP., p. 152. Vism., p. 118.
2. PP., p. 147. Vism., p. 114.
3. PP., p. 147. "Samādhi kāmacchandassa paṭipakkho, pīti byāpādassa,

Thus each *jhāna* factor is seen as having the specific task of eliminating a particular obstruction to the *jhāna*. To correlate these obstructions with the five *jhāna* factors they are collected into a scheme of five hindrances.

The same principle also serves to explain the rationale behind the coupling that takes place in two of the hindrances, "sloth and torpor" and "restlessness and worry." As we saw the five hindrances break down under analysis into seven separate mental states: sensual desire, ill will, sloth, torpor, restlessness, worry, and doubt. The reason the seven are reduced by synthesis to five again lies in the economy required to set the *jhāna* factors and hindrances in direct opposition. Since there are five *jhāna* factors the defilements they oppose must likewise be five. Sloth and torpor on the one side, and restlessness and worry on the other, readily lend themselves to the required coupling. For sloth and torpor share the common feature of mental indisposition, restlessness and worry the common feature of disturbing the mind. Thus it is natural that a single *jhāna* factor should be capable of opposing and silencing the two hindrances in each set. According to the method cited in the *Visuddhimagga*, sloth and torpor are both countered by applied thought, restlessness and worry by happiness. In this way the mutual exclusion of hindrances and *jhāna* factors becomes the ground for the grouping of the hindrances into a fivefold set.

Seclusion from the Hindrances

Kinds of Seclusion

The stock passage describing the attainment of the first *jhāna*, with which we began the present chapter, says that the *jhāna* is attained by one who is "secluded from sense pleasures, secluded from unwholesome states of mind." Now that we have determined the purport of the phrase "unwholesome states of mind" to be the five hindrances, we must inquire into the meaning of the word "seclusion" (*viveka*). The *Visuddhimagga*, in its

---

vitakko thinamiddhassa, sukhaṁ uddhaccakukkuccassa, vicāro vicikicchaya ti [ ] Petake vutta." Vism., p. 114.

N.B. *The Path of Purification's* "happiness" is our "rapture" (pīti), and *The Path of Purification's* "bliss" is our' 'happiness" (*sukha*). The other differences in translation are more obvious, and can be checked in Appendix 3.

gloss of this passage, explains that there are three kinds of seclusion relevant to the present context—namely, bodily seclusion (*kāyaviveka*), mental seclusion (*cittaviveka*), and seclusion by suppression (*vikkhambhaṇaviveka*).[1] These three terms allude to two distinct sets of exegetical categories, which must be considered to bring their meaning to light.

The first two terms pertain to a threefold arrangement made up of bodily seclusion, mental seclusion, and "seclusion from the substance" (*upadhi viveka*). The first means physical withdrawal from active social engagement into a condition of solitude for the purpose of devoting time and energy to spiritual development. The second, which generally presupposes the first, means the seclusion of the mind from its entanglement in defilements; it is in effect equivalent to concentration of at least the access level. The third, "seclusion from the substance," is *nibbāna*, liberation from the elements of phenomenal existence. The achievement of the first *jhāna* does not depend on the third, which is its outcome rather than prerequisite, but it does require physical solitude and the separation of the mind from defilements, hence bodily and mental seclusion.

The third type of seclusion pertinent to the context, seclusion by suppression, belongs to a different scheme generally discussed under the heading of "abandonment" (*pahāna*) rather than "seclusion." This scheme records five kinds of abandoning: abandoning by suppression, by substitution of opposites, by cutting off, by tranquilization and by deliverance.[2]

[1] Abandoning by suppression occurs when the hindrances are excluded from the mind by the force of concentration, particularly evident on occasions of *jhāna*. It is illustrated by the pressing down of weeds in water by means of a porous pot. [2] Abandoning by substitution of opposites means the replacement of unwholesome states by wholesome ones, the usual instance cited being the abandoning of erroneous notions by particular factors of insight knowledge. [3] Abandoning by cutting off is the eradication of the fetters by the supramundane paths in such a way that they can never arise again, like a tree struck by a thunder-

1. Vism., p. 113.

2. In Pali: Vikkhambhanappahānaṁ, tadaṅgappahānaṁ, samucchedappahānaṁ, paṭippassaddhippahānaṁ, nissaranappahānaṁ. See Pts., p. 26.

bolt. [4] Abandoning by tranquilization is the subsiding of defilements at the moments of "fruition" following the noble paths. And [5] abandoning by deliverance is *nibbāna*, the ultimate release from all conditioned phenomena.[1]

The type of abandoning relevant to the attainment of *jhāna* is abandoning by suppression. The work of suppressing the hindrances begins with the first efforts to concentrate the mind upon one of the prescribed objects such as the *kasiṇas*. As the meditator fixes his mind on the initial object, a point is reached where he can apprehend the object as clearly with his eyes closed as with them open. This visualized object is called the "learning sign" (*uggahanimitta*). As he concentrates on the learning sign, his efforts call into play the embryonic *jhāna* factors, which grow in force, duration, and prominence as a result of the meditative exertion. These factors, being incompatible with the hindrances, function as their precise antidotes, so that their repeated cultivation excludes the hindrances, attenuates them, and holds them at bay. With continued practice the "learning sign" gives rise to a purified luminous reproduction of itself called the "counterpart sign" (*paṭibhāga nimitta*). The manifestation of the counterpart sign marks the complete suppression of the hindrances and the attainment of access concentration (*upacārasamādhi*). All three events—the suppression of the hindrances, the arising of the counterpart sign, and the entrance upon access concentration—take place at precisely the same moment, without interval.[2] And though previously the process of mental cultivation may have required the elimination of different hindrances at different times, when access is achieved they all subside together:

> Simultaneously with his acquiring the counterpart sign his lust is abandoned by suppression owing to his giving no attention externally to sense desires (as object). And owing to his abandoning of approval, ill will is abandoned too, as pus is with the abandoning of blood. Likewise stiffness and torpor is abandoned through exertion of energy, agitation and worry is abandoned through devotion to peaceful things that cause no remorse; and uncertainty about the Master who teaches the way, about the way, and about the fruit of the way, is abandoned

1. Vism., pp. 596-97. MN. A. 1:24-25.
2. See PP., p. 130-131. Vism., p. 102.

through the actual experience of the distinction attained. So the five hindrances are abandoned.[1]

Though the mental factors determinative of the *jhāna* are present in access concentration, they do not as yet possess sufficient strength to give this state the full qualification of the first *jhāna*. They are strong enough only to exclude the hindrances and hold them at bay. With continued practice, however, the nascent *jhāna* factors grow in strength until they gain sufficient force to issue in the first *jhāna*. Thus, starting from the distracted condition of the untrained mind, a yogin begins developing concentration. This initial practice arouses certain mental factors which counter the hindrances and unify the mind upon its object. The complete suppression of the hindrances marks the achievement of access concentration with the attainment of *jhāna* lying close at hand. When, through further application, these factors gain the power to make the mind become immersed in its object, the *jhāna* is actually attained.

The Causal Arising of the Hindrances

The five hindrances, the Buddha teaches, are like all other phenomena causally conditioned, arising and subsiding in correlation with other things which serve as their supports. When these supports are present the hindrances spring up and grow, when the supports are removed they fade away and disappear. Since the hindrances depend on other factors for their origination and cessation, an understanding of these factors is essential to their abandoning. For this reason the Buddha has taken special care to provide an exact account of the genetic groundwork of the hindrances, an account which proceeds at both the general and particular level, laying bare the causes for the hindrances as a group and for each member of this group individually.

In the Aṅguttara Nikāya, the Buddha includes the five hindrances in a sequence of conditions nourishing and sustaining ignorance, itself the fundamental root of *saṁsāra*:

> Ignorance, monks, has its nutriment, I say, it is not without nutriment. And what is the nutriment for ignorance? 'The five hindrances' should be the reply. The five hindrances,

1. PP., p. 196. Vism., p. 155.

> monks, have their nutriment, I say, they are not without nutriment. And what is the nutriment for the five hindrances? 'The three types of misconduct' should be the reply. The three types of misconduct also have their nutriment...non-restraint of the sense faculties. Non-restraint of the sense faculties also has its nutriment...lack of mindfulness and discernment. Lack of mindfulness and discernment also has its nutriment...unwise consideration. Unwise consideration also has its nutriment... lack of faith. Lack of faith also has its nutriment...not listening to the true Dhamma. Not listening to the true Dhamma also has its nutriment...not associating with superior men.[1]

As this statement points out, the five hindrances while "nourishing" ignorance are nourished in turn by the three types of misconduct (bodily, verbal, and mental), non-restraint of the senses, lack of mindfulness and self-composure, unwise consideration, and so on. Through unwise consideration a man fails to control his mind. Lacking mindfulness he allows his senses to roam unchecked in their objective fields, seeking sensual gratification. Obsessed by sense stimuli, he engages in the three types of misconduct, thereby reinforcing the hindrances, which then maintain the ignorance that holds him in bondage.

In this causal genesis a crucial role is played by "unwise consideration" (*ayoniso manasikāra*). Unwise consideration is "inexpedient reflection, reflection on the wrong track", generally explained as reflection which apprehends its object through the four "perversions" (*vipallāsa*), considering the impermanent as permanent, pain as pleasure, non-self as self, and the foul as beautiful.[2] Calling attention to the instrumental role of unwise consideration in causing the arising and growth of all five hindrances collectively, the Buddha states that as a result of such wrong reflection the unarisen hindrances arise and the arisen ones increase.[3] However unwise consideration functions not only as a collective cause for the hindrances as a group, but also as a specific cause for each of the hindrances individually. For acts of unwise consideration always take on particular forms, with differences determined by the variations in its objects and mode

1. GS. 5:79. AN. 5:113.
2. Soma Thera, *The Way of Mindfulness*, p. 116.
3. SN. 5:93-94.

of occurrence. These differences in the forms of unwise consideration are correlated with the hindrances in such a way that unwise consideration to one thing becomes a cause for one hindrance, unwise consideration to something else the cause for another hindrance. Thus the Buddha says:

> Just as this body, monks, is sustained by nutriment, stands in dependence on nutriment, and does not stand without nutriment, in the same way the five hindrances are sustained by nutriment, stand in dependence on nutriment, and do not stand without nutriment.
>
> [1] What, monks, is the nutriment for the arising of unarisen sensual desire, and for the growth and expansion of sensual desire that has already arisen? There is, monks, the beautiful appearance of things. Habitual unwise consideration of that is the nutriment for the arising of unarisen sensual desire, and for the growth and expansion of sensual desire that has already arisen.
>
> [2] And what, monks, is the nutriment for the arising of unarisen ill will, and for the growth and expansion of ill will that has already arisen? There is, monks, the repulsive appearance of things. Habitual unwise consideration of that is the nutriment for the arising of unarisen ill will...
>
> [3] And what, monks, is the nutriment for the arising of unarisen sloth and torpor...? There is, monks, discontent, drowsiness, langour, surfeit after meals, and sluggishness of mind. Habitual unwise consideration of them is the nutriment for the arising of unarisen sloth and torpor......
>
> [4] And what, monks, is the nutriment for the arising of unarisen restlessness and worry... ? There is, monks, non-tranquillity of mind. Habitual unwise consideration of that is the nutriment for the arising of unarisen restlessness and worry.
>
> [5] And what, monks, is the nutriment for the arising of unarisen doubt......? There are, monks, matters which are grounds for doubt. Habitual unwise consideration of them is the nutriment for the arising of unarisen doubt...[1]

Specifically, then, sensual desire arises through unwise conside-

1. SN. 5:64-65.

ration of the attractive appearance of things, ill will through unwise consideration of the repulsive features of things, sloth and torpor through unwise consideration of states conducive to lethargy, restlessness and worry through unwise consideration of disturbing states, and doubt through unwise consideration of dubious matters.

The Elimination of the Hindrances

Once the genetic basis for the rise and growth of the hindrances becomes clear, the way to counteract and eliminate them follows as a matter of course. Since the hindrances occur in dependence on specific causes and conditions, their control and conquest require simply that their generative causes be removed. Though the actual achievement of such a stoppage may require diligent effort, it is the fundamental optimism of Buddhism that the qualities needed to overcome the hindrances are not beyond man's capacity for development, provided only that he is given the proper methodology. It is the purpose of the Buddha's discipline to provide precisely that methodology.

The final eradication of the hindrances is effected exclusively by the four supramundane paths. To reach the path the development of insight (*vipassanā*) is indispensable, since insight into the true characteristics of phenomena issues in the supramundane wisdom of the path. But in order for insight to arise, the hindrances have to be attenuated to a degree where they no longer disrupt the process of contemplation.

The canonical texts offer two basic approaches to the preliminary overcoming of the hindrances. One is the suppression of the hindrances by the development of serenity (*samatha*), either access concentration or *jhāna*; the other is their elimination in the course of developing insight. The former is described in the discourses of the Buddha expounding the stages of the "gradual training," the latter in the discourses on the practice of *satipaṭṭhāna*, "the foundations of mindfulness."[1]

Two different approaches are offered because of the differing mental dispositions of disciples. Disciples of a contemplative bent generally incline to first attain concentration by suppressing the

1. For the gradual training, see DN., 1:47-86. MN., 1:175-84; 271-80. For the way of mindfulness, see DN. 2:290-315 and MN. 1:55-63.

hindrances through *jhāna* and then move on to the development of insight. These are called practitioners of the vehicle of serenity (*samathayānika*) who develop "insight preceded by serenity." Other disciples, of an intellectual bent, are generally disposed to strive immediately for insight, leaving until later the task of deepening concentration. These are called practitioners of the vehicle of insight (*vipassanāyānika*) who develop "serenity preceded by insight." Both types must eventually cultivate insight by practising the foundations of mindfulness, since insight-wisdom is needed to reach the supramundane path. They differ, not with respect to the inclusion of insight, but in the sequence they follow to develop it. The practitioner of serenity attains *jhāna*, then cultivates insight, and finally reaches the path. The practitioner of insight reaches the path directly by cultivating insight without relying on a foundation of *jhāna*.

We will now consider in turn each of the two approaches to the overcoming of the hindrances, taking first the approach of the gradual training, in which the attainment of serenity is emphasized, and then the approach of the foundations of mindfulness, which emphasizes the direct development of insight. Finally we will briefly note the way the hindrances are eradicated by the four supramundane paths.

The Way of the Gradual training

We saw above that the hindrances are maintained by a series of conditions beginning with failure to follow after superior men and continuing on through not listening to the true Dhamma, lack of faith, unwise consideration, absence of mindfulness and self-possession, non-restraint of the senses, and engagement in the three types of misconduct. The gradual training, as taught for example in the Sāmaññaphala Sutta, provides the way to reverse this originative pattern. The appearance in the world of the Buddha and his teaching of the doctrine, with which the presentation begins, make available the opportunity to follow after superior men and to hear the true Dhamma. The gain of faith in the teaching leads to commitment to the training, which proceeds according to a graded step-by-step structure designed to lead the practitioner gradually to the goal of liberation.

The most elementary step along the path is the observance of moral discipline. The moral precepts, varying in range from the five precepts for the laity to the full code of Vinaya rules for monks, have the purpose of inculcating restraint of body and speech. Since the unwholesome mental states motivating bodily and verbal misconduct grow stronger when such actions are indulged in, to overcome the defilements it is necessary to begin by controlling their coarser expressions by way of physical and verbal activity. This control is exercised by acting in conformity with the rules of conduct. By careful observance of the moral code, the disciple can eliminate the bodily and verbal modes of misconduct which nourish the five hindrances, thereby weakening their outer impulsive force.

The mere observance of moral rules, however, is not sufficient to combat the hold of the defilements upon the interior processes of the mind. There the defilements must be dealt with at their own level by being subjected to a thoroughgoing mental discipline. This training begins with the restraint of the senses (*indriya saṁvara*). Seeing a visible form with the eye, or cognizing any object with any sense faculty, the disciple does not seize upon its general appearance or details, but controls, guards, and masters his sense faculties. Since misapprehension of sensually attractive and repulsive objects can become a ground for attachment and aversion, the meditator has to avoid fascination with sense objects, confining his attention to the bare facts without elaborating upon them through subjective commentary. Then, endowed with this self-restraint, the disciple develops mindfulness and discernment (*satisampajañña*) in all his activities, movements, and modes of deportment. By examining everything he does with full awareness and clear comprehension, he can prevent these activities from becoming bases for the arising of the hindrances. To avoid attachment and aversion with respect to the physical supports of life, he is further enjoined to cultivate contentment (*santuṭṭhi*) with a bare minimum of robes, food, medicine, and shelter.

These preliminary trainings in morality, restraint of the senses, mindfulness and discernment, and contentment provide the necessary preparation for the cultivation of the higher consciousness through the practice of meditation. Once he has fulfilled these preliminaries the disciple is prepared to go into solitude to develop the *jhānas*, and it is here that he meets the hindrances in direct confrontation. The elimination of the hindrances requires that the meditator first honestly appraises his inner condition by way of introspective self-scrutiny. When sensuality, ill will, and the other hindrances are present, he must recognize that they are present. Then, when their presence has been detected, what is required is knowledge of their appropriate antidotes. Since all the hindrances arise, as we saw, through unwise consideration, it follows that the most efficient general way to overcome them is to alter the manner in which things are attended to. This means, in effect, to replace unwise consideration with wise consideration (*yonisomanasikāra*). By correcting the subtle cognitive distortions which supply the hindrances with food for growth, the constant cultivation of wise consideration removes the hindrances and holds them at bay. Thence the Buddha says that for one who gives wise consideration to things, the unarisen hindrances do not arise and the arisen hindrances are abandoned.[1]

Just as each hindrance has its individual nutriment in the particular kind of unwise consideration corresponding to its own unique operative mode, so each hindrance has its "non-nutriment" (*anāhāra*), the cause for its elimination, in the appropriate kind of wise consideration. Wise consideration of the repulsive feature of things (*asubhanimitta*) is the non-nutriment for sensual desire. Wise consideration of the mental liberation of loving kindness (*mettācetovimutti*) counteracts illwill; wise consideration of the elements of effort (*ārambhadhātu*), exertion (*nikkamadhātu*), and striving (*parakkamadhātu*) counteracts sloth and torpor; wise consideration of tranquility (*cetaso vūpasama*) counteracts restlessness and worry ; and wise consideration of wholesome and unwholesome states (*kusalākusaladhamma*) counteracts doubt.[2]

In the commentaries the Buddha's miscellaneous suggestions on the elimination of the hindrances are organized into a systematic exposition of six measures conducive to the vanquishing of each hindrance. Sensual desire is to be abandoned by:

> Taking up the sensuously inauspicious subject of meditation; application for the development of the jhana on the sensuously inauspicious subject of meditation; the guarded state of the controlling faculties of sense; moderation in food; the sympathy and support of good men in the endeavour; and stimulating talk that helps the accomplishment of the object in view.

1. SN. 5:85.
2. *Ibid.*, 105-106.

Ill will or anger is overcome by the following six measures:

> Taking up the practice of the love subject of meditation; applying oneself to the development of jhana on the thought of love; reflection on one's action as one's own property; abundance of wise consideration; sympathetic and helpful companionship of the good; and stimulating talk that assists the development of the thought of love and the overthrow of anger.

The six things leading to the conquest of sloth and torpor are:

> The seeing of the reason of sloth and torpor in the fact of eating too much, or gluttony; the changing of the postures completely; reflection on the perception of light; staying in the open; sympathetic and helpful companionship of the good: and stimulating talk that assists in dispelling sloth and torpor.

The six things conducive to eliminating restlessness and worry are :

> Knowledge; questioning; understanding of disciplinary rules; association with those more experienced and older than oneself in the practice of things like virtue; sympathetic and helpful companionship; and stimulating talk that helps the rejection of mental agitation and worry.

And the following six measures lead to the transcendence of doubt:

> The state of being learned in the Buddha's teaching; of inquiring about the Buddha, the Teaching, and the Order of Real Saints; of understanding thoroughly the nature of the Discipline; of being decided about the truth of the Buddha, the Teaching, and the Order of the Real Saints; sympathetic and helpful companionship; and stimulating talk that helps to dispel doubt.[1]

The suppression of hindrances effected by these methods is necessary not only as a preliminary for entering upon *jhāna,* but also to ensure the ability to extend the attainment and make it last long. Even if a meditator can overcome the hindrances by force of sheer concentration, if he has not weakened their grip on the subliminal layers of the mind by right reflection and mental

1. Soma Thera, *Way of Mindfulness,* pp. 117-126. MN. A. 1:286-90.

application, they will tend to break through the absorption and dispel his concentration. Therefore, as the *Visuddhimagga* explains, his enjoyment of *jhāna* will be short and superficial:

> When a bhikkhu enters upon a jhana without (first) completely suppressing lust by reviewing the dangers in sense desires, etc., and without (first) completely tranquillizing bodily irritability by tranquillizing the body, and without (first) completely removing stiffness and torpor by bringing to mind the elements of initiative, etc., and without (first) completely abolishing agitation and worry by bringing to mind the sign of serenity, etc., and without (first) completely purifying his mind of other states that obstruct concentration, then that bhikkhu soon comes out of that jhana again, like a bee that has gone into an unpurified hive, like a king who has gone into an unclean park.[1]

The Way of Mindfulness

In the Satipaṭṭhāna Sutta, the "Discourse on the Foundations of Mindfulness,"[2] the Buddha proposes a different approach to overcoming the hindrances, one which utilizes mindful observation of the hindrances themselves as a method for loosening their hold. This approach presupposes the same basic set of preliminaries observed in the gradual training: moral discipline, restraint of the senses, mindfulness and discernment, and contentment. However, instead of employing a variety of techniques to counteract the hindrances with the aim of reaching *jhāna*, the method of mindfulness proceeds directly to the contemplation of mental and bodily phenomena with the aim of arousing insight. The diverse phenomena of body and mind are classified into four "foundations of mindfulness": the body (*kāya*), feelings (*vedanā*), states of mind (*citta*), and mental objects (*dhamma*). The confrontation with the hindrances enters into the last set, the contemplation of mental objects (*dhammānupassanā*) where it comes as the first exercise in this group:

> Herein, monks, a monk dwells contemplating mental objects in mental objects with regard to the five hindrances. And how does

1. PP., p. 157. Vism., p. 122.
2. DN. 2:290-315. MN. 1:55-63.

a monk dwell contemplating mental objects in mental objects with regard to the five hindrances? Herein, monks, when sensual desire is present in him a monk understands: 'There is sensual desire in me.' When there is no sensual desire present in him he understands: 'There is no sensual desire present in me.' He understands how unarisen sensual desire arises, how the arisen sensual desire is abandoned, and how the abandoned sensual desire does not arise again in the future. He understands the same with regard to ill will, sloth and torpor, restlessness and worry, and doubt.[1]

Since it is impossible for a meditator to completely avoid situations tending to provoke the hindrances into activity, he requires a technique which enables him to deal with them effectively at the causal level—to prevent them from arising if possible, or to eliminate them swiftly and surely if they should arise. Mindful observation provides him with just such a technique. Through bare attention to the hindrances, he is able to gain clear comprehension of their individual nature and to discern their causes and conditions. Contemplation of the hindrances is a means both to calm and insight. By directly facing each hindrance that presents itself, the meditator divests it of the destructive power it exercises when it escapes undetected. Repeated introspective self-examination, performed with complete sincerity, gives him the self-knowledge required to transform and purify the direction of his mental life. In this way mindfulness of the hindrances becomes a means to the development of concentrated calm.

The same contemplation, when directed towards the hindrances as bare instances of phenomena exhibiting the universal features of phenomena, becomes a means for gaining insight (*vipassanā*). By observing the rise and fall of the mental processes associated with the hindrances, the meditator gains insight into the fact of impermanence (*anicca*). By attending to their restless nature and disturbing effects, he sees the truth of suffering (*dukkha*). And by viewing the hindrances as mere impersonal events, devoid of any substance or ego-oriented reference point, he comes to an appreciation of the truth of selflessness (*anattā*). If these insights are pursued and developed to the deeper levels they imply, they could even issue in the attainment of the supra-

1. DN. 2:300-301 (Condensed.)

mundane path. In this way the method of mindfulness is able to transform even obstacles to meditation into integral parts of the meditative process.

In the practice of insight meditation no deliberate effort is made to develop concentration. Since the practitioner does not confine his attention to a single object, the arising of concentration at the access or absorption level is impossible. Insight meditation involves the contemplation of the constantly changing flow of phenomena; its object is shifting from moment to moment, as one phenomenon passes away to be replaced by the next. Thus the stability of a single focal point essential to attaining *jhāna* is absent.

Nevertheless, the practice of insight does produce a spontaneous kind of concentration existing concurrently with itself. This kind of mental unification, called "momentary concentration" (*khaṇika samādhi*), comes into being through the fixity with which the mind attends to the changing phenomena. As the mind examines undistractedly the phenomenal process, the successive moments of contemplation acquire a concentrative power equal to the task of suppressing the hindrances. Though it does not possess the force needed to attain *jhāna*, this momentary concentration arisen through insight-practice is sufficiently strong to prevent the hindrances from disturbing contemplation and to allow the wisdom of insight to arise. Thus even without developing *jhāna* the practitioner of bare insight can build up concentration moment by moment, giving him enough mental unification to serve as a basis for insight and attainment of the path.

In sum, the practitioner of serenity first suppresses the hindrances by access concentration or *jhāna*, then begins to develop insight. The practitioner of bare insight begins by contemplating the four foundations of mindfulness. He incidentally develops momentary concentration which eliminates the hindrances, then he arouses insight.

The Eradication of the Hindrances

In the *jhāna* the hindrances are abandoned only by way of suppression. Though inactive, they still remain as dormancies in the mental continuum, capable of cropping up again if sufficiently stimulated. The actual eradication of the hindrances requires the wisdom of the supramundane paths, which abandons the hindrances by cutting them off at the root. This abandonment by cutting off (*samucchedappahāna*) is accomplished with respect to different hindrances by different paths in the four stages of supramundane development. According to the *Visuddhimagga*, the first path, the path of stream-entry (*sotāpattimagga*), cuts off the hindrance of doubt. The second, the path of the once-returner (*sakadāgāmi magga*), weakens all the hindrances but cuts off none. The third, the path of the non-returner (*anāgāmi magga*), cuts off the hindrances of sensual desire, ill will, and worry. And the fourth, the path of arahatship (*arahatta magga*), cuts off the remainder —sloth and torpor and restlessness.[1] Thus it is only the arahat who has completely overcome all the hindrances. In the arahat, the Buddha explains, "these five hindrances are abandoned, cut down at the root, made like a palmtree stump, made something that has ceased to be, so as not to grow again in future time."[2]

The Benefits of Abandoning the Hindrances

From the perspective of Pali Buddhism, the reduction and elimination of the five hindrances is essential not only to the attainment of *jhāna*, but to all aspects of man's moral and spiritual development. The hindrances represent an entire spectrum of defiled mental states, inclusive of the unwholesome roots, the floods, bonds, cankers, clinging, ties and fetters. They are compared to a debt, a disease, imprisonment, slavery, and a desert road, and obscure a man's vision so that he can perceive neither his own good, the good of others, or the good of both.[3] Under their influence he will do what he should not do and neglect what he ought to do.[4] They corrupt the mind and weaken wisdom, cause spiritual blindness and ignorance, destroy wisdom, lead to vexation, and distract from *nibbāna*.[5] Just as gold impaired by five impurities—iron, copper, tin, lead, and silver—is not pliant and wieldy, lacks radiance, is brittle, and cannot be wrought well, so the mind, corrupted by the five hindrances, "is not pliant and wieldy, lacks radiant lucidity and firmness and cannot

1. PP., p. 802. Vism., p. 589.
2. SN. 5:327.
3. DN. 1:73. SN. 5:121-22.
4. AN. 2:67.
5. SN. 5:94, 97.

concentrate well upon the eradication of the taints."[1] Therefore the Buddha can say of them: "Rightly speaking, bhikkhus, one would call the five hindrances 'a heap of unwholesome states'; for indeed the five hindrances are one entire heap of unwholesome states."[2]

The abandonment of the hindrances marks the beginning of freedom: "But when these five hindrances have been abandoned, the bhikkhu looks upon himself as freed from debt, rid of disease, released from prison, a free man, and in a secure place."[3] With the hindrances abandoned, there is no limit to the possibilities for spiritual growth. Just as gold free from the five impurities will be pliant and supple, radiant and firm, and can be wrought well, so, the Buddha says:

> If the mind is freed of these five impurities, it will be pliant and supple, will have radiant lucidity and firmness, and will concentrate well upon the eradication of the taints. To whatever state realizable by the higher mental faculties one may direct the mind, one will, in each case, acquire the capacity of realization, if the (other) conditions are fulfilled.[4]

The abandonment of the five hindrances is the precondition, not only for the attainment of *jhāna*, but for all other higher achievements. It is by the abandoning of the hindrances that the four *Brahmavihāras* become possible, as the meditator must purge his mind of the hindrances prior to suffusing the world with the sublime emotions of loving kindness, compassion, sympathetic joy, and equanimity.[5] Before teaching a receptive disciple the Four Noble Truths, the Buddha always made sure that his mind was "ready, malleable, devoid of the hindrances"[6] in order to ensure his ability to grasp this profound doctrine, inaccessible to a defiled mind. Freedom from the hindrances is thus a requisite for the arising of the "eye of Dhamma," the direct insight into the truth which leads to the first level of liberation, the stage of

1. Nyanaponika Thera, *The Five Mental Hindrances And Their Conquest*, p. 2. An. 3:16.
2. SN. 5:145.
3. DN. 1:73.
4. Nyanaponika, *Five Mental Hindrances*, pp. 2-3. AN. 3:17-18.
5. DN. 3:49-50.
6. DN. 1:110. MN. 1:380.

stream-entry. Those who have entered the stream and are training to attain "supreme security from bondage" dwell having abandoned the five hindrances.[1] It is when his mind has become "concentrated, purified, clarified, free from blemish, devoid of taints, malleable, and workable, steady, imperturbable," that the disciple can direct it to attain the triple knowledge—the recollection of former lives, the knowledge of the passing away and reappearance of beings, and the knowledge of the destruction of the cankers.[2] All who reach liberation first abandon the hindrances:

> All those who are emancipated from the world, who were emancipated or will be emancipated, are emancipated by abandoning the five hindrances which are corruption sof the mind and weakening of wisdom, by establishing their minds well in the four foundations of mindfulness and developing correctly the seven factors of enlightenment.[3]

Even the perfectly enlightened Buddhas of the past, present, and future awaken to supreme, perfect enlightenment by having first abandoned the five hindrances.[4] Thus the Buddha can prescribe his teaching for the destruction of these impediments: "It is for the direct knowledge of these five hindrances, for the full understanding, destruction, and abandoning of them, that the Noble Eightfold Path should be developed."[5]

1. SN. 5:327.
2. MN. 1:182.
3. AN. 5:195.
4. DN. 2:83.
5. SN. 5:60.

Chapter IV

THE FIRST JHĀNA AND ITS FACTORS

The attainment of *jhāna*, as we said at the beginning of the last chapter, can be understood from two points of view: one is the abandoning of the states obstructive to its attainment, the other the acquisition of the states constituting its attainment, its *jhāna* factors. In the case of the first *jhāna* the factors are the five mental states: applied thought (*vitakka*), sustained thought (*vicāra*), rapture (*pīti*), happiness (*sukha*), and one-pointedness of mind (*cittass' ekaggatā*). Four of these are mentioned in the formula for the attainment given in the texts; the fifth, one-pointedness, is added elsewhere.[1] Having led the mind to the *jhāna*, these five remain there as its defining factors, giving it a distinct shape and character. Thence to understand the first *jhāna* it is necessary to approach it via a study of its factors.

In the present chapter we will examine in detail each of the five factors belonging to the first *jhāna*, paying special attention to the specific qualities and functions these phenomena possess in the structure of the attainment as opposed to their occurrence elsewhere. Then we will take a general overview of the *jhāna* itself in order to make it clear that the first *jhāna* is not just a chance combination of unconnected factors but an organic unity of its coordinates. This will be followed by a look at the place of the *jhāna* in the process of consciousness, the cognitive series used to show the dynamic nature of experience. We will conclude the chapter with some remarks on the ways of perfecting the first *jhāna*, a necessary prelude to the higher development of concentration.

Vitakka: A. *General*

The word *vitakka*, derived from the Pali root *tak* (Skt. *tark*) meaning "to think," frequently appears in the texts in conjunction with the other word *vicāra*, which derives from the root *car* (P. & Skt.) meaning "to move." The two together signify two

1. For the formula, see Chapter III, p. 28.

interconnected but distinct aspects of the thought process. We will translate *vitakka* consistently as "applied thought" or simply "thought", *vicāra* as "sustained thought."

In an important passage from the Cūḷavedalla Sutta the wise bhikkhuni Dhammadinnā describes *vitakka* and *vicāra* together as "activity of speech" (*vacīsaṁkhāra*), giving as the reason: "Having first had applied thought and sustained thought, one subsequently breaks out into speech; therefore applied thought and sustained thought are activity of speech."[1] The commentary defines "activity of speech" as that which "causes, creates, or activates speech."[2] The subcommentary explains that *vitakka* and *vicāra* are said to activate speech because "the mind without *vitakka* and *vicāra* is unable to make a verbal sound."[3] Since the inner verbal formulation of ideas precedes and governs their articulation through the apparatus of verbal expression, the mainsprings of intelligible speech turn out to be the key factors in the thinking process.

In the suttas and the Abhidhamma *vitakka* is defined as "application of mind" (*cetaso abhiniropana*), which the *Aṭṭhasālinī* glosses as meaning that *vitakka* applies the mind to the object.[4] The same work singles out application of mind as the primary characteristic of *vitakka*, illustrating it with a brief analogy:

> It (*vitakka*) has the characteristic of the application of the mind to the object. For it mounts the mind onto the object. Just as someone ascends the king's palace in dependence on a relative or friend dear to the king, so the mind ascends the object in dependence on *vitakka*.[5]

This function of applying the mind to the object seems to be the unifying element underlying the different modes in which *vitakka* occurs, giving it a single quality despite the diversity of its applications. In an illuminating discussion, Shwe Zan Aung shows how the directing of the mind and its concomitants to an object is the elemental meaning of *vitakka*, applicable in every case where its operation is discernible. Aung explains:

1. MN. 1:111-12.
2. *Ibid.*, 1:301.
3. MN. T. 2:383.
4. MN. 3:73. Dhs., p. 18. Dhs. A., p. 187.
5. Dhs. A., p. 157.

> [In cognition of sense objects] the element of *vitakka* is present as a directing of concomitant elements to a sensible object. In imagination *vitakka* directs to an image; in conception, to an idea; in symbolical conception, to a concept; in judgments (*vinicchaya-vīthi*), to a proposition; in reasoning (*takkavīthi*), alluded to, but not discussed in my Essay (it belongs to the province of logic), to a syllogism or an inference. In doubt, *vitakka* is a directing now to one object, now to another, back again, etc. In distraction *vitakka* is a directing of mind to several objects one after another. In first *jhāna*, *vitakka* is a directing of mind to the 'after-image' etc., and in transcendental consciousness, *vitakka* is a directing of mind to *nibbāna*, the Ideal. So engaged it is called *sammā-saṁkappa*, perfect aspiration.[1]

In the processes of discursive thinking, thought-conception, and imagination the operation of *vitakka* may be more conspicuous than in other cognitive processes. But wherever it occurs its directive function is at work, becoming especially clear in the first *jhāna*, where verbal thinking is not prominent but *vitakka* remains.

Unwholesome Applied Thought

In itself *vitakka* is neither unwholesome (*akusala*) nor wholesome (*kusala*). It is merely the intrinsically indeterminate function of directing the mind and its concomitants onto the object. Its moral quality is determined by its associated factors, especially its underlying roots. When it is associated with the unwholesome roots—greed (*lobha*), hatred (*dosa*), and delusion (*moha*)—it becomes unwholesome applied thought (*akusala-vitakka*). When it is associated with the wholesome roots—non-greed (*alobha*), non-hatred (*adosa*), and non-delusion (*amoha*)—it becomes wholesome applied thought (*kusalavitakka*).

Unwholesome thoughts are enumerated in the suttas as threefold: thoughts of sensuality (*kāmavitakka*), thoughts of ill will (*byāpāda-vitakka*), and thoughts of harming (*vihiṁsāvitakka*). The former is thought rooted in the factor of greed; the latter two are differing expressions of thought rooted in hatred or aversion. Unwholesome thoughts are also called unwholesome

1. *Compendium*, p. 238.

intentions (*akusalasaṁkappa*), the words *vitakka* and *saṁkappa* being used interchangeably. Thus there are three unwholesome intentions—namely, intentions for sense pleasure, for ill will, and for harming. In describing his practice during his search for enlightenment the Buddha explains that he divided his thoughts into two categories, the wholesome and the unwholesome. On the unwholesome side he placed thoughts of sensuality, thoughts of ill will, and thoughts of harming. Whenever one of these thoughts would arise in him he would dispel it by reflecting that these thoughts lead to the harm of oneself, to the harm of others, and to the harm of both; they are destructive of wisdom, conduce to vexation, and lead away from *nibbāna.* He then explains that whenever one frequently thinks and ponders on these unwholesome thoughts, the mind inclines to them and makes them habitual.[1]

Beyond these three, there are other minor types of unwholesome thoughts spoken of in an unspecified way as "evil unwholesome states" (*papakā akusalā dhammā*). The Buddha declares that the suppression and elimination of all unwholesome thoughts and intentions is one of the essential disciplines of the spiritual life. A monk in training

> ...reflecting wisely, does not give in to an arisen thought of sense pleasures; he abandons it, dispels it, puts an end to it, extinguishes it. He does not give in to an arisen thought of ill will...to an arisen thought of harming...to the evil unwholesome states that arise from time to time; he abandons them, dispels them, puts an end to them, extinguishes them.[2]

In striving for *jhāna*, a yogin has to eliminate all unwholesome thoughts. These will be the *vitakkas* associated with the five hindrances. The thought associated with the first hindrance, sensual desire, is clearly thought of sense pleasures. Thoughts of ill will and thoughts of harming cluster around the hindrance of ill will. The thoughts connected with the remaining hindrances can be seen as comprised in the "evil, unwholesome states" which a monk has to overcome in the course of his training. The texts record several minor distracting thoughts as thoughts about relatives, thoughts about one's district, and thoughts

1. MN. 1:115-18.
2. MN. 1:11.

about one's reputation.[1] The Buddha declares that all unwholesome thoughts cease without remainder in the first *jhāna*, the practice for eliminating unwholesome thoughts being the four right endeavors—the endeavor to abandon arisen unwholesome states, to prevent unarisen unwholesome states from arising, to arouse unarisen wholesome states, and to develop arisen wholesome states.[2]

Wholesome Applied Thought

Wholesome applied thought (*kusalavitakka*) occurs at three levels: [a] the wholesome thought of ordinary morally virtuous states of consciousness, [b] the wholesome thought of the first *jhāna*, and [c] the wholesome thought of the supramundane path.

Ordinary wholesome thought :

Applied thought becomes wholesome in association with the three wholesome roots of non-greed, non-hatred, and non-delusion. Wholesome thoughts that do not directly involve a higher spiritual experience are analyzed in the suttas as threefold: thoughts of renunciation (*nekkhammavitakka*), thoughts of benevolence (*abyāpādavitakka*), and thoughts of harmlessness (*avihiṁsāvitakka*). These three are the direct antitheses of the three unwholesome thoughts. The thought of renunciation opposes the thought of sensuality, the thought of benevolence the thought of ill will, and the thought of harmlessness the thought of harming. Wholesome thoughts are also spoken of under the name "wholesome intentions" (*kusalasaṁkappa*), which are of the same threefold nature. The Buddha explains that when he was a Bodhisatta he established a category of wholesome thoughts into which he put the three thoughts of renunciation, benevolence, and harmlessness. He understood that these thoughts conduce neither to the harm of oneself, to the harm of others, nor to the harm of both, that they lead to the growth of wisdom, to freedom from vexation, and to the attainment of *nibbāna*. Moreover, he declares, by thinking and pondering on the thought of renunciation one can expel thoughts of sensuality ; by thinking thoughts of

1. AN. 1:254.
2. MN. 2:27.

benevolence one can expel thoughts of ill will; and by thinking thoughts of harmlessness one can expel thoughts of harming.[1]

In the Vitakkasaṇṭhāna Sutta the Buddha recommends five methods of using wholesome thoughts to overcome unwholesome thoughts, here classified by way of their roots as connected with desire, hatred, and delusion. One method involves applying a wholesome thought to eliminate the unwholesome thought directly opposed to it :

> Like an experienced carpenter or carpenter's apprentice, striking hard at, pushing out, and getting rid of a coarse peg with a fine one, should the bhikkhu in order to get rid of the adventitious object, reflect on a different object which is connected with skill. Then the evil unskilful thoughts connected with desire, hate and delusion are eliminated; they disappear. By their elimination, the mind stands firm, settles down, becomes unified, and concentrated, just within (his subject of meditation).[2]

The other four ways of overcoming unwholesome thoughts are: [1] pondering on their disadvantages, [2] trying not to pay any attention to them, [3] reflecting on the removal of the [thought] source of those thoughts, and [4] with clenched teeth and tongue pressing the palate, restraining, subduing, and beating down the evil mind by the good mind.

This advice is given to a bhikkhu who is training himself to attain the higher consciousness (*adhicitta*), an equivalent term for *jhāna*. When unwholesome thoughts arise from time to time hindering his progress, he can develop wholesome thoughts to overcome them. The commentary explains that he should reflect on an unlovely object in order to overcome lustful thought connected with living beings and on impermanence in order to overcome thoughts of desire connected with inanimate objects. He should cultivate loving kindness in order to overcome aversion towards living beings and on the primary elements of matter (*dhātumanasikāra*) to overcome aversion towards inanimate objects.[3]

1. MLS. 1:150. MN. 1:116.
2. Soma Thera, *The Removal of Distracting Thoughts*, p. 1. MN. 1:119.
3. Reflection on materiality (*dhātumanasikāra*) means the analysis of material objects into the primary elemental modes of solidity, cohesion, heat,

Wholesome Applied Thought in Jhāna

The general function of *vitakka,* as we have seen, is to direct the mind and its associated factors onto the object. In *jhāna* this function becomes stronger and more pronounced than on other occasions. In the *jhānic* consciousness it would perhaps be more exact to say that *vitakka* thrusts its concomitants into the object rather than that it directs them onto it. The *Visuddhimagga* thus states that in *jhāna* the function of *vitakka* is "to strike at and thresh—for the meditator is said, in virtue of it, to have the object struck at by applied thought, threshed by applied thought."[1]

In the context of *jhāna, vitakka* is qualified by another term, *appanā,* meaning absorption. The *Milindapañha* gives this quality of absorption as the salient characteristic of *vitakka* : "*Vitakka,* your majesty, has the characteristic of absorption. Just as a carpenter drives (*appeti*) a well-fashioned piece of wood into a joint so *vitakka* has the characteristic of absorption."[2] While ordinary *vitakka* can be said to apply the mind merely to the surface of the object, *vitakka* on occasions of *jhāna* penetrates into the depths or interiority of the object. Thus *vitakka* at the level of absorption is compared to a solid body, which sinks to the bottom of water and remains fixed there, the *vitakka* of ordinary consciousness to a hollow ball which stays under the water when held down by pressure but rises to the surface when the pressure is removed.

The object of *jhāna* into which *vitakka* thrusts the mind and its concomitants is the counterpart sign (*paṭibhāganimitta*). We already met this object in our discussion of the suppression of the hindrances, but its nature must now be further clarified. When a meditator begins his practice for the attainment of *jhāna,* he takes a preliminary object such as a colored or elemental *kasiṇa* and concentrates on it until he is able to visualize it with his eyes closed as clearly as when he looks at it with eyes open. Whenever he notices that the object is not clear he should open his eyes and look at the object again until he is able to build up a

and vibration. This analysis into impersonal elements removes the personal reference from the experience and thence deprives the mind of a sufficient ground for aversion.

1. PP., p. 148. Vism., p. 114.
2. Milp., p. 62.

clear mental impression of its mode of appearance. Then, remembering the appearance of the object, he should shut his eyes again and repeat the process of visualization as long as is required. When the object comes into focus when he attends to it with eyes shut as clearly as it does when he looks at it with open eyes the learning sign (*uggahanimitta*) is said to have arisen. At this point the yogin should leave off the physical object and focus solely on the learning sign, developing it by striking at it over and over with applied thought and sustained thought.

As he practices thus the *jhāna* factors grow in strength, each suppressing its respective hindrance. Applied thought, as we saw, counters the hindrance of sloth and torpor, eventually reducing it to a state of complete suppression. When the hindrances are suppressed and the defilements subside the mind enters access concentration. At this time the learning sign is replaced by the counterpart sign. The *Visuddhimagga* explains the difference between the two signs thus :

> In the learning sign any fault in the kasina is apparent. But the counterpart sign appears as if breaking out from the learning sign, and a hundred times, a thousand times, more purified, like a looking-glass disk drawn from its case, like a mother-of-pearl dish well washed, like the moon's disk coming out from behind a cloud, like cranes against a thunder cloud. But it has neither colour nor shape; for if it had, it would be cognizable by the eye, gross, susceptible of comprehension [by insight] and stamped with the three characteristics. But it is not like that. For it is born only of perception in one who has obtained concentration, being a mere mode of appearance.[1]

The counterpart sign is the object of both access concentration and *jhāna*. The difference between the latter two consists, not in their object, but in the strength of their respective *jhāna* factors. In the former the *jhāna* factors are still weak and not yet fully developed, in the latter they are strong enough to actually thrust the mind into the object with the force of full absorption. In this process applied thought is the factor most responsible for bringing about the mind's absorption in the counterpart sign.

Since applied thought in *jhāna* is associated with the wholesome

1. PP., p. 130. Vism., p. 102.

roots, it will take form as a wholesome thought of renunciation, of benevolence, and of harmlessness. Its occurrence in these modes stems from the abandonment of the hindrances of sensual desire and ill will, the defilements responsible for the three unwholesome thoughts of sensuality, ill will, and harming. Since applied thought is needed to directly counter the hindrance opposite to itself, it performs the task of suppressing sloth and torpor. And since it has the general function of directing the mind to the object, it also thrusts the mind into the counterpart sign, keeping it fixed and focussed there with the intensity of absorption-concentration.

Wholesome Applied Thought in the Noble Path

The highest form of wholesome *vitakka* is the *vitakka* included in the Noble Eightfold Path. The Noble Eightfold Path, with its eight factors, operates at two levels—the mundane and the supramundane. The mundane (*lokiya*) path is developed on occasions of wholesome consciousness when the aspirant is striving to reach penetration of the Four Noble Truths and to eradicate defilements. The supramundane (*lokuttara*) path arises when the practice is fully mature. When this path arises it penetrates the four truths by realizing *nibbāna* as its object, simultaneously eradicating defilements.

Wholesome applied thought figures on both levels of the noble path as *sammāsaṁkappa*, "right intention," the second factor of the path. At the mundane stage it is the threefold wholesome thought of renunciation, benevolence, and harmlessness. At the supramundane level it is the directive factor of consciousness which thrusts the mind upon its object, *nibbāna*, the unconditioned element. Mundane right intention, though meritorious, is still described as subject to the cankers (*sāsava*) and resulting in the continuation of existence (*upadhivepakkha*). Supramundane right intention, in contrast is noble (*ariya*) and cankerless (*anāsava*), a factor of the supramundane path. The Buddha defines it as "the thought, applied thought, intention, absorption, focussing, application of mind, activity of speech in the ariyan state of consciousness, the cankerless state of consciousness of one endowed with the noble path developing the noble path."[1] Right intention

1. "Katamo ca bhikkhave, sammāsaṁkappo ariyo anāsavo lokuttaro

of this kind is still a wholesome thought of renunciation, benevolence, and harmlessness, since it is associated with non-greed and non-hatred. Its primary characteristic, however, being its ability to lead the mind into absorption on *nibbāna*, it is this aspect which the Buddha emphasizes in his definition.

Vicāra

Although the word *vicāra* and its derivatives almost invariably appear in the suttas in conjunction with the word *vitakka* and its derivatives, the use of two distinct terms and the occasional recognition that one can occur without the other suggest that they represent different aspects of the thought-process. Since *vicāra* always comes after *vitakka* it would seem to be a more developed phase of thought, and this suspicion is borne out by the analysis given in the Abhidhamma and commentaries. To capture this difference in nuance we render *vicāra* as "sustained thought". The commentaries explain sustained thought thus :

> Sustained thinking (*vicārana*) is sustained thought (*vicāra*); continued sustainment (*anusañcarana*) is what is meant. It has the characteristic of continued pressure on (occupation with) the object. Its function is to keep conascent [mental] states [occupied] with that.

It is manifested as keeping consciousness anchored [on that object].[1] From this explanation several features of *vicāra* emerge. Firstly, by way of etymology, *vicāra* connotes continued movement; thus it is the mind's continued movement upon the object. Secondly, by way of function, *vicāra* performs the task of fixing the mind and its states upon the object; it keeps them anchored there, sustaining the work of mental application effected by *vitakka*. And thirdly, *vicāra* plays the role of examination. By securing the mind's focus on the object it enables the mind to inspect, examine, and investigate the object's properties.

The commentaries spell out the differences between *vitakka* and *vicāra* by describing the former as the first impact of the mind

---

maggaṅgo ? Yo kho, bhikkhave, ariyacittassa anāsavacittassa ariyamaggassa samaṅgino ariyamaggaṁ bhāvayato takko vitakko saṁkappo appanā vyappanā cetaso abhiniropanā vacīsaṁkhāro, ayaṁ bhikkhave sammāsaṁkappo ariyo anāsavo lokuttaro maggaṅgo". MN. 3:73.

1. PP., p. 148. Vism., p. 114. Dhs. A., p. 158.

on the object, the gross and inceptive phase of thought which is like the striking of a bell, and the latter as the act of anchoring the mind on the object, the subtle phase of continued pressure which is like the ringing of the bell.[1] Buddhaghosa gives five additional analogies to illustrate the relationship between *vitakka* and *vicāra*. [1] *Vitakka* is analogous to the movement of a bird taking off into the air by flapping its wings, *vicāra* to its moving through the air gracefully and leisurely with outspread wings. [2] *Vitakka* is comparable to a bee's flying towards a flower, *vicāra* to its buzzing around the flower. [3] *Vitakka* is like the hand that holds firmly a tarnished metal dish that has to be cleaned; *vicāra* is like the other hand that rubs it with powder, oil, and a woolen pad. [4] *Vitakka* is like the supporting hand of a potter when he is making a pot, *vicāra* like the hand that moves back and forth. [5] *Vitakka* is like the compass pin that stays fixed to the center when one is drawing a circle, *vicāra* like the pin that revolves around.[1]

These similes make it clear that despite their constant concomitance, *vitakka* and *vicāra* perform different tasks, the former enjoying a functional priority over the latter. *Vitakka* brings the mind to the object, *vicāra* fixes and anchors it there. *Vitakka* focusses the mind on the object, *vicāra* examines and inspects what is focussed on. *Vitakka* brings a deepening of concentration by again and again leading the mind back to the same object, *vicāra* sustains the concentration achieved by keeping the mind anchored on that object. In their union they are indispensable for the achievement and stabilization of the first *jhāna*.

Pīti

The third *jhāna* factor present in the first *jhāna* is *pīti*, usually translated "joy" or "rapture."[2] In the suttas *pīti* is sometimes said to arise from another aligned quality called *pāmojja*, transla-

1. PP., p. 148. Vism., p. 115.

2. The Venerable Nanamoli, in his translation of the *Visuddhimagga*, renders *pīti* by "happiness", but this rendering seems misleading since most translators use "happiness" as an English equivalent for *sukha*, the quality of pleasurable feeling present in the *jhāna* as its fourth factor. We will render *pīti* by "rapture", thus maintaining the connection of the term with ecstatic meditative experience.

ted as "joy" or "gladness," which springs up with the abandonment of the five hindrances. When the disciple sees the five hindrances abandoned in himself "gladness arises within him; thus gladdened, rapture arises in him; and when he is rapturous his body becomes tranquil."[1] Tranquility in turn leads to happiness, on the basis of which the mind becomes concentrated, entering the first *jhāna*. Thus we can see that rapture precedes the actual arising of the first *jhāna*, but persists through the remaining stages and continues on as a *jhāna* factor up to the third *jhāna*.

For an analytic treatment of *pīti* we must turn to the Abhidhamma piṭaka and the commentaries. The Vibhaṅga defines the *jhāna* factor of rapture as "gladness, joy, joyfulness, mirth, merriment, exultation, exhilaration, and satisfaction of mind."[2] The commentaries pinpoint *pīti* in terms of its verbal derivation, characteristic, function, and manifestation: "It refreshes (*pīnayati*), thus it is [rapture]. It has the characteristic of endearing. Its function is to refresh the body and the mind, or its function is to pervade (thrill with rapture). It is manifested as elation."[3]

Rapture is closely associated with happiness (*sukha*), but remains different in nature. Happiness is a feeling and thus belongs to the aggregate of feelings (*vedanākkhandha*). Rapture, on the other hand, belongs to the aggregate of mental formations (*saṅkhārakkhandha*). It is not hedonic but directive, referring to the object of consciousness. Shwe Zan Aung explains that "*pīti* abstracted means interest of varying degrees of intensity, in an object felt as desirable, or as calculated to bring happiness."[4] When defined in terms of agency *pīti* is that which creates interest in the object; when defined in terms of its nature it is the interest created in the object. The Abhidhamma subcommentaries state: "It is said that *pīti* has, as its characteristic mark, grasping the object qua desirable."[5] Because it creates a positive interest in the object, the *jhāna* factor of rapture is able to counter and suppress the hindrance of ill will, a state of aversion implying a negative evaluation of the object.

1. DN. 1:73.
2. Vbh., p. 267.
3. PP., p. 149. Vism., p. 115.
4. *Compendium*, p. 243.
5. "Ārammanaṁ kallato gahaṇa lakkhanā ti vuttaṁ." *Three Ṭīkās* p. 75. [quoted in *Compendium*, p. 243].

The commentaries grade rapture into five categories: minor rapture, momentary rapture, showering rapture, uplifting rapture, and pervading rapture.[1] Of these five types, minor rapture is said to be able to raise the hairs on the body. Momentary rapture is like lightning produced moment by moment. Flooding rapture descends on the body and disappears like the waves breaking on the seashore. Transporting rapture is able to lift the physical body and cause it to move from one place to another. All-pervading rapture pervades the whole body. To illustrate the power of uplifting rapture, the commentaries relate the story of the elder Mahātissa, who "aroused uplifting [rapture] with the Enlightened One as object, and rose into the air like a painted ball bounced off a plastered floor." They also relate the story of a young girl who aroused uplifting rapture while contemplating the thought of a shrine and travelled to the shrine through the air, arriving before her parents who went there by foot.

The five kinds of rapture are evidently ranked in degrees of intensity, minor rapture representing the weakest degree and all-pervading rapture the strongest. The five in sequence bring about the gradual perfection of concentration:

> Now this fivefold [rapture], when conceived and matured perfects the twofold tranquillity, that is, bodily and mental tranquillity. When tranquillity is conceived and matured, it perfects the twofold bliss, that is, bodily and mental bliss. When bliss is conceived and matured, it perfects the threefold concentration, that is, momentary concentration, access concentration, and absorption concentration.[2]

Minor rapture is generally the first to appear in the progressive development of meditation, coming into being as defilements subside and the meditator experiences indications of successful concentration. Momentary rapture comes next. Though stronger in its impact than the earlier grade, momentary rapture, as its name indicates, is still ephemeral and cannot be sustained for long. Showering rapture runs through the body, producing a great thrill but without leaving a lasting impact. Uplifting rapture is more sustained but still tends to disturb concentration.

1. In Pali : *khuddhikā pīti, khaṇikā pīti, okkantikā pīti, ubbegā pīti,* and *pharaṇā pīti.* PP., p. 149. Vism., pp. 115-16. Dhs. A., p. 158.
2. PP., p. 150. Vism., p. 117.

The form of rapture most conducive to the deepening of concentration is all-pervading rapture, which is said to suffuse the whole body, so that it becomes like a full bladder or like a mountain cavern inundated with a mighty flood of water. The *Visuddhimagga* states that what is intended by the *jhāna* factor of rapture is this all-pervading rapture, "which is the root of absorption and comes by growth into association with absorption."[1]

Sukha

The next *jhāna* factor is *sukha* (happiness). The word "*sukha*" is used both as a noun meaning "happiness," "ease," "bliss," or "pleasure," and as an adjective meaning "blissful" or "pleasant." As a factor of the first *jhāna*, *sukha* signifies pleasant feeling. The word is explicitly defined in this sense in the Vibhaṅga's analysis of the first *jhāna*: "Therein, what is happiness ? Mental pleasure, mental happiness, the felt pleasure and happiness born of mind-contact, pleasurable and happy feeling born of mind-contact—this is called 'happiness'."[2] The *Visuddhimagga* explains that happiness in the first *jhāna* has the characteristic of gratifying, the function of intensifying associated states, and as manifestation, the rendering of aid (to its associated states).[3]

To understand precisely the nature of the happiness present in the first *jhāna*, a brief discussion of the Buddhist analysis of feeling is necessary. Feeling (*vedanā*) is a mental factor present in all types of consciousness, a universal concomitant of experience. It has the characteristic of being felt, the function of experiencing, and as manifestation the gratification of the mental factors. It is invariably said to be born of contact (*phassa*), which is the coming together (*saṅgati*) of a sense object, a sense faculty, and the appropriate type of consciousness. When these three coalesce consciousness makes contact with the object. It experiences the affective quality of the object, and from this experience a feeling arises keyed to the object's affective quality.[4]

1. PP., p. 151. Vism., p. 117.
2. "Tattha katamaṁ sukhaṁ ? Yaṁ cetasikaṁ sukhaṁ cetasikaṁ sātaṁ cetosamphassajaṁ sātaṁ sukhaṁ vedayitaṁ cetosamphassajā sātā sukhā vedanā." Vibh., pp. 83-84.
3. PP., p. 151. Vism., p. 117.
4. MN 3:242-43.

Since contact is of six kinds by way of the six sense faculties, feeling is also of six kinds corresponding to the six kinds of contact from which it is born. There is feeling born of eye-contact, feeling born of ear-contact, feeling born of nose-contact, etc. Feeling is also divided by way of its affective tone either into three or five classes. On the threefold division there is pleasant feeling (*sukhavedanā*), painful feeling (*dukkhavedanā*), and neither pleasant nor painful feeling (*adukkhamasukhā vedanā*), i.e., neutral feeling. The pleasant feeling may be subdivided into bodily pleasant feeling (*kāyika-sukha*) called "pleasure" (*sukha*) and mental pleasant feeling (*cetasika-sukha*) called "joy" (*somanassa*). The painful feeling may also be subdivided into bodily painful feeling (*kāyika-dukkha*) called "pain" (*dukkha*) and mental painful feeling (*cetasikasukha*) called "displeasure" (*domanassa*). In this system of classification the neutral feeling is called "equanimity' (*upekkhā*). Thus on the fivefold division we find the following five types of feeling: pleasure, joy, pain, displeasure, and equanimity.[1] According to the Abhidhamma, pleasure and pain are found only in association with body-consciousness, joy and displeasure only in association with mind-consciousness, and equanimity in association with both mind-consciousness and the other four classes of sense consciousness.[2]

The Vibhanga statement that the *sukha* of the first *jhāna* is mental happiness born of mind-contact means that it is a form of joy or *somanassa.* The Buddha enumerates contrasting types of mental happiness: the happiness of the household life and that of monastic life, the happiness of sense pleasures and that of renunciation, happiness with attachments and taints and happiness without attachments and taints, worldly happiness and spiritual happiness, the happiness of concentration and happiness without concentration, etc.[3] Happiness associated with greed and directed to pleasurable forms, sounds, smells, tastes, and tangibles is sensual happiness (*kāmasukha*). Happiness associated with the wholesome roots produced by the renunciation of sensual enjoyments is spiritual happiness (*nirāmisasukha*) or the happiness of renunciation (*nekkhammasukha*). The happiness of *jhāna* is a

1. MN. 1:398-400.
2. Narada, *Manual,* pp. 143 ff.
3. AN. 1:80-81.

spiritual happiness born of seclusion from sense pleasures and the hindrances (*pavivekasukha*). It is also a happiness of concentration (*samādhisukha*).

The Buddha shows that happiness is causally conditioned. It arises in the sequence of conditions issuing in liberation. In this sequence it follows rapture (*pīti*) and tranquility (*passaddhi*) and leads to concentration (*samādhi*). The Upanisā Sutta says: "Gladness is the supporting condition for rapture; rapture is the supporting condition for tranquility, tranquility for happiness, happiness for concentration."[1] The commentary explains that "gladness" (*pāmojja*) represents the initial forms of rapture, "*pīti*" the stronger forms. "Tranquility" (*passaddhi*) is the calm that emerges through the subsiding of defilements; the happiness (*sukha*) to which it leads the commentary calls "the happiness preceding absorption"[2] and the subcommentary "the happiness pertaining to the access to *jhāna*."[3] The resulting concentration is the *jhāna* forming a basis for insight (*pādakajjhāna*). From this we can infer that the happiness included in this causal sequence is the nascent *jhāna* factor of *sukha*, which begins to emerge in the access stage and reaches full maturity in the actual *jhāna* itself. But since happiness is always present whenever rapture is present, it follows that happiness must have arisen at the very beginning of the sequence. In the stage bearing its name it only acquires special prominence, not a first appearance. When happiness gains in force, it exercises the function of suppressing its direct opposite, the hindrance of restlessness and worry, which causes unhappiness through its agitating nature.

Pīti and *sukha* link together in a very close relationship, so that it may be difficult to distinguish them. Nevertheless the two are not identical states. *Sukha* always accompanies *pīti* but *pīti* does not always accompany *sukha*: "Where there is *pīti* there is *sukha* but where there is *sukha* there is not necessarily *pīti*."[4] In the third *jhāna* there is *sukha* but no *pīti*. *Pīti*, as we noted, belongs to the aggregate of mental formations, *sukha* to the aggregate of feelings. The *Aṭṭhasālini* explains *pīti* as "delight in the attaining of the

1. SN. 2:30.
2. "Appanāya pubbabhāgasukhaṁ." SN. A. 2:50.
3. "Upacārajjhānasahitasukhaṁ." SN. T. 2:65.
4. "Yattha pīti tattha sukhaṁ yattha sukhaṁ tattha na niyamato pīti." Vism., p. 117. Dhs. A., p. 160.

desired object" and *sukha* as "the enjoyment of the taste of what is acquired," illustrating the difference by means of a vivid simile :

> Rapture is like a weary traveller in the desert in summer, who hears of, or sees water or a shady wood. Ease [happiness] is like his enjoying the water or entering the forest shade. For a man who, travelling along the path through a great desert and overcome by the heat, is thirsty and desirous of drink, if he saw a man on the way, would ask, 'Where is water ?' The other would say, 'Beyond the wood is a dense forest with a natural lake. Go there, and you will get some'. He hearing these words would be glad and delighted, and as he went would see lotus leaves, etc., fallen on the ground and become more glad and delighted. Going onwards, he would see men with wet clothes and hair, hear the sounds of wild fowl and pea-fowl, etc., see the dense forest of green like a net of jewels growing by the edge of the natural lake, he would see the water lily, the lotus, the white lily, etc., growing in the lake, he would see the clear transparent water, he would be all the more glad and delighted, [118] would descend into the natural lake, bathe and drink at pleasure and, his oppression being allayed, he would eat the fibres and stalks of the lilies, adorn himself with the blue lotus, carry on his shoulderst he roots of the mandalaka, ascend from the lake, put on his clothes, dry the bathing cloth in the sun, and in the cool shade where the breeze blew ever so gently lay himself down and say: 'O bliss ! O bliss !' Thus should this illustration be applied : The time of gladness and delight from when he heard of the natural lake and the dense forest till he saw the water is like rapture having the manner of gladness and delight at the object in view. The time when, after his bath and drink he laid himself down in the cool shade, saying, 'O bliss ! O bliss !', etc., is the sense of ease [happiness] grown strong, established in that mode of enjoying the taste of the object.[1]

Rapture and happiness co-exist in the first *jhāna*, thence the commentarial simile should not be taken to imply that they are mutually exclusive. Its purport is to suggest that rapture gains

1. *Expositor,* 1:155-56. Dhs. A., pp. 160-61.

prominence before happiness, for which it helps provide a causal foundation.

In the description of the first *jhāna*, rapture and happiness are said to be "born of seclusion." The Vibhaṅga elaborates: "They are born, well born, come into existence, come well into existence, appear in this seclusion. Therefore 'born of seclusion' is said."[1] The rapture and happiness born of seclusion, the Buddha states, suffuse the whole body of the meditator in such a way that there is no part of his body which remains unaffected by them :

> Monks, secluded from sense pleasures...a monk enters and dwells in the first *jhāna*. He steeps, drenches, fills and suffuses his body with the rapture and happiness born of seclusion, so that there is no part of his entire body that is not suffused with this rapture and happiness. Just as a skilful bath-attendent or his apprentice might strew bathing powder in a copper basin, sprinkle it again and again with water, and knead it together so that the mass of bathing soap would be pervaded, suffused, and saturated with moisture inside and out yet would not ooze moisture, so a monk steeps, drenches, fills and suffuses his body with the rapture and happiness born of seclusion, so that there is no part of his entire body that is not suffused with this rapture and happiness born of seclusion.[2]

Ekaggatā

Unlike the previous four *jhāna* factors, *ekaggatā* or one-pointedness is not specifically mentioned in the standard formula for the first *jhāna*, nor for that matter, in the formulas for any *jhāna* except the second. This omission, however, should not be taken to imply that the other *jhānas* lack one-pointedness, for no *jhāna* is worthy of the name without this salient element. One-pointedness is, in fact, included as a *jhāna* factor by the Mahāvedalla Sutta, where the venerable Sāriputta states : "The first *jhāna*, friend, is five-factored. Herein, when a monk has attained the first *jhāna* there is applied thought, sustained thought, rapture, happi-

1. Vibh., p. 267.
2. AN. 3:25. DN. 1:74.

ness, and one-pointedness of mind. Thus, friend, the first *jhāna* is five-factored."[1] Further, in the Anupada Sutta one-pointedness is also said to be present in the first *jhāna*, coming fifth in a list of constituents immediately preceded by the four familiar factors.[2] The Abhidhamma too grants one-pointedness the status of a *jhāna* factor. The Vibhaṅga, in its chapter on the *jhānas*, states immediately after the standard *jhāna* formula: "(First) *jhāna*: applied thought, sustained thought, rapture, happiness, one-pointedness of mind."[3] The *Abhidhammattha Saṅgha*, a late compendium of Abhidhmma philosophy, defines the first *jhāna* consciousness in exactly the same way.[4] Buddhaghosa gives commentarial sanction to this position by citing the Vibhaṅga to corroborate the inclusion of one-pointedness as a *jhāna* factor.[5] Thus the suttas, the Abhidhamma, and the commentaries—our three authorities—all recognize one-pointedness to be a *jhāna* factor. Perhaps the prominence of one-pointedness in the attainment of *jhāna* was so evident that it was felt unnecessary to mention it separately in the formula.

One-pointedness of mind is a universal mental concomitant present in all states of consciousness. It is the factor by virtue of which the mind is conscious of one and only one object at a time, without being distracted by a multiplicity of objects. As its name indicates, it brings the mind to a single point, namely, the point occupied by the object of mental activity. In unwholesome states of consciousness, however, one pointedness is not strong, as its stabilizing function is constantly being undermined by the defilements. It gains full strength in wholesome or moral states of consciousness, especially in the *jhānas*. The *Aṭṭhasālini* explains :

> As by sprinkling a dusty place with water and smoothing it, the dust subsides only for a short time and again resumes its original condition whenever it is dry, so in the immoral portion, one-pointedness of mind is not strong. And as when we sprinkle a place with water poured from pots and dig it up with spades and cement it by beating, pounding and kneading, an image

1. MN. 1:294.
2. MN. 3:25.
3. Vibh., p. 274.
4. Nārada, *Manual*, p. 42.
5. Vism., p. 119.

is reflected there as in a burnished glass, and the reflection is true any moment though a hundred years were to pass, so in moral [consciousness], one-pointedness of mind is strong.[1]

As a *jhāna* factor one-pointedness is always directed to a wholesome object. It serves to ward off unwholesome influences, in particular the hindrance of sensual desire. As the hindrances are absent in *jhāna* one-pointedness acquires special strength, based on the previous sustained effort of concentration. Its stabilizing function is reinforced by the cooperation of the other *jhāna* factors—by applied thought thrusting the mind upon the object, by sustained thought keeping it anchored there, by rapture and happiness encouraging its interest and satisfaction in the object. Since one-pointedness in *jhāna* directs the other factors to the work of unification, it is called the "faculty of concentration (*samādhindriya*). Because it picks up a stabilizing power which cannot easily be overcome by distracting influences, it is also called the "power of concentration" (*samādhibala*). It brings the mind to a state of serenity (*samatha*) which helps mature the other spiritual faculties and acts as a foundation for liberating insight (*vipassanā*).

One-pointedness is used in the Pali texts as a synonym for concentration (*samādhi*). In fact, as we pointed out above, concentration is defined explicitly in the *Visuddhimagga* as wholesome one-pointedness of mind.[2] Concentration has the characteristic of non-distraction, the function of eliminating distractions, non-wavering as its manifestation, and happiness as its proximate cause.[3] The statement that happiness is the proximate case of concentration alludes to the causal sequence of spiritual development already discussed. When the yogī sees that the five hindrances are abandoned in him gladness (*pāmojja*) springs up. Out of gladness rapture (*pīti*) arises. Rapture produces tranquility of body and mind, tranquility produces happiness, and happiness in turn conduces to concentration. This concentration exercises the task of overcoming sensual desire, the most subtle type of excitement.

1. *Expositor*, 1:190. Dhs. A., p. 188.
2. "Kusalacittass'ekaggatā." Vism., p. 68.
3. *Ibid.*

An Overview of the First Jhāna

The five states designated by the Buddha as the factors of the first *jhāna* should not be understood to be the only mental phenomena present in the *jhāna*. The first *jhāna* contains a great number of mental concomitants functioning in unison as coordinate members of a single state of consciousness. Already the Anupada Sutta lists, as additional components of the first *jhāna*, the following phenomena : contact, feeling, perception, volition, consciousness, desire, decision, energy, mindfulness, equanimity, and attention.[1] In the Abhidhamma literature this list is extended still further. The Dhammasaṅgani, the primary text of the canonical Abhidhamma, states that on the occasion of the first *jhāna* consciousness about sixty mental states are present. Since these represent a smaller number of factors spread out with repetitions over twelve general categories, the synoptical *Abhidhammattha Saṅgaha* reduces them to a set of thirty-three distinct concomitants. Seven—contact, feeling, perception, volition, one-pointedness, the life-faculty, and attention—are factors common to all states of consciousness. Six—applied thought, sustained thought, decision, energy, rapture, and desire—are general non-universal variables. There are present as well the nineteen beautiful factors (*sobhana*) which accompany all wholesome mental states: faith, mindfulness, shame, moral dread, non-attachment, non-hatred, equanimity, tranquility of the (mental) body and the mind, lightness of the (mental) body and the mind, pliancy of the (mental) body and the mind, adaptability of the (mental) body and the mind, proficiency of the (mental) body and the mind, and rectitude of the (mental) body and the mind.[2] In addition the faculty of wisdom (*paññindriya*) is always present in *jhāna*. The two illimitables, compassion (*karuṇā*) and sympathetic joy (*muditā*), may also be present individually, thus bring-

1. In Pali : *Phasso vedanā saññā cetanā cittaṁ chando adhimokkho viriyaṁ sati upekkha manasikāro*. MN. 3:25.

2. Narada, *Manual*, pp. 77-78. "Phasso, vedanā, saññā, cetanā, ekaggatā, jīvitindriyaṁ, manasikāro, vitakko, vicāro, adhimokkho, viriyaṁ, pīti, chando; saddhā, sati, hiri, ottappaṁ, alobho, adoso, tatramajjhattatā, kāyapassaddhi, cittapassaddhi, kāyalahutā, cittalahutā, kāyamudutā, cittamudutā, kāyakammaññatā, cittakammaññatā, kāyapaguññatā, citta paguññatā, kāyujjukatā, cittujjukatā." Ibid., p. 78. See also pp. 131-32.

ing the total of states possible in the first *jhāna* up to thirty-five. The divine abodes of loving kindness (*mettā*) and equanimity (*upekkhā*) are covered by the factors of non-hatred and equanimity, of which they represent certain intensifications.

Nevertheless only five of these states—applied thought, sustained thought, joy, happiness and one-pointedness—are called the factors of the first *jhāna*. The reason is that "when these are arisen *jhāna* is said to be arisen." The *jhāna* is not something apart from these factors which possesses them but the constellation of these factors themselves :

> But just as 'The army with the four factors' and 'music with the five factors' and 'The path with the eight factors (eightfold path)' are stated simply in terms of their factors, so this too should be understood as stated simply in terms of its factors, when it is said to have 'five factors' or 'possess five factors'.[1]

None of the factors, taken in separation from the rest, can constitute the first *jhāna*. For the *jhāna* to arise they all must be present together, exercising their special *jhānic* functions of inhibiting the hindrances opposed to themselves and of bringing the mind into absorption on the object. The five mental phenomena are only *jhāna* factors by virtue of these special functions. Ordinary applied thought (*vitakka*), for example, is not a *jhāna* factor if it does not counter sloth and torpor. Sloth and torpor and applied thought can co-exist in many ordinary states of consciousness, but when applied thought is being developed towards attaining *jhāna* it expels and excludes the hindrance of sloth and torpor. Therefore the applied thought in *jhāna* is of a high quality and specialized function supporting concentration. Similarly for doubt and sustained thought. Sustained thought can be present in the mind while one is in a state of doubt, but as long as doubt is present sustained thought cannot become a *jhāna* factor. When sustained thought is directed to *jhāna* then it shuts out doubt. The same applies to the other three factors. No matter how strong rapture, happiness, and one-pointedness might become in a mind obsessed by the hindrances, they do not constitute the first *jhāna* until the hindrances are eliminated.

Each *jhāna* factor serves as support for the one which succeeds

1. PP., p. 152-53. Vism., p. 118.

it. Applied thought must direct the mind to the object in order for sustained thought to anchor it there. Sustained thought supports the arising of rapture since it is only when the mind is anchored on the object that it can develop the interest needed for rapture to occur. As rapture grows and matures it brings to maturity happiness. This spiritual happiness, by providing an alternative to the fickle pleasures of the senses, encourages the growth of one-pointedness. Desire for sensual pleasure unsettles the mind, preventing the arising of concentration. As the mind begins to find rapture and happiness in a wholesome meditation object, sensual desire is reduced permitting concentration to become stronger. In this way, as Nāgasena explains, all the other wholesome states incline, slope, and lead towards concentration, which stands at their head like the apex on the roof of a house.[1]

In order for a state of mind to qualify as a first *jhāna* state of consciousness the five *jhānic* factors must not only be able to inhibit and occlude the five hindrances, but must also be able to thrust the mind into the object with the intensity of absorption. If the factors are present only in part, if they are all present but lack sufficient strength to exclude the hindrances, if they can exclude the hindrances but cannot put the mind into absorption, the state of consciousness is not the first *jhāna*. But when they arise together performing their individual functions in the production of absorption, the first *jhāna* has arisen complete in its possession of five factors. The *Visuddhimagga* explains this cooperative endeavor culminating in *jhāna* thus :

> But applied thought directs the mind onto the object; sustained thought keeps it anchored there. Happiness [rapture] produced by the success of the effort refreshes the mind whose effort has succeeded through not being distracted by those hindrances; and bliss [happiness] intensifies it for the same reason. Then unification aided by this directing onto, this anchoring, this refreshing and this intensifying, evenly and rightly centers the mind with its remaining associated states on the object, consisting in unity. Consequently possession of five factors should be understood as the arising of these five, namely applied thought, sustained thought, happiness [rapture], bliss [happiness], and unification of mind. For it is

1. Milp., pp. 38-39.

when these are arisen that jhāna is said to be arisen, which is why they are called the five factors of possession.[1]

The Jhāna Thought-Process

The commentaries and later analytical treatises of the Theravāda tradition connect the process of *jhāna* attainment with a special account of the cognitive process (*cittavīthi*) based upon the Abhidhamma. The Abhidhamma analyzes experience into a succession of discrete, causally connected occasions of consciousness called *cittas* or *citt'uppādas*. Each *citta* endures for only a small fraction of a second, undergoing three stages: arising (*uppāda*), duration (*ṭhiti*), and dissolution (*bhaṅga*). *Cittas* succeed one another with inconceivable rapidity, so much so that it is impossible for an average person to note the distinct mental moments. Experience as we know it is a coarse fusion of a sequence of *cittas* indiscernible in their uniqueness and discreteness as they rise and fall away.

According to the Abhidhamma philosophy, *cittas* do not occur in isolation but as parts of a series. These series are of two types. One is the passive stream of consciousness which functions as the underlying "limb of becoming," the life-continuum (*bhavaṅga*). The second type is the process of active consciousness, by which clear perceptions are made, thoughts and volitions generated, and actions performed. This active series is called the cognitive process (*cittavīthi*).

The life-continuum is made up of a succession of *cittas* proceeding through beginningless time. With each new life the continuum springs up in the mother's womb at the moment of conception (in the case of human or animal life), rooted in ignorance, supported by the desire to exist and given its specific form and character by the generative *kamma* of the past. Through the course of a lifetime it continues to function whenever the mind is free from active thought processes. It is most conspicuous in deep sleep, but it also occurs very briefly innumerable times during waking life between occasions of active perception and cognition.

When a sensory datum or idea impinges on the mind, the

1. PP., p. 152. Vism., p. 118.

passive flow of the life-continuum is interrupted. The mind then enters a phase of active consciousness, after which it returns to its passive state. The process of *jhāna* attainment occurs as such an active process of cognition. When the mind has been freed from the hindrances and fully prepared for the attainment of absorption, the mind which has subsided into the life-continuum is stimulated to break out from it by the force of previous intention. This break consists of three moments. The first is simply the past moment of the life-continuum (*atītabhavaṅga*); the second is the vibration of the continuum (*bhavaṅga calana*), caused by the decisive intention; the third is the cutting off or arrest of the passive stream of consciousness (*bhavaṅga upaccheda*), as active consciousness is about to supervene. Immediately after this arrest moment the mind, well-impressed with the counterpart sign of the meditation subject, rises up in active form, adverting to the object through the "mind-door" (*manodvāra*) as a datum of internal perception.

Following the act of adverting, there takes place the most important part of the cognitive process—a succession of highly active occasions of consciousness called *javanas*. We will translate *javana* as "impulsion." As the hindrances have been suppressed the four or five impulsions that arise in the *jhānic* process following the advertance are associated with unusually intense applied thought, sustained thought, rapture, happiness, and one-pointedness. The first impulsion in this series is called "the preliminary work" (*parikamma*), since it prepares the mind for the first *jhāna*. In the case of a quick-witted meditator, the moment of preliminary work is skipped over and the series begins with the next moment. The second impulsion is called "access" (*upacāra*) as it brings the mind to the neighborhood of *jhāna*. The third, called "conformity" (*anuloma*), qualifies the mind further for the *jhāna*. The fourth, called "change-of-lineage" (*gotrabhū*), is the act by which the stream of consciousness crosses over from the sense-sphere plane (*kāmāvacara*) to the *jhānic* plane. These four moments gain the general designation "access concentration" (*upacārasamādhi*), though technically speaking only one is singled out as the moment of access. Immediately after this sequence the *jhāna* consciousness arises. On the occasion of initial attainment it lasts for only one great thought-moment. Then the *jhāna* thought passes away and the mind returns to the passive state of the life-continuum, since the first *jhāna* consciousness is close to the passive continuum.

This process can be made more vivid by the following diagram:

A										B						
1	2	3	4	5	6	7	8	9	10	11	12	13	14	15	16	17
...	...	...	...	...	...	...	...	...	...	...	...	...	...	...	...	...
bh	l	ch	m	p	u	a	g	jh	bh	bh	bh	bh	bh	bh	bh	bh

Here line *A* represents the four great thought moments preceding the *jhāna* process. This comprises the past life-continuum (bh), its vibration (l), its cutting off (ch), and the mind's advertance to the counterpart sign through the mind-door (m). Line *B* represents the lapsing of the mind back into the passive life-continuum after the *jhāna* attainment is over. *P* represents the moment of preliminary work (*parikamma*), *u* the moment of access (*upacāra*), *a* the moment of conformity (*anuloma*), and *g* the moment of change-of-lineage. The following *jh* represents the first *jhāna*. After this the mind relapses into the life-continuum (*bhavaṅga*) which is represented by *bh* repeated seven times. The groups of three dots in each *citta* represent the arising (*uppāda*), duration (*ṭhiti*), and dissolution (*bhaṅga*) of each thought moment.[1]

It is evident from this diagram that on the occasion of initial attainment *jhāna* lasts only for a single thought moment. Unless the meditator masters this attainment by the five ways of mastery to be explained he cannot sustain it. But when he has mastered the *jhāna*, a succession of *jhāna* thought-moments will continue on for as long as he determined before entering the attainment. Therefore if we were to represent this situation diagramatically we would find a repetition of *jh* rather than *bh* after the first *jh* in our diagram.

Perfecting the First Jhāna

The elevated forms of concentration, as we mentioned, are divided into two basic stages, access concentration (*upacāra-*

1. For a more detailed account of the cittavīthi see Nārada, *Manual*, pp. 214-19; Vism., pp. 111-12; Compendium, pp. 54-55.

samādhi) and absorption concentration (*appanāsamādhi*). Access concentration is obtained when the hindrances have been suppressed and the mind has become focussed on the counterpart sign. Absorption concentration develops later when the *jhāna* factors become manifest in full force. The difference between access and absorption lies in the relative strength of the *jhāna* factors. In access the factors are still weak, so that concentration is intermittent. Just as a young child, lifted to its feet, stands for a while and then falls down, the mind in access remains focussed on the sign for a short while and then falls away. In absorption the *jhāna* factors are strong and fully developed; thus the mind can remain continuously in concentration just as a healthy man can remain standing on his feet for a whole day and night.

Absorption concentration is the concentration of the four *jhānas* and access the concentration immediately preceding entrance upon the *jhānas*. Once the meditator gains access and the counterpart sign appears to him, he still has to strive to attain absorption. To develop his practice the *Visuddhimagga* recommends several essential measures based on the testimony of the ancients. He has to live in a suitable dwelling place, rely upon a suitable alms resort, avoid profitless talk, associate only with spiritually-minded companions, make use only of suitable food, live in a congenial climate, and maintain his practice in a suitable posture.[1]

Beyond these measures the earnest yogī should rely on the ten kinds of skill in absorption.[2] The first is "making the basis clean," which means that he should clean his lodging and his physical body so that they conduce to clear meditation. The second is "balancing the spiritual faculties" (*indriyasamattapaṭipādana*). Of the five spiritual faculties, faith must be balanced with wisdom and energy with concentration; the fifth faculty, mindfulness, is always useful and has no opposite counterpart. Third, the yogin must be skilful in producing and developing the sign of concentration. Measures four through seven involve exerting the mind (*paggaha*) on an occasion when it is slack and needs to be exerted, restraining it (*niggaha*) on an occasion when it is agitated and needs to be restrained, encouraging it (*sampahaṅsa*)

1. PP., pp. 132-34. Vism., pp. 103-104.
2. PP., pp. 134-40. Vism., pp. 104-110.

when it is restless or dejected and needs encouragement, and looking at the mind with equanimity (*ajjhūpekkhanā*) when all is proceeding well and interference is not needed. As an eighth measure, the yogī should avoid distracting persons, as a ninth he should approach people experienced in concentration and lastly he should be firm in his resolution to achieve concentration.

After attaining the first *jhāna* a few times the meditator is not advised to set out immediately striving for the second *jhāna*. This would be a foolish and profitless spiritual ambition. Before he is prepared to make the second *jhāna* the goal of his endeavor he must first bring the first *jhāna* to perfection. If he is too eager to reach the second *jhāna* before he has perfected the first he is likely to fail to gain the second and find himself unable to regain the first. The Buddha compares such a meditator to a foolish cow who, while still unfamiliar with her own pasture, sets out for new pastures. She gets lost in the mountains without gaining food or drink and cannot find her way back home.[1]

The perfecting of the first *jhāna* involves two steps: the extension of the sign and the achievement of the five masteries. The 'extension of the sign' (*nimittavaḍḍhana*) means extending the size of the counterpart sign, the object of the *jhāna*. Before entering *jhāna* the meditator mentally determines the boundaries to which he wishes to extend the sign ; then he should enter the *jhāna* and try to expand the sign to those boundaries. Beginning with a small area, the size of one or two fingers, he gradually learns to broaden the sign until the mental image can be made to cover the world-sphere or even beyond.[2]

Following this the meditator should try to acquire five kinds of mastery over the *jhāna*: mastery in adverting, mastery in attaining, mastery in resolving, mastery in emerging, and mastery in reviewing.[3] Mastery in adverting is the ability to advert to the *jhāna* factors one by one after emerging from the *jhāna*, wherever he wants, whenever he wants, and for as long as he wants. Mastery in attaining is the ability to enter upon *jhāna* quickly, mastery in resolving the ability to remain in the *jhāna* for exactly

1. AN. 4:418-19.

2. PP., pp. 158-59. Vism., p. 123.

3. The five are respectively : *Āvajjanavasī, samāpajjanavasī, adhiṭṭhānavasī, vuṭṭhānavasī,* and *paccavekkhanavasī*. For a discussion see Vism., pp. 124-25. PP., pp. 160-61. The canonical source is the Pts., pp. 96-97.

the pre-determined length of time, mastery in emerging the ability to emerge from the *jhāna* quickly, without difficulty, and mastery in reviewing the ability to review the *jhāna* and its factors with retrospective knowledge (*paccavekkhanañāṇa*) immediately after adverting to them. When the yogī has achieved this fivefold mastery, then he is ready to strive for the second *jhāna*.

Chapter V

THE HIGHER JHĀNAS

Having dealt at length with the first *jhāna*, we can now turn to the remaining three members of the tetrad—the second, third, and fourth *jhānas*. As before, taking the stock descriptive formulas of the Pali Canon as our starting point, we will examine these *jhānas* in terms of their process of attainment, factors, and additional concomitants. Our discussion will emphasize in particular the dynamic nature of the course by which the *jhānas* are achieved. The attainment of the higher *jhānas*, we will see, is a process whereby the grosser factors are successively eliminated and the subtler ones brought to greater prominence. From our examination it will become clear that the *jhānas* link together in a graded sequence of development, the lower serving as basis for the higher, the higher refining and purifying states already present in the lower. Finally we will close by considering the relationship between the fourfold scheme of *jhānas* used in the suttas and the fivefold scheme introduced in the Abhidhamma.

The Second Jhāna

The Attainment of the Second *Jhāna*

The formula for the attainment of the second *jhāna* runs as follows :

> With the subsiding of applied thought and sustained thought he enters and dwells in the second *jhāna*, which has internal confidence and unification of mind, is without applied thought and sustained thought, and is filled with rapture and happiness born of concentration.[1]

Like the first *jhāna*, the second *jhāna* is attained by eliminating the factors to be abandoned and by developing the factors of

1. "Vitakka vicārānaṁ vūpasamā ajjhattaṁ sampasādanaṁ cetaso ekodibhāvaṁ avitakkaṁ avicāraṁ samādhijaṁ pītisukhaṁ dutiyajjhānaṁ upasampajja viharati." DN. 1:74.

possession. In this case, however, the factors to be abandoned are the two initial factors of the first *jhāna* itself—applied thought and sustained; the factors of possession are the three remaining *jhāna* factors—rapture, happiness, and one-pointedness. Hence the formula begins "with the subsiding of applied thought and sustained thought," and then goes into the *jhāna*'s positive endowments.

Before he can enter upon the practice for reaching the second *jhāna* the meditator must first perfect the first *jhāna* through the five kinds of mastery.[1] Then, after achieving such mastery, he enters the first *jhāna*, emerges from it, and begins contemplating its defective features. These defects are two: first the attainment is threatened by the nearness of the hindrances, and second its factors are weakened by the grossness of applied and sustained thought.[2] The former we might call the defect of proximate corruption, the latter the inherent defect. Though the first *jhāna* is secluded from the hindrances, it is only a step removed from the non-*jhānic* consciousness and thus provides only a mild safeguard against the hindrances. If the yogin is not mindful his contacts with sense objects can incite unwise reflection and thereby bring the hindrances into activity once again. To ensure himself of further protection from the hindrances the meditator realizes that the deeper absorption of the higher *jhānas* is needed.

The inherent defect of the first *jhāna* is its inclusion of applied thought and sustained thought. When striving for the first *jhāna* these two factors helped in the struggle against the hindrances, applied thought directing the mind onto the object, sustained or anchoring it there and preventing it from drifting away. But after mastering the first *jhāna* the meditator comes to see that applied and sustained thought are relatively gross. Not only are they gross in themselves, but also by reason of their grossness, they weaken the other factors. The rapture, happiness and one-pointedness associated with applied and sustained thought, he sees, are not as powerful and peaceful as they would be if they were freed from this association. Hence he regards applied and sustained thought as impediments needing to be eliminated. As the Buddha explains in the Poṭṭhapāda Sutta, what the medi-

1. See Ch. IV p. 104.
2. PP., p. 161. Vism., p. 125.

tator previously perceived as subtle and actual subsequently appears to him to be gross and harmful.[1] Then he eliminates it by attaining a higher *jhāna*.

The meditator thus comprehends that in spite of his mastery of the first *jhāna*, his progress is not fully satisfactory; the first *jhāna*—the cherished object of his early striving—itself turns out to be defective, corrupted by the proximity of the hindrances and by the grossness of its factors. He then calls to mind his theoretical knowledge of the second *jhāna*. He reflects that this *jhāna* is free from applied thought and sustained thought, that it is therefore more tranquil, subtle, and sublime than the first. While applied thought and sustained thought appear gross, rapture, happiness, and one pointedness appear peaceful. By so reflecting the meditator ends his attachment to the first *jhāna* and engages in renewed striving with the aim of reaching the second *jhāna*.

The meditator applies his mind to his meditation subject—a *kasiṇa* or the breath—repeatedly concentrating on it with the intention of overcoming applied and sustained thought. When his practice is sufficiently matured the second *jhāna* arises equipped with its three factors—rapture, happiness, and one-pointedness.

The thought process by which the second *jhāna* is attained is similar to that for the first. First there occur the three moments of the life-continuum—the past moment, vibration, and cutting off. This is followed by the mind-door adverting consciousness, the four preparatory moments—preliminary work, access conformity, and change-of-lineage—and then the moment of the second *jhāna*. Again, in the case of a quick-witted meditator, the moment of preliminary work is bypassed. There is, however, one important difference between the first and second *jhānas* concerning the relation of their access moments to the *jhānas* themselves. In the case of the first *jhāna* the access moments have the same factorial constitution as the *jhāna* moments. The difference concerns only their intensity. But in the case of the second *jhāna* the access and *jhāna* moments differ in their actual makeup. Whereas the second *jhāna* moment is free from applied and sustained thought, the latter are still present in all four preliminary

1. DN. 1:178-203.

moments. Only in the moment of full absorption are they totally eliminated. The same is also true for the remaining higher *jhānas*.

After stating that the yogin enters and abides in the second *jhāna* through the subsiding of applied and sustained thought (*vitakkavicārānaṁ vūpasamā*), later in the descriptive formula the Buddha says that the *jhāna* is "without applied thought and sustained thought" (*avitakkaṁ avicāraṁ*). This phrase appears at first sight to be an unnecessary repetition of the former, but the *Visuddhimagga* defends this choice of wording, showing that the second phrase is not redundant but fulfills a different function. The commentator points out that the opening phrase is stated, firstly, in order to show directly that the second *jhāna* is attained through the surmounting of the gross factors of the first *jhāna*; secondly, to show that the internal confidence and unification of mind, mentioned immediately afterwards, come about with the act of stilling applied and sustained thought; and thirdly, to show that this *jhāna* is without applied and sustained thought, not through their bare absence as in the higher *jhānas* or in elementary sense consciousness, but through their actual stilling. But the first phrase does not state blankly that the second *jhāna* is devoid of applied and sustained thought. To make this latter meaning explicit a separate phrase is needed; hence the words "without applied thought and sustained thought."[1]

Because the second *jhāna* is free from applied and sustained thought it is called the "noble silence."[2] As we saw applied thought and sustained thought are the primary mental factors causing vocal activity (*vacisaṅkhāra*). Therefore, when these springs of verbal activity come to a stop inner mental verbalization also subsides, replaced by a profound inward silence of the mind. Since this stilling of thought occurs at the level of the second *jhāna*, the *jhāna* acquires the name "noble silence" (*ariyo tunhībhāvo*).

Internal Confidence (*ajjhattaṁ sampasādanaṁ*)

With the subsiding of applied thought and sustained thought the meditator gains internal confidence (*ajjhattaṁ sampasādanaṁ*).

1. PP., pp. 163-64. Vism., p. 130.
2. See SN. 2:273.

The word *sampasādana,* which we translate as "confidence," has two connotations: one is faith in the sense of belief, trust, or conviction; the other is tranquility. Both these meanings are relevant to the second *jhāna.* On the one hand the meditator gains stronger faith in the Buddha and his teaching as he sees the effectiveness of his practice; on the other, as a result of this confidence, he gains tranquility.

The Vibhaṅga explicitly defines internal confidence as faith: "'Confidence' : faith, the placing of faith, trust, conviction."[1] Since, according to the Abhidhamma, faith is present in every wholesome state of consciousness, it must also be present in the first *jhāna.* However, in the first *jhāna* the meditator's faith lacks full clarity and serenity due to the disturbing activity of applied thought and sustained thought and thus cannot be called "confidence". The *Visuddhimagga* explains :

> The first *jhāna* is not fully confident owing to the disturbance created by applied and sustained thought, like water ruffled by ripples and wavelets. That is why, although faith does exist in it, it is not called 'confidence'.[2]

When applied and sustained thoughts are made to subside the mind of the meditator becomes very clear and peaceful, and his faith takes on the quality of confidence. To indicate this maturation of faith the term "internal confidence" is mentioned in the description of the second *jhāna* but not in that of the first.

Unification of Mind (*cetaso ekodibhāvaṁ*)

The texts and commentaries equate unification of mind with one-pointedness and concentration. Though concentration is present already as a factor of the first *jhāna,* it only gains special mention in the formula for the second *jhāna* since it is here that it first acquires eminence. The concentration of the first *jhāna,* being subject to the disturbing influence of applied thought and sustained thought, is still imperfect. But in the second *jhāna,* with these gross factors suppressed and the mind purified by inner confidence one-pointedness becomes stronger and more

1. Vibh., p. 268.
2. PP., p. 163. Vism., pp. 126-27.

stable. The *Visuddhimagga* explains the eminence of this mental unification in its etymological account of the term :

> Here is the construction of the meaning in that case. Unique (*eka*) it comes up (*udeti*), thus it is single (*ekodi*); the meaning is, it comes up as the superlative, the best, because it is not overtopped by applied and sustained thought, for the best is called 'unique' in the world. Or it is permissible to say that when deprived of applied and sustained thought it is unique, without companion. Or alternatively: it evokes (*udeyati*) associated states, thus it is an evoker (*udi*); the meaning is, it arouses. And that is unique (*eka*) in the sense of best, and it is an evoker (*udi*), thus it is a unique evoker (*ekodi*=single). This is a term for concentration.[1]

Concentration (*samādhi*)

This *jhāna*, or the rapture and happiness of this *jhāna*, are said to be "born of concentration" (*samādhijaṁ*). The concentration that gives birth to this *jhāna* can be understood in two ways—either as the earlier stages of concentration leading up to the second *jhāna*, or as the mental factor of concentration immediately associated with the second *jhāna* itself.[2] To reach the second *jhāna* the meditator had to pass through three earlier degrees of concentration—the preliminary concentration of his initial endeavor, access concentration and the absorption concentration of the first *jhāna*. All three of these stages can be seen as the concentration giving birth to the second *jhāna*. Alternatively, the concentration giving birth to the *jhāna* can be identified with the one-pointedness contained in the second *jhāna* itself. As in the case of the phrase "unification of mind," special emphasis is placed on this concentration to show its secure establishment following the cessation of applied and sustained thought, which hinder advanced concentration by activating discursive thinking. The *Visuddhimagga* points out, in regard to the concentration of the second *jhāna*, that "it is only this concentration that is quite worthy to be called 'concentration' because of its complete confidence and

1. PP., pp. 162-63. Vism., p. 126.
2. *Ibid.*, p. 105.

extreme immobility due to absence of disturbance by applied and sustained thought."[1]

Rapture and Happiness (*pītisukhaṁ*)

Rapture and happiness in the first *jhāna*, as we saw, are described as born of seclusion (*vivekajaṁ pītisukhaṁ*). In contrast, the rapture and happiness of the second *jhāna* are said to be born of concentration (*samādhijaṁ pītisukhaṁ*). The pre-*jhānic* condition for the arising of rapture and happiness in the first *jhāna* is seclusion, which means the suppression of the five hindrances in access concentration. The preliminary condition for the arising of rapture and happiness in the second *jhāna* is the concentration of the first *jhāna*. Thus when rapture and happiness are said to be "born of concentration," this can be taken to indicate that their source is the first *jhāna* concentration. However, the phrase can also be understood to mean that they are born from the concomitant concentration of the second *jhāna*, as the *Visuddhimagga* allows. Because they are not weakened by the gross factors of applied and sustained thought, the rapture and happiness of the second *jhāna* are more peaceful and profound than those of the first. The Buddha says that this rapture and happiness born of concentration suffuse the meditator's entire body just as the cool current of a spring would suffuse a pool with water.[2]

General Remarks on the Second *Jhāna*

As the first *jhāna* has five factors, the second *jhāna* has three—rapture, happiness, and one-pointedness. The two factors present in the first *jhāna* but absent in the second are the two gross elements which have been made to subside—applied thought and sustained thought. Unlike the first *jhāna* formula, which does not mention one-pointedness explicitly, the formula for the second *jhāna* refers to it twice—one time directly under the synonymous term "unification of mind" (*ekodibhavaṁ*) and once obliquely by calling the rapture and happiness "born of concen-

1. PP., p. 164. Vism., p. 127.
2. DN. 1:74-75.

tration" (*samādhijaṁ*). Even though the three factors of the second *jhāna* are the same in nature as those in the first, they are still different in quality, acquiring a subtler, more peaceful, and more exquisite tone as a consequence of the elimination of the gross elements.

Whereas all the states mentioned in the first *jhāna* formula are *jhāna* factors, the present formula includes "internal confidence." This indicates that the constituency of the *jhāna* is wider than its basic factors. The Anupada Sutta, already referred to, gives the following expanded list of states included in the second *jhāna* : internal confidence, rapture, happiness, one-pointedness of mind, contact, feeling, perception, volition, consciousness, desire, decision, energy, mindfulness, equanimity, and attention.[1] The Dhammasaṅgani lists close to sixty states, including all those present in the first *jhāna* except applied and sustained thought and their equivalents.[2] The *Abhidhammattha Saṅgaha*, too, mentions thirty-three possible constituents of the second *jhāna*, i.e. all those of the first *jhāna* except applied thought and sustained thought.[3]

The Third Jhāna

The Attainment of the Third *Jhāna*

To attain the third *jhāna* the meditator must apply the same method he used to ascend from the first to the second. After mastering the second *jhāna* in the five ways already described, he enters it, emerges, and reflects upon its defects. He sees that this attainment is threatened by the two flaws, the defect of proximate corruption and the inherent defect. The defect of proximate corruption is the nearness of applied and sustained thought. If these should arise they will disrupt the serenity and powerful concentration of the second *jhāna* and bring the mind back down to the first *jhāna* or to lower states of consciousness. The inherent defect is the presence of rapture (*pīti*), a relatively gross factor which weakens the other *jhāna* factors remaining in the mind. As the Buddha says: "Whatever there is in it pertaining to rapture, of mental excitation, that appears to be gross."[4]

1. MN. 3:26.
2. Dhs., p. 44.
3. Narada, *Manual*, pp. 131-32. See above Ch. IV., pp. 94-95.
4. DN. 1:37.

Since the meditator finds that the second *jhāna* is insecure and corrupted by rapture, he cultivates an attitude of indifference towards it. He intensifies his attention to happiness (*sukha*) and one-pointedness (*ekaggatā*), considering them as more peaceful and sublime. Putting away attachment to the second *jhāna*, he focusses his mind on gaining the third *jhāna*, which appears superior for the reason that it possesses happiness and mental unification free from the disturbing influence of rapture. He again renews concentration on his meditation object with the aim of ascending to the higher *jhāna*. When his practice matures, he attains the third *jhāna* with its factors of happiness and one-pointedness. In the attainment the mind passes through the same stages of the thought-process as in the earlier *jhānas*. But here applied thought, sustained thought, and rapture are present in the moments of access, only disappearing on the actual occasion of full absorption.

The standard formula for the third *jhāna* appears in the suttas as follows :

> With the fading away of rapture, he dwells in equanimity, mindful and discerning; and he experiences in his own person that happiness of which the noble ones say: 'Happily lives he who is equanimous and mindful'—thus he enters and dwells in the third *jhāna*.[1]

The formula indicates that the third *jhāna* contains, besides the *jhāna* factors, three additional mental concomitants not included among the *jhāna* factors. These three are equanimity (*upekkhā*), mindfulness (*sati*), and clear comprehension or discernment (*sampajañña*). Therefore a peculiarity of this formula is that it mentions three mental properties which are not *jhāna* factors and does not mention one-pointedness, which along with happiness is a factor.

We will now discuss in turn the three additional mental concomitants and the two *jhāna* factors mentioned in the formula.

1. "Pītiyā ca virāgā upekkhako ca viharati sato ca sampajāno, sukhaṁ a kāyena paṭisaṁvedi yaṁ taṁ ariyā ācikkhanti 'upekkhako satimā sukha-vihārī ti tatiyaṁ jhānaṁ upasampajja viharati." DN. 1:75.

Equanimity (*upekkhā*)

The Pali word for equanimity, *upekkhā* (Skt. *upekṣā*), is formed from the prefix *upa* and the root *ikh* (Skt. *ikṣ*) meaning "to see". The commentaries on the *jhāna* formula gloss the clause "dwells in equanimity" (*upekkhako viharati*) thus:

> He dwells in equanimity: it watches [things] as they arise (*upapattito ikkhati*), thus it is equanimity (upekkhā—or on-looking); it sees fairly, sees without partiality (*a-pakkhapātita*), is the meaning. A possessor of the third *jhāna* is said to dwell in equanimity since he possesses equanimity that is clear, abundant and sound.[1]

The word *upekkhā* or "equanimity" occurring in the Pali texts has a wide range of meanings. The *Visuddhimagga* isolates ten, partly over-lapping, kinds of equanimity found in the canon. These are as follows :

> [1] Six-factored equanimity, [2] equanimity as a divine abiding, [3] equanimity as an enlightenment factor, [4] equanimity of energy, [5] equanimity about formations, [6] equanimity as a feeling, [7] equanimity about insight, [8] equanimity as specific neutrality, [9] equanimity of *jhāna*, and [10] equanimity of purification.[2]

To gain a clear understanding of the equanimity included in the third *jhāna* it will be helpful to consider each briefly in turn.

[1] Six-factored equanimity is the arahat's unbiased responses, free of attachment and aversion, towards pleasant and unpleasant sense objects—forms, sounds, smells, tastes, tangibles, and mental data—experienced through the six senses. [2] Equanimity as a divine abiding is the socially directed meditative state marked by the transcending of approval and resentment towards living beings, the sublime attitude of impartiality which looks upon all beings equally without preferences or dis-

1. PP., p. 166. Vism., p. 129.

2. In Pali the ten are : [1] chalaṅgupekkhā, [2] brahmavihārupekkhā, [3] bojjhaṅgupekkhā, [4] viriyupekkhā, [5] saṅkhārupekkhā, [6] vedanupekkhā, [7] vipassanupekkhā, [8] tatramajjhattupekkhā, [9] jhānupekkhā, and [10] parisuddhi upekkhā. The following summary is based on PP., pp. 166-67. Vism., pp. 129-30.

crimination. [3] Equanimity as an enlightenment factor is the balanced frame of mind developed in practising the path to liberation; it comes last in the seven factors of enlightenment, preceded by the enlightenment factors of mindfulness, investigation, energy, rapture, tranquility, and concentration. [4] Equanimity of energy is the balanced application of energy by avoiding over-exertion and laxity. [5] Equanimity about formations signifies the wisdom which looks with detached indifference upon the phenomena that come within its view, free from clinging. In the case of serenity meditation it consists in detachment from the eight sets of factors to be surmounted by the eight attainments (the four *jhānas* and four *āruppās*). In the case of insight meditation it is the mental composure that evolves for the purpose of gaining the paths and fruits.[1] [6] Equanimity as a feeling is neutral feeling, i.e. feeling which is neither painful nor pleasant (*adukkhamasukhā vedanā*). [7] Equanimity about insight is indifference towards further investigating the characteristics of phenomena after these characteristics have been seen with insight knowledge. [8] Specific neutrality (*tatramajjhattatā*) is the mental factor responsible for maintaining balance among the component factors in the beautiful (*sobhana*) states of consciousness. The commentaries define it as the "equal efficiency of conascent states."[2] According to the Abhidhamma specific neutrality is present in every beautiful state of consciousness, giving balance and harmony to the virtuous mind. As a particular mental factor (*cetasika*), specific neutrality can assume different forms in different contexts. In fact, as we will see below, it appears as six of the ten kinds of equanimity being outlined here. [9] Equanimity of *jhāna*, as the name implies is the equanimity present in the *jhāna*. And [10] purification equanimity is the equanimity of the fourth *jhāna*, purified of all obstructions.

These ten kinds of equanimity can be reduced to four basic factors. Equanimity about formations and equanimity about insight are modes of wisdom (*paññā*), the wisdom that looks at things with detached indifference. Equanimity of energy and equanimity of feeling are, respectively, the mental factors of

1. See Pts. pp., 60-65.
2. PP., pp. 167, 527. "Sahajātānaṁ samavāhitabhūtā" Vism., pp. 130, 395.

energy (*viriya*) and feeling (*vedanā*). The remaining six are modes of specific neutrality (*tatramajjhattatā*). The *Vimativinodani* points out how this single versatile factor can fulfill different roles under different circumstances :

> The same centeredness (of mind) is called the six-factored equanimity of an arahat as it does not abandon the natural state of purity when desirable or undesirable objects of the six kinds come into focus in the six doors; equanimity as a divine abiding, as it maintains the balanced state of mind towards all beings; equanimity as an enlightenment factor, as it balances the associated mental states; specific equanimity of *jhāna* as it unbiasedly balances the great happiness in the third, *jhāna*; and purification equanimity, as it purifies all mental factors in the fourth *jhāna*. Thus it is said to be six-fold owing to circumstantial differences.[1]

The kind of *upekkhā* referred to in the third *jhāna* formula by the phrase "he abides in equanimity" is the equanimity of *jhāna*, a form of specific neutrality. Since the latter is present in all wholesome states of consciousness, it must have been present as well in access concentration and in the two lower *jhānas*. But it is only mentioned first in the third *jhāna* formula since it is here that it first gains prominence, the fading away of rapture allowing it to become evident.

Nevertheless, though equanimity is referred to twice in the formula, it is not cited as a *jhāna* factor for the third *jhāna*. Only two mental states are designated as third *jhāna* factors, namely, happiness and one-pointedness. Thus in the Vibhaṅga's treatment of the third *jhāna*, though equanimity is included among the prominent components of the *jhāna*, the *jhāna* itself is said to be a two-factored attainment comprising happiness and one-pointedness.[2] The reason is that only those phenomena present in a meditative attainment which oppose the hindrances and aid mental unification are counted as *jhāna* factors. These are the five mentioned in the Mahāvedalla Sutta, plus neither painful-nor-pleasant feeling, a factor of the fourth *jhāna*.

The statement that both happiness and equanimity are present

1. Vimv. T., 1:73-74.
2. See Vibh., pp. 270, 275.

in the third *jhāna* might create the impression that two different feelings are present simultaneously. Such confusion is due to misinterpreting this equanimity as equanimous feeling (*vedan' upekkhā*). Equanimous feeling and specific neutrality, though often concomitant, are distinct mental factors. The latter, which belongs to the aggregate of mental formations (*saṅkhārakkhandha*), is an attitude of reflective impartiality towards sense objects, beings, or formed phenomena. Equanimous feeling, which belongs to the aggregate of feelings (*vedanākkhandha*), is feeling which is neither painful nor pleasant. Whereas specific neutrality is a morally beautiful mental factor present only in wholesome or indeterminate states of consciousness, equanimous feeling is a variable which can be present in any kind of consciousness—wholesome, unwholesome, or indeterminate. Since the moral wholesome quality of *jhānic* equanimity or specific neutrality can enter into association with either pleasant or indifferent feeling, there is no difficulty in admitting the simultaneous presence of equanimity and happiness.

Mindfulness and Discernment

Mindfulness (*sati*) and discernment (*sampajañña*) are two mental states which work hand in hand to facilitate progress in the spheres both of serenity and insight. Mindfulness means the remembrance of an object, in the context of meditation the contant bearing of the meditation subject in the mind. Because mindfulness is a very clear and steady state, it is said to have the characteristic of "not floating away" (*apilāpanatā*).[1] The *Aṭṭhasālini* compares mindfulness to the king's treasurer who reminds the king of everything he has in his treasury: mindfulness reminds the meditator of both his good and bad qualities, and also reminds him to avoid the bad and cultivate the good.[2] Discernment is in nature the same as wisdom (*paññā*), which has illuminating and understanding as characteristics.[3] The *Aṭṭhasālini* states that discernment has the characteristic of non-delusion,

1. Dhs. A., p. 188.
2. Ibid., pp. 164-65.
3. "Obhāsana lakkhaṇā paññā, pajānana lakkhaṇā ca." Ibid., p. 165.

the function of scrutinizing, and the manifestation of examination.[1]

Mindfulness and discernment are most conspicuous in insight meditation, but they contribute as well to the attainment of *jhāna*. Though they are mentioned for the first time in the formula for the third *jhāna*, this should not be taken to imply that they appear for the first time only here. They occur as well in the first two *jhānas*, but because these *jhānas* are comparatively gross they do not reveal the functions of mindfulness and discernment with sufficient clarity to merit attention. These functions become evident when the mind reaches the subtlety of the third *jhāna*. The two are particularly needed to avoid a return of rapture. The *Aṭṭhasālini* points out that just as a suckling calf, removed from the cow and left unguarded, again approaches the cow, so the happiness of the third *jhāna* tends to veer towards rapture if unguarded by mindfulness and discernment.[2] Once rapture arises the third *jhāna* is lost. It is mindfulness and discernment which hold the *jhānic* mind on happiness rather than rapture, to which the mind naturally tends to cling in their absence. In order to emphasize this function they perform, the two are mentioned here rather than in the descriptions of the preceding *jhānas*.

Happiness

The feeling experienced in the third *jhāna* is happiness free from rapture (*nippītikasukha*), which the Buddha says suffuses the meditator's body in the way the waters of a pond suffuse a lotus flower growing in its depths.[3] The formula for the third *jhāna* says of the meditator that "he experiences happiness with his body" (*sukhaṁ ca kāyena paṭisaṁvedeti*). The word "body" (*kāya*) could be misinterpreted if we are not careful about its usage in this particular context, leading us to the wrong conclusion that the happiness belonging to the *jhāna* is pleasant bodily feeling. The happiness is still mental pleasure (*cetasika sukha*)

1. "Asammohalakkhaṇaṁ sampajaññaṁ. Tiraṇarasaṁ; pavicaya paccupaṭṭhānaṁ." Ibid. p. 219.
2. Ibid. p. 219.
3. DN. 1:75.

or joy (*somanassa*), as in the first two *jhānas*. The word "body" here means the mental body (*nāmakaya*), that is, the group of mental factors associated with consciousness. However, the happiness of the mental body also overflows and produces physical pleasure. For the meditator's mind, saturated with happiness, originates certain types of subtle material phenomena which cause bodily pleasure even after the meditator has emerged from *jhāna*. The *Visuddhimagga* explains:

> Now as to the clause 'he feels bliss [happiness] with his body', here although in one actually possessed of the third jhana there is no concern about feeling bliss [happiness], nevertheless he would feel the bliss [happiness] associated with his mental body, and after emerging from the jhana he would also feel bliss [happiness] since his material body would have been affected by the exceedingly superior matter originated by that bliss [happiness] associated with the mental body. It is in order to point to this meaning that the words, 'he feels bliss [happiness] with his body' are said.[1]

One-pointedness

The second component factor of the third *jhāna* is one-pointedness of mind (*ekaggatā*). Though one-pointedness is not mentioned by name in the third *jhāna* formula, it is explicitly classed as a *jhāna* factor in the Vibhaṅga.[2] Moreover, the mind in the third *jhāna* is full of happiness, and the mind suffused with happiness, as we saw earlier, gains concentration, identical with one-pointedness. Therefore one-pointedness must be present here. One-pointedness is mentioned only in the formula for the second *jhāna* since it there acquires novel intensity due to the subsiding of applied and sustained thought.

In terms of the Abhidhamma analysis, the third *jhāna* consciousness includes all the mental phenomena originally present in the first *jhāna* consciousness except applied thought, sustained thought, and rapture. Thus it contains a minimum of thirty concomitants of consciousness, and can further include compassion and

1. PP., p. 169. Vism., p. 132.
2. Vibh., p. 275.

sympathetic joy separately at times when these qualities are developed to the *jhānic* level.[1]

After attaining the third *jhāna*, the yogin proceeds to perfect it through the five types of mastery, and then prepares himself for the next step.

The Fourth Jhāna

The Attainment of the *Jhāna*

Having achieved the fivefold mastery over the third *jhāna*, the meditator enters it, emerges from it, and reviews its constituting factors. When he reviews the *jhāna* the meditator sees the defect of proximate corruption—that the attainment is threatened by the nearness of rapture which though suppressed with the achivement of the third *jhāna*, still threatens to swell up again due to its natural association with happiness.

The inherent defect of the third *jhāna* is happiness itself which the meditator sees to be a relatively gross factor that weakens the entire attainment. As he reflects equanimous feeling and one-pointedness appear more subtle, peaceful, and secure, and the fourth *jhāna* more desirable because it is constituted by these two factors.

Then, taking as his object the same counterpart sign he took for the earlier attainments, the meditator repeats his concentration for the purpose of abandoning the gross factor of happiness and attaining the higher *jhāna*. When his practice matures the mind enters upon the thought-process culminating in absorption of the fourth *jhāna*. First the life-continuum (*bhavaṅga*) vibrates and gets cut off, after which there arises the mind-door adverting with the counterpart sign as object. This is followed by four or five impulsions (*javana*) on the same object, the last of which is an impulsion of the fourth *jhāna*. The three or four impulsions of the preliminary stage retain applied thought and sustained thought, but because the *jhāna* to follow involves neither-painful-nor-pleasant feeling, the preliminary impulsions, too, involve the same feeling. Thus they are devoid of rapture and happiness, as these are incompatible with neither-painful-nor-pleasant feeling.[2]

1. Narada, *Manual*, pp. 131-32.
2. PP., pp. 170-71.

The Four Conditions

The standard suttanta description of the fourth *jhāna* is as follows:

> With the abandoning of pleasure and pain, and with the previous disappearance of joy and grief, he enters and dwells in the fourth *jhāna*, which has neither-pain-nor-pleasure and has purity of mindfulness due to equanimity.[1]

The first part of this formula states four preliminary conditions needed for attaining the fourth *jhāna*: [1] the abandoning of pleasure, [2] the abandoning of pain, [3] the disappearance of joy, and [4] the disappearance of grief.[2] To understand these four conditions it is first necessary to determine the precise meaning of the four feelings they involve.

[1] *Pleasure* (*sukha*)

When we discussed the word *sukha* in the context of the first *jhāna* we noted that it has both a general and a narrow application. In a general sense *sukha* signifies happiness or pleasant feeling, covering both bodily pleasant feeling (*kāyika sukha*) and mental pleasant feeling (*cetasika sukha*). In a narrow sense it signifies exclusively bodily pleasant feeling; it is then contrasted with mental pleasant feeling, which is denoted by another word, *somanassa*, here translated "joy". Now the *sukha* spoken of as a factor of the first three *jhānas* is mental pleasant feeling, that is, *somanassa* or joy. As we saw, the Vibhaṅga defines the *sukha* of these *jhāna* as "mental pleasure, mental happiness, the felt pleasure and happiness born of mind-contact, pleasurable and happy feeling born of mind-contact."[3] But in the fourth *jhāna* description the *sukha* which is said to be abandoned as a pre-requisite for the *jhāna* has undergone a shift in meaning: it now signifies bodily pleasure or physical happiness (*kāyikasukha*). Thus the Vibhaṅga defines the *sukha* intended in the phrase *sukhassa ca pahānā*, "with the abandoning of pleasure," as follows:

1. "Sukhassa ca pahānā dukkhassa ca pahānā pubbeva somanassadomanassānaṁ atthaṅgamā adukkhamasukhaṁ upekkhasatipārisuddhiṁ catuttham jhānaṁ upasampajja viharati." DN. 1:75.
2. See MN. 1:296.
3. Vibh., p. 267.

> Therein, what is happiness [pleasure]? Bodily pleasure; bodily happiness, the felt pleasure and happiness born of body-contact, pleasurable and happy feeling born of body-contact—this is called "happiness" [pleasure].[1]

Mental pleasure, or happiness, will be indicated later in the formula by the word *somanassa*.

[2] *Pain* (*dukkha*)

We see from the formula that the attainment of the fourth *jhāna* presupposes the prior abandonment of *dukkha* or pain. Like the word *sukha* the word *dukkha* has a twofold meaning in relation to feelings: on the one side it signifies all unpleasurable feeling, physical and mental; on the other it signifies exclusively bodily pain. When it is used to signify bodily pain it is contrasted with *domanassa*, "grief", which then means mental unpleasurable feeling. In the present context *dukkha* bears the narrower meaning of bodily painful feeling, as the Vibhaṅga explains: "Therein, what is pain? Bodily displeasure, bodily pain, the felt displeasure and pain born of body-contact, unpleasurable and painful feeling born of body-contact—this is called pain."[2]

[3] *Joy* (*somanassa*)

The joy that is made to disappear prior to the attainment of the fourth *jhāna* is mental happiness, the feeling present as *sukha* in the first three *jhānas*. The Vibhaṅga says: "Therein, what is joy? Mental pleasure, mental happiness, the felt pleasure and happiness born of mind-contact, pleasurable and happy feeling born of mind contact—this is called joy."[3]

[4] *Grief* (*domanassa*)

Grief is the opposite of joy, i.e., mental unpleasurable feeling. According to the Vibhaṅga: "Therein, what is grief? Mental displeasure, mental pain, the felt displeasure and pain born of mind-contact, the unpleasurable and painful born of mind-contact—this is called grief."[4]

1. Ibid., p. 270.
2. Ibid., p. 271.
3. *Ibid.*, p. 271.
4. *Ibid.*

The fourth *jhāna* is said to arise following the abandonment of pleasure and pain and the disappearance of joy and grief. This statement seems to suggest that all four feelings first disappear prior to the attainment of the fourth *jhāna*. Such an interpretation, however, is not correct. The Buddha says that the faculty of pain (*dukkhindriya*) ceases without remainder when the first *jhāna* is attained, the faculty of grief (*domanassindriya*) when the second *jhāna* is attained, the faculty of pleasure (*sukhindriya*) when the third *jhāna* is attained, and the faculty of joy (*somanassindriya*) when the fourth *jhāna* is attained.[1] Thus three of the four conditions for the fourth *jhāna* are fulfilled with the attainment of the first three *jhānas*, and only the fourth, the disappearance of joy, with the actual entrance upon the fourth *jhāna*.

The *Visuddhimagga* qualifies the Buddha's statement further with the assertion that the four feelings—pain, grief, pleasure, and joy—actually cease at the moments of access to the first, second, third, and fourth *jhānas*, respectively. However, they only undergo "reinforced cessation" (*atisayanirodhattā*) with the attainment of the *jhāna* itself, which is why the Buddha says that in the *jhāna* they "cease without remainder" (*aparisesaṁ nirujjhati*).[2] Thus bodily pain, which ceases in the first *jhāna* access, can arise again prior to *jhāna* on account of insect bites, an uncomfortable seat, cold, heat, etc. But in the *jhāna* the whole body is suffused with bliss due to pervasion by rapture, and the pain-faculty then completely ceases, beaten out by opposition. Therefore the reinforced cessation of the pain-faculty takes place only with absorption in the first *jhāna*, not with access.

Similarly, the grief faculty initially ceases in the second *jhāna* access, but can arise again when the body is weary and the mind vexed due to applied and sustained thought. But at the level of second *jhāna* absorption, where applied and sustained thought are absent, mental grief does not reappear. The bodily pleasure-faculty, which ceases in the third *jhāna* access, can reappear when the meditator's body is pervaded by the subtle materiality originated by consciousness, but it does not arise in the third *jhāna* absorption where the rapture producing such materiality has ceased. Likewise, the faculty of joy which has ceased in the fourth

1. SN. 5:213-15.
2. Vism., p. 134. PP., p. 172.

jhāna access could be reawakened due to the proximity of the third *jhānic* happiness, but not in the fourth *jhāna* absorption where it is fully suppressed by equanimity.

When three other feelings have been abandoned earlier, the question comes up why all four feelings are collected together and negated here, in the description of the fourth *jhāna*. The *Visuddhimagga* gives four reasons for grouping them. The first is to make it easier to grasp the nature of neither-painful-nor-pleasant feeling, which being subtle and difficult to recognize has to be apprehended by negating the alternatives, like a refractory cow that has to be caught by gathering all the cows in a pen and releasing the others one by one. The second reason is to show the condition for the neither-painful-nor-pleasurable mind-deliverance, which is the abandonment of the other four feelings. A third reason is to recommend this *jhāna* by showing its freedom from the grosser types of feeling. And a fourth is to show that greed and hatred are very far away owing to the absence of pleasure and pain, their proximate causes.[1]

New Elements in the *Jhāna*

The fourth *jhāna* formula introduces several new terms and phrases which have not been used in the formulas for the preceding *jhānas*. First of all, it introduces a new feeling. This is the feeling of neither-pain-nor-pleasure (*adukkhamasukha*), which remains after the other four types of feeling have been eliminated.

Neither-painful-nor-pleasant feeling, also called equanimous feeling (*upekkhāvedanā*), replaces happiness as the concomitant feeling of the *jhāna*. It also figures as an actual *jhāna*-factor. Thus this *jhāna* has two factors: neither-painful-nor-pleasant feeling and one-pointedness of mind. Previously the ascent from one *jhāna* to the next was marked by the progressive elimination of the coarser *jhāna*-factors without any replacement. But in the move from the third to fourth *jhāna* there takes place a substitution. While one-pointedness remains constant, equanimous feeling enters to replace happiness, which has been abandoned.

Simultaneously with the progressive elimination and refinement of *jhāna* factors, there has occurred in the description of each suc-

1. PP., pp. 173-74. Vism., p. 135.

ceeding *jhāna* the introduction of several new and complex elements. The second *jhāna* formula introduced confidence and mental unification, the third *jhāna* formula equanimity, mindfulness, and discernment. Consistent with this we now find in the move to the fourth *jhāna*, besides the abandonment of the grosser feelings and the addition of a new feeling, a new phrase composed of already familiar terms suggesting a new element—"purity of mindfulness due to equanimity." The Pali compound *upekkhāsatipārisuddhi* is explained by the Vibhaṅga in a way that makes it plain that the relation between the two terms is causal, not merely copulative: "This mindfulness is cleared, purified, clarified by equanimity; hence it is said to have purity of mindfulness due to equanimity."[1] The *Visuddhimagga* also supports this interpretation: "For the mindfulness in this *jhāna* is quite purified, and its purification is effected by equanimity, not by anything else."[2]

The equanimity which purifies the mindfulness, according to the Vibhaṅga, is not neither-painful-nor-pleasant feeling, but mental neutrality (*majjhattatā cittassa*), the same as "specific neutrality" (*tatramajjhattatā*) discussed above.[3] Thus this *jhāna* has two kind of equanimity—[1] equanimous feeling, the affective tone which inclines neither towards pleasure nor pain, and [2] specific neutrality, the mental attitude of sublime impartiality free from attachment and aversion. Though the two are different factors, the one belonging to the aggregate of feelings (*vedanākkhandha*) and the other to the aggregate of mental formations (*sankhārakkhandha*), their concomitance is not fortuitous; for as specific neutrality becomes more and more refined it naturally tends to come into association with equanimous feeling, its hedonic counterpart.

Of the two, as we have seen, it is equanimity as specific neutrality that purifies mindfulness. Though both equanimity as specific neutrality and mindfulness are present in the earlier three *jhānas*, none among these is said to have purity of mindfulness due to equanimity. The reason is that the equanimity in the preceding *jhānas* is not purified, and thus cannot purify mindfulness and

1. Vibh., p. 271.
2. PP., p. 174. Vism., p. 136.
3. Vibh., p. 271.

the other conascent states. In the other *jhānas* equanimity lacks clarity and distinctness because it is overshadowed by the opposing states and because it lacks association with equanimous feeling. The *Visuddhimagga* illustrates this with a vivid simile :

> ... just as, although a crescent moon exists by day but is not purified or clear since it is outshone by the sun's radiance in the daytime or since it is deprived of the night, which is its ally owing to gentleness and owing to helpfulness to it, so too, this crescent moon of equanimity consisting in specific neutrality exists in the first jhāna, etc., but it is not purified since it is outshone by the glare of the opposing states consisting in applied thought, etc., and since it is deprived of the night of equanimity as feeling for its ally; and because it is not purified, the conascent mindfulness and other states are not purified either, like the unpurified crescent moon's radiance by day. That is why no one among these [first three *jhānas*] is said to have purity of mindfulness due to equanimity.[1]

But in the fourth *jhāna* the "crescent moon of specific neutrality" is completely pure because it is not outshone by the opposing states and because it appears against the background of equanimous feeling. Itself pure, it is able to purify mindfulness and the other associated factors, just as a purified crescent moon is able to send forth a purified radiance.

So pervasive is the purity reached in the fourth *jhāna* that to illustrate it the Buddha no longer uses the image of one thing suffusing another, as he did for the happiness and rapture of the earlier *jhānas*. Instead he employs the image of one thing covering another, that is, a white cloth covering a man's whole body from top to bottom :

> Suppose a man were sitting wrapt in white cloth covering his whole body from head to toes, so that there were not a single spot of his body that is not covered by the white cloth. Similarly the bhikkhu sits pervading his whole body with a pure and lucid mind so that not a single spot of his entire body is left unpervaded by that pure and lucid mind.[2]

1. PP., p. 175. Vism., p. 136.
2. DN. 1-76.

The Abhidhammic system counts thirty factors in the fourth *jhāna*. From the original set of thirty-three, applied thought, sustained thought, and rapture are excluded, and the feeling is changed to neither-pain-nor-pleasure. Compassion and sympathetic joy do not unite with the *jhāna*, as they require association with pleasant feeling while this *jhāna* contains neutral feeling exclusively.

The Fivefold Scheme of the Jhānas

Whereas the suttas arrange the *jhānas* into a fourfold system, the texts of the Abhidhammapiṭaka present them in two ways—in terms of the familiar fourfold system of the suttas and also in terms of a fivefold system. The fourfold presentation of *jhāna* becomes fivefold through the separate rather than simultaneous elimination of applied thought (*vitakka*) and sustained thought (*vicāra*). In the fivefold system the factorial constitution of the five *jhānas* is as follows :

First *jhāna*: applied thought, sustained thought, rapture, happiness, one-pointedness. Second *jhāna*: sustained thought, rapture, happiness, one-pointedness. Third *jhāna*: rapture, happiness, one-pointedness. Fourth *jhāna*: happiness, one-pointedness. Fifth *jhāna*: neither painful-nor-pleasant feeling, one-pointedness.[1]

In following the fivefold system a meditator who has mastered the first *jhāna* and aspires to go higher reviews its factors and finds only applied thought to be gross. Thus he endeavors to eliminate only applied thought, and attains a second *jhāna* which is devoid of applied thought (*avitakkaṁ*) but still associated with sustained thought (*vicāramattaṁ*). This second *jhāna* of the fivefold scheme is the addition which is not present in the fourfold scheme. After mastering the second *jhāna*, the meditator finds sustained thought to be gross, eliminates it, and attains a third *jhāna* which is identical with the second *jhāna* of the fourfold system. The fourth and fifth *jhānas* of the fivefold system are the same as the third and fourth *jhānas* of the fourfold system, respectively.

The two different systems answer to the differing capacities of meditators for progressing along the scale of mental unification.

1. See Narada, *Manual*, pp. 42-44.

This difference in capacity could stem either from their differing abilities to comprehend applied thought and sustained thought simultaneously or from their differing abilities to abandon them simultaneously. The progress of one following the fourfold method is more rapid, as he eliminates two factors in moving from the first to second *jhāna*. Yet both start from the same place, move through the same range of spiritual experience, and (providing they succeed in reaching the highest *jhāna* in their respective systems) arrive in the end at the same destination.

The two meditators can be compared to two mountain climbers. Both start out at the foot of a mountain at the same time and reach the same initial rest station at the same time. But then their rates of progress may show a difference. The stronger may continue on more quickly, bypass the second rest station, and go right on to the third before stopping, while the weaker will advance more slowly and have to make separate stops at the second and third stations. Both will stop at the fourth and at the fifth station at the top. Thus for both mountain climbers their position is the same when starting out at the bottom of the mountain, at the first station, and when reaching the top. They differ only in their rates of progress and in the number of stops they have to make to arrive at the top. Similarly for the two meditators of the fourfold and fivefold systems. Their first *jhāna* is the same, and their final achievement is the same. But the follower of the fivefold system has made an additional stop passed over by the follower of the fourfold system. This stop is the added second *jhāna* of the fivefold system, free from applied thought but having sustained thought.

The fivefold reckoning of *jhāna* first appears in the Abhidhammapiṭaka and remains as a distinctive feature of the "Abhidhamma method," yet this system has a definite basis in the suttas. Though the suttas always speak of four *jhānas*, they divide concentration (*samādhi*) into three types: a concentration with applied thought and sustained thought, a concentration without applied thought but with sustained thought, and a concentration without either applied thought or sustained thought.[1] Thus in the Aṅguttara Nikāya the Buddha declares:

1. The Pali for the three is : *savitakko savicāro samādhi*, *avitakkavicāramatto samādhi*, and *avitakko avicāro samādhi*.

> When, monk, this concentration has been thus developed and cultivated by you, then you should develop this concentration with applied and sustained thought, without applied thought but with sustained thought only, and without either applied or sustained thought.[1]

The commentary to the Aṅguttara Nikāya glosses this as attaining fourfold and fivefold *jhāna*. The *Aṭṭhasālini* explains that while the fourfold scheme of *jhānas* includes concentration with both applied and sustained thought and without either of the two, it does not deal with that concentration having only sustained thought; thence an additional *jhāna* necessitating a fivefold system is required to deal with it.[2]

In the Abhidhammattha Saṅgaha the five *jhānas* are presented only in skeletal form, in terms of their defining factors. The canonical Dhammasaṅgaṇi and the Vibhaṅga, however, present them with full formulas. In their formulas for the second *jhāna* of the fivefold system these two Abhidhamma treatises differ in some interesting respects. The Dhammasaṅgaṇi formula runs as follows: "He enters and abides in the second *jhāna*, which is without applied thought, has only sustained thought, and is filled with rapture and happiness born of concentration."[3] The Vibhaṅga formula states:

> Quite secluded from sense pleasures, secluded from unwholesome states of mind, he enters and dwells in the second *jhāna* which is accompanied only by sustained thought with rapture and happiness born of seclusion.[4]

Thus the Vibhaṅga version includes a phrase about seclusion from sense pleasures and unwholesome states, while the Dhammasaṅgaṇi version omits this and instead simply describes the *jhāna*. Again, the two differ in the way they qualify the rapture and happiness existing in the *jhāna*. The Dhammasaṅgaṇi says

1. AN. 4:301.
2. Dhs. A., p. 224.
3. "Avitakkaṁ vicāramattaṁ samādhijaṁ pītisukhaṁ dutiyaṁ jhānaṁ upasampajja viharati." Dhs., p. 47.
4. "Vivicceva kāmehi vivicca akusalehi dhammehi avitakkaṁ vicāramattaṁ vivekajaṁ pītisukhaṁ dutiyaṁ jhānaṁ upasampajja viharati." Vibh. p. 275.

they are "born of concentration" (*samādhijaṁ pītisukhaṁ*), the Vibhaṅga that they are born of seclusion (*vivekajaṁ pītisukhaṁ*).

The preliminary phrase in the Vibhaṅga version appears to be an inappropriate repetition of the beginning of the first *jhāna* formula, and thus can perhaps be dismissed as an editorial error made by the ancient redactors of the text. The second difference between the two works, that concerning the cause of rapture and happiness, may also be due to an editorial oversight, but is more difficult to resolve. When explaining the phrase *samādhijaṁ* in connection with the second *jhāna* of the tetradic scheme, the *Visuddhimagga* said that "born of concentration" could be understood to mean that the rapture and happiness of the second *jhāna* are born of the first *jhāna* concentration, or born of the associated second *jhāna* concentration. It then added:

> It is only this concentration [of the second *jhāna*] that is quite worthy to be called 'concentration' because of its complete confidence and extreme immobility due to absence of disturbance by applied and sustained thought.[1]

Now if we accept the idea that the concentration responsible for producing the rapture and happiness of the second tetradic *jhāna* is the first *jhāna* concentration, then it follows logically that the rapture and happiness of the second *jhāna* in the fivefold scheme can also be born of the same concentration. Thus the reading of the Dhammasaṅgaṇi would be correct. However, we also have to take account of the *Visuddhimagga's* remark that the word "concentration" is only fully appropriate in the absence of disturbance by applied and sustained thought. Then, because sustained thought is present in the pentadic second *jhāna*, it is questionable whether the phrase "born of concentration" can belong to the formula. In this case the preference would go to the Vibhaṅga reading. Due to the ambiguity of interpretative method, the difference seems impossible to settle with complete definiteness, and must just be left for the present as unresolved.

Concluding Remarks

From our inquiry two important points emerge concerning the dynamics of *jhāna* attainment. First, the ascent from one *jhāna*

1. PP., p. 164. Vism., p. 127.

to another is signalled by a progressive elimination of *jhāna* factors. The first *jhāna*, as we saw, has five factors. In moving to the second *jhāna* two factors, applied thought and sustained thought, are abandoned, in moving to the third rapture is abandoned, and in moving to the fourth happiness is abandoned, replaced by neither-painful-nor-pleasant feeling. This process of elimination, we can assume, involves concurrently an intensification of concentration, whereby the energy that was diffused among the coarser and more numerous *jhāna* factors comes to be invested in the subtler and fewer factors, enabling the concentration to gain in depth and intensity.

The second point to be noticed is that in the formulas for each of the ascending *jhānas* new elements were mentioned, most of which did not correspond to any *jhāna* factors. The second *jhāna* formula added "internal confidence," the equivalent of faith. The third *jhāna* formula added equanimity, mindfulness, and discernment, and the fourth added "purification of mindfulness due to equanimity." These elements, though not themselves *jhāna* factors, are still deserving mention. The *jhāna* factors are the states which directly exercise the *jhānic* functions of countering the hindrances and unifying the mind on the object. But beyond these can be found, in each *jhāna*, a number of other factors which contribute to the distinctive character of the attainment, and these have been selected for inclusion in its descriptive formula. This procedure helps make it clear that the *jhānas* are not abstract states completely susceptible to schematic analysis, but living experiences with a vitality and directness that elude mere intellectual treatment.

Chapter VI

BEYOND THE FOUR JHĀNAS

Following the attainment of the fourth *jhāna* there are several options open to a meditator. These can be grouped together into three basic categories. One is the attainment of the four *āruppas*, immaterial *jhānas* involving further concentration and refinement of mental serenity. A second—which as we will see generally presupposes the immaterial *jhānas*—is the development of the *abhiññās*, higher faculties of knowledge in some cases issuing in supernormal powers. A third alternative is the cultivation of wisdom, which brings the destruction of the defilements and emancipation from *saṁsāra*. In the present chapter we will explore the first and second of these three alternatives, closing with some remarks concerning the relationship between *jhānas* and rebirth. Then in the next two chapters we will examine the place of *jhāna* in the development of wisdom leading to final deliverance.

Throughout the following discussion it should be borne in mind that the attainment of the immaterial *jhānas* and the exercise of supernormal powers are not essential to achieving the ultimate Buddhist goal, the realization of *nibbāna*. What is essential is the practice of the Noble Eightfold Path, which does not necessarily include the *āruppas* and *abhiññās*. However, because these latter two sets of practices can contribute to the growth of calm and insight and embellish the spiritual perfection of a yogin, the Buddha included them in his discipline. There they have remained as options open for meditators inclined to develop them.

The Four Immaterial Jhānas

Beyond the four *jhānas* lie four higher attainments in the scale of mental unification. In the suttas these are referred to as the four *āruppas*, "immaterial states," or as the "peaceful immaterial liberations transcending material form."[1] In the commentaries

1. "Santā vimokkhā atikkamma rūpe āruppā." MN. 1:33.

they come to be called the immaterial *jhānas* (*arūpajjhānāni*); the lower four attainments are named, in contrast, the four fine material *jhānas* (*rūpajjhānāni*) or simply the four *jhānas*. The immaterial *jhānas* are individually designated, not by numerical names like their predecessors, but by the names of their objective spheres: the base of boundless space, the base of boundless consciousness, the base of nothingness, and the base of neither perception nor non-perception.[1] They receive the designation "formless" or "immaterial" for two reasons: [1] because they are achieved by surmounting all perceptions of material form (*rūpa*), even of the subtle material form of the counterpart sign which serves as the object for the fine material *jhānas*; and [2] because they are the subjective counterparts of the immaterial planes of existence.

Before turning to consider the immaterial *jhānas* individually, some important remarks are called for concerning their "internal constitution." We saw in the previous chapter that the movement from any lower *jhāna* to its successor involves the elimination of the coarser *jhāna* factors. The refinement of consciousness that occurs through this movement thus hinges upon actual changes being effected in the composition of the states of consciousness corresponding to the *jhānas*. However, in ascending from the fourth fine material *jhāna* to the first immaterial *jhāna*, and then from one immaterial *jhāna* to another, no changes in the compositional factors of consciousness are required. In other words, the fourth fine material *jhāna* and all four formless attainments have precisely the same kinds of factors entering into their internal constitution. The factors in each higher attainment are subtler than those in its predecessors, more peaceful and more sublime, but they do not differ in number or in their essential nature. The climb from one formless attainment to another is brought about by changing the object of concentration, not by eliminating or replacing component factors. For this reason the treatises of the Abhidhammapiṭaka, such as the Dhammasaṅgaṇi and the Vibhaṅga, treat the four *āruppas* as modes of the fourth *jhāna*, combining the formula for each with the general formula for the fourth *jhāna*. All five states—the fourth fine

1. In Pali : *Ākāsanañcāyatana, viññāṇañcāyatana, ākiñcaññāyatana,* and *nevasaññānāsaññāyatana.*

material *jhāna* and the four immaterial *jhānas*—contain the same basic constellation of mental concomitants (*cetasikas*) and the same two *jhāna* factors, namely one-pointedness and neither-painful-nor-pleasant feeling. Thence from the standpoint of the Abhidhamma, which defines a class of consciousness (*citta*) by its components, the four types of consciousness belonging to the four formless attainments are modes of the fourth *jhāna* consciousness according to the fourfold scheme, and of the fifth *jhāna* consciousness according to the fivefold scheme.

The First Āruppa : The Base of Boundless Space

The four formless attainments must be achieved in sequence, beginning with the base of boundless space and culminating in the base of neither perception nor non-perception. The motivation which initially leads a yogin to seek the immaterial states is a clear recognition of the dangers posed by gross physical matter. As it is said in the Majjhima Nikāya:

> It is in virtue of matter that wielding of sticks, wielding of knives, quarrels, brawls and disputes take place; but that does not exist at all in the immaterial state, and in this expectation he enters upon the way of dispassion for only material things, for the fading and cessation of only those.[1]

He might also become repelled by matter as a result of considering the numerous afflictions to which the physical body is vulnerable, such as eye diseases, ear diseases, and so forth. Aspiring to escape from these dangers connected with material form, the meditator must first attain the four *jhānas* of the fine material sphere. He then enters the fourth *jhāna*, taking as his object any of the *kasiṇas* except the limited space *kasiṇa*. By achieving the fourth fine material *jhāna* the meditator has risen above gross matter but still has not completely transcended all material form, which includes the self-luminous counterpart sign, the object of his *jhāna*. To reach the formless attainments he must desire to surmount as well the materiality of the *kasiṇa*. Such a desire can be induced by contemplating the *kasiṇa* materiality as the counterpart of gross matter, sharing to some extent its defects. Buddhaghosa illustrates how this is done by means of a simile. If a timid man is pursued by a snake in the forest he will flee

1. PP., p. 354. MN. 1:410.

from it as fast as he can. If he should later see something resembling the snake, such as a palm leaf with a streak painted on it, a creeper, a rope, or a crack in the ground, he would become fearful and anxious and would not want to look at it. The time the meditator was frightened by seeing the danger in gross matter is like the time the man saw the snake. When the meditator escapes gross matter by reaching the fourth *jhāna*, this is like the time the man flees from the snake. The time the meditator observes the subtle matter of the *kasiṇa* to be the counterpart of gross matter and wants to surmount it is like the time the man sees the object resembling a snake and is afraid to look at it.[1]

Once he has generated a strong desire to reach the immaterial *jhānas* the meditator must achieve the fivefold mastery over the fourth *jhāna*. Then, after emerging from the *jhāna*, he perceives its defects and the benefits in the higher attainment. The defects are: [1] that the fourth *jhāna* has an object consisting in material form and hence is still connected with gross matter; [2] that it is close to happiness, a factor of the third *jhāna*; and [3] that it is coarser than the immaterial attainments. On the other hand, the meditator sees the base of boundless space as more peaceful and sublime than the fourth *jhāna* and as more safely removed from materiality.

By reflecting on its defects the meditator ends his attachment to the fourth *jhāna* and sets out to reach the base of boundless space. To do so he does not make any effort to eliminate *jhāna* factors, as both the fourth fine material *jhāna* and the four immaterial *jhānas* have the same factorial constitution—one-pointedness and neutral feeling. The method for attaining this first formless *jhāna* is to mentally extend the *kasiṇa* "to the limit of the world-sphere, or as far as he likes," and then to remove the *kasiṇa* by attending exclusively to the space it covered without adverting to the *kasiṇa*.

The original *kasiṇa* which provided the preliminary sign (*parikammanimitta*) for concentration was, as we saw, a disc-like object, in the case of the earth *kasiṇa* a disc filled with reddish-brown clay. When practising preliminary concentration the meditator kept focusing his mind upon this disc until there appeared the learning sign (*uggahanimitta*), a mental image apprehended as

1. PP., pp. 354-55. Vism., p. 272.

clearly as the physical object. Concentration on the learning sign gave rise to the counterpart sign (*paṭibhāganimitta*), the conceptualized image used as the object for access concentration and the fine material *jhānas*. After entering each *jhāna*, the meditator learned to extend the sign outwards by degrees, making the visualized *kasiṇa* cover increasingly larger areas up to a world-system or more. Now, to reach the base of boundless space, the meditator must remove the *kasiṇa* by attending exclusively to the space it has been made to cover without attending to the *kasiṇa*:

> When he is removing it, he neither folds it up like a mat nor withdraws it like a cake from a tin. It is simply that he does not advert to it or give attention to it or review it; it is when he neither adverts to it nor gives attention to it nor reviews it but gives his attention exclusively to the space touched by it [regarding that] as 'Space, space', that he is said to 'remove the *kasiṇa*'.[1]

Taking as his object the space left after the removal of the *kasiṇa*, the yogin adverts to it as "boundless space, boundless space," or simply as "space, space," striking at it with applied and sustained thought. He cultivates this practice again and again, repeatedly developing it until the concept reaches maturity. When his development is fully matured, then the consciousness pertaining to the base of boundless space arises with boundless space as its object. It is the first wholesome consciousness of the immaterial sphere, and appears in the cognitive series in the same place that the first *jhāna* appeared in its own thought-process. In the prior moments of the series, the three or four moments of access concentration are always associated with equanimous feeling and pertain to the sense sphere; the fourth or fifth moment, the moment of absorption, pertains to the immaterial sphere.

The standard formula for the base of boundless space, as presented in the suttas, is as follows:

> With the complete surmounting of perceptions of matter, with the disappearance of perceptions of resistance, with non-attention to perceptions of variety, [aware of] 'unbounded

1. PP., p. 355. Vism. p. 272.

space', he enters upon and dwells in the base consisting of boundless space.[1]

There are four phrases in this formula worth discussing separately: [1] with the complete surmounting of perceptions of matter (*sabbaso rūpasaññānaṁ samatikkamā*); [2] with the disappearance of perceptions of resistance (*paṭigha saññānaṁ atthagamā*); [3] with non-attention to perceptions of variety (*nānattasaññānaṁ amanasikārā*); and [4] unbounded space (*ananto ākāso*).

[1] "*With the complete surmounting of perceptions of matter*" (*sabbaso rūpasaññānaṁ samatikkamā*)

The phrase "perceptions of matter," according to the commentaries, means both the perceptions of the fine-material *jhānas* and their objects, the *kasiṇas*.[2] We saw that in developing the fine-material *jhānas* the meditator began with a coarse physical object, shifted his focus to the subtle counterpart sign, and ascended from the first to the fourth *jhāna* by abandoning various mental factors while retaining the same object. But now he must give up, not only the perceptions of material form belonging to the four *jhānas*, but also the object of these perceptions—the fine material form of the counterpart sign—since it is impossible to attain the base of boundless space without overcoming all perceptions of material form.

[2] "*With the disappearance of perceptions of resistance*" (*paṭighasaññānaṁ atthagamā*)

The word patigha, which we translate here as "resistance," generally signifies aversion, repugnance, or anger. In this place, however, it is used to mean sensory impact, the striking (*gha*= *han*) against one another (*paṭi*) of the sense organs and their respective sense objects. Perceptions of resistance are thus sensory perceptions, perceptions of the five outer sense objects. It should be noted that only perception through the five physical senses is excluded from the base of boundless space. No mention

1. PP., p. 356. "Sabbaso rūpasaññānaṁ samatikkamā paṭighasaññānaṁ atthagamā nānatta saññānaṁ amanasikārā ananto ākāsoti ākāsanañcāyatanaṁ upasampajja viharati." Dn. 1:183.

2. PP., pp. 357-58. Vism., p. 273.

is made of the disappearance of *dhammasaññā*, perception of mental objects, for the reason that this type of perception remains. Although sensory perceptions are also absent in the four *jhānas*, their disappearance is accentuated here to emphasize the fading away of attachment to material form and to arouse a greater interest in the formless *jhānas*.[1]

[3] "*With non-attention to perceptions of variety*" (*nānattasaññānaṁ amanasikārā*)

According to the Vibhaṅga, "perceptions of variety" are the non-sensory perceptions of those who are not absorbed in a meditative attainment.[2] When the text lays down non-attention, to perceptions of variety as a condition for reaching the base of boundless space, this means that the yogin must not advert to perceptions having diversified objects, since to attend to them or review them is obstructive to the attainment.

According to the *Visuddhimagga*, the phrase "with the surmounting of perceptions of matter" signifies the abandonment of all fine material-sphere states and the other two phrases the abandonment of and non-attention to all sense-sphere consciousness and its concomitants.[3]

[4] "*Unbounded space*" (*ananto ākāso*)

The "unbounded space" which the meditator becomes aware of is the space left by the removal of the *kasiṇa* after the latter has been extended boundlessly. The space is called "unbounded" or "endless" (*ananta*) because neither a beginning boundary nor a terminal boundary can be perceived for it. The meditator "enters upon and dwells in the base of boundless space" in the sense that after reaching that attainment he abides in the *jhāna* which has the base of boundless space as its object.

The Second *Āruppa* : The Base of Boundless Consciousness (*viññāṇañcāyatana*)

To attain the second immaterial *jhāna* the yogin must gain mastery over the base consisting of boundless space; then he

1. PP., p. 358. Vism., p. 274.
2. Vibh., p. 272.
3. PP., p. 359. Vism., p. 275.

must discern its defects. The first immaterial state is defective, firstly, because it is still close to the fine material *jhānas*, and secondly, because it is not as peaceful as the base of boundless consciousness. By reflecting on these defects he develops indifference to the lower attainment and turns his attention to the higher one.

To develop the second *āruppa* the meditator focuses upon the consciousness that occurred pervading the boundless space of the first *āruppa*. Thus the second *āruppa* takes as its object the consciousness pertaining to the first. Since space objectified by the first *āruppa* was boundless, the consciousness of this object also contained an aspect of boundlessness, and it is to this boundless consciousness that the aspirant for the second *āruppa* adverts. He is not to attend to it merely as boundless, but as "boundless consciousness" or simply as "consciousness." As he does so the hindrances are suppressed and the mind enters access concentration. He continues to cultivate this sign again and again, until the consciousness belonging to the base of boundless consciousness arises in absorption. The cognitive series should be understood as in the previous attainment, with the appropriate changes made to fit the case.

The formula for the attainment of the base consisting of boundless consciousness reads thus : "By completely surmounting the base consisting of boundless space, [aware of] 'unbounded consciousness', he enters upon and dwells in the base consisting of boundless consciousness."[1] According to the word-commentary on this passage, the phrase "base consisting of boundless space" signifies both the first immaterial *jhāna* and its object. The surmounting of the base means the overcoming, of both the *jhāna* and its object together, since the base of boundless consciousness is to be entered and dwelt in by passing beyond both aspects of the base of boundless space.

To be aware of "unbounded consciousness" is to give attention to the consciousness that occurred pervading the space left by the removal of the *kasiṇa*. Thus the object of this *jhāna* is the consciousness that had pervaded boundless space in the previous *jhāna*. The boundless consciousness which pervaded boundless

1. PP., p. 361. "Sabbaso ākāsānañcāyatanaṁ samatikkamā, anantaṁ viññāṇaṁ ti viññāṇañcāyatanaṁ upasampajjā viharati." Vibh., p. 273.

space is itself the base consisting in boundless consciousness, and the *jhāna* as well, because it is founded upon this base, derivatively comes to be called by the same name.

The Third *Āruppa*: The Base of Nothingness (*akiñcaññāyatana*)

To attain the next *āruppa*, the base of nothingness, the meditator who has mastered the base of boundless consciousness must perceive this attainment as defective due to its proximity to the base of boundless space and its grossness compared to the next higher *jhāna*. By recognizing these defects the meditator removes his attachment to the base of boundless consciousness; then he should advert to the base of nothingness as more peaceful. To concentrate on the base of nothingness the meditator must

> give attention to the [present] non-existence (*abhāva*), voidness (*suññata*), secluded aspect (*vivittākāra*) of that same [past] consciousness belonging to the base consisting of boundless space which became the object of [the consciousness belonging to] the base consisting of boundless consciousness.[1]

In other words, to attain the base of nothingness the yogin has to focus upon the present absence or non-existence of the consciousness belonging to the base consisting of boundless space. He is advised to advert to it over and over, thinking to himself "There is not, there is not" or "void, void," etc. When his practice matures there arises in absorption a consciousness belonging to the base of nothingness, making the non-existence of the consciousness of boundless space its object.

Though both the base of boundless consciousness and base of nothingness are concerned objectively with the consciousness of the base of boundless space, they relate to it in opposite ways. The second *āruppa* objectifies it positively, focussing upon the consciousness of boundless space in terms of its content and appropriating its boundlessness for itself. The third *āruppa*, in contrast, relates to the consciousness of the base of boundless space negatively. It excludes this consciousness from awareness, making the absence or non-existence of this consciousness its object. As the *Visuddhimagga* explains:

1. PP., p. 362. Vism., p. 277.

Suppose a man sees a community of bhikkhus gathered together in a meeting hall or some such place and then goes elsewhere; then after the bhikkhus have risen at the conclusion of the business for which they had met and have departed, the man comes back, and as he stands in the doorway looking at that place again, he sees it only as void, he sees it only as secluded, he does not think 'so many bhikkhus have died, so many have left the district', but rather he sees only the nonexistence thus, 'this is void, secluded'—so too, having formerly dwelt seeing with the jhana eye belonging to the base consisting of boundless consciousness the [earlier] consciousness that had occurred making the space its object, [now] when that consciousness has disappeared owing to his giving attention to the preliminary work in the way beginning 'there is not, there is not', he dwells seeing only its non-existence, in other words its departedness when this consciousness has arisen in absorption.[1]

The texts describe the attainment of the third *āruppa* with a standard formula: "By completely surmounting the base consisting of boundless consciousness, [aware that] 'There is nothing', he enters upon and dwells in the base consisting of nothingness."[2] According to the commentary on this formula, the "base of boundless consciousness" which must be surmounted is both the second immaterial *jhāna* and its object. The phrase "there is nothing" is explained in the Vibhaṅga thus: " 'There is nothing': he makes that same consciousness non-existent, makes it absent, makes it disappear, sees that 'there is nothing', hence 'There is nothing' is said."[3] To make "that same consciousness" (i.e. the consciousness belonging to the base of boundless space) non-existent means not to advert to it or attend to it, but to attend only to its non-existence or absence. By so doing, the yogin "enters and dwells in the base consisting of nothingness." The base consisting of nothingness, which is the foundation for the third formless *jhāna*, is "a term for the disappearance of the consciousness belonging to the base consisting of boundless space."[4]

1. PP., p. 363. Vism., p. 277.
2. PP., p. 363. "Sabbaso viññāṇañcāyatanaṁ samatikkamma, n'atthi kiñci ti ākiñcaññāyatanaṁ upasampajja viharati ti." Vibh., p. 254.
3. Vibh., p. 273, PP., p. 364.
4. PP., p. 364. Vism., p. 278.

The Fourth *Āruppa*: The Base of Neither Perception nor Non-perception (*nevasaññā nāsaññāyatana*)

If the yogin wants to go further and reach the fourth and final *āruppa* attainment, the base of neither perception nor non-perception, he must first achieve fivefold mastery over the base of nothingness. Then he should contemplate the defectiveness of that attainment and the superiority of the base of neither perception nor non-perception. He can also reflect upon the unsatisfactoriness of perception, thinking: "Perception is a disease, perception is a boil, perception is a dart...this is peaceful, this is sublime, that is to say, neither perception nor non-perception."[1] In this way he ends his attachment to the base of nothingness and arouses a desire to attain the base of neither perception nor non-perception.

The base of neither perception nor non-perception has as its object the four mental aggregates that constitute the attainment of the base of nothingness—that is, the aggregates of feeling, perception, mental formations, and consciousness. Just as the second *āruppa* took as its object the consciousness belonging to the first *āruppa*, so the fourth *āruppa* takes as its object the consciousness and associated states belonging to the third *āruppa*. Focussing on the four mental aggregates of the base of nothingness, the meditator adverts to the base as "peaceful, peaceful," reviewing it and striking at it with applied and sustained thought. As he does so the hindrances are suppressed, the mind enters access concentration, and then passes into absorption pertaining to the base of neither perception nor non-perception. The process of attainment is described in the canon thus: "By completely surmounting the base consisting of nothingness he enters and dwells in the base consisting of neither perception nor non-perception."[2]

Though the yogin, as the formula points out, attains the base of neither perception nor non-perception by passing beyond the base of nothingness, it still should be borne in mind that this fourth attainment has the third as its object. The yogin reached the fourth *āruppa* by focussing upon the base of nothingness as

1. PP., p. 265. MN. 2-231
2. PP., : p. 365. "Sabbaso ākiñcaññāyatanaṁ samatikkamma nevasaññā nāsaññāyatanaṁ upasampajja viharati ti." Vibh., p. 254.

"peaceful, peaceful."[1] To the question this may arouse as to how the meditator can overcome the base of nothingness if he attends to it as peaceful the *Visuddhimagga* provides an answer. Although the meditator attends to the third *āruppa* as peaceful he has no desire to attain it, since he has reflected upon the base of neither perception nor non-perception as more peaceful and sublime. Buddhaghosa gives the example of a king who, when he sees craftsmen at work while proceeding along a city street, might admire their skill but would not want to become a craftsman himself, since he is aware of the superior benefits of kingship.[2]

The name "base of neither perception nor non-perception" suggests the abstruse nature of this *jhāna*. The *jhāna* receives this name because on the one hand it lacks gross perception and on the other retains a subtle perception. Lacking gross perception, it cannot perform the decisive function of perception—the clear discernment of objects—and thus cannot be said to have perception (*neva saññā*). But yet this attainment retains an extremely subtle perception and thus cannot be said to be without perception (*nāsaññā*). To make plain this ambivalent character of the *jhāna* it is named "the base of neither perception nor non-perception." Because perception as well as all the other mental factors such as feeling, consciousness, contact, and the rest, continue here reduced to the finest subtlety this *jhāna* is also named "the attainment with residual formations" (*saṅkhārāvasesa samāpatti*).[3]

The commentaries illustrate the method of naming this attainment by means of the following anecdote. A novice smeared a bowl with oil and an elder monk asked him to bring the bowl to serve gruel. The novice replied, "Venerable sir, there is oil in the bowl." Then the monk told him, "Bring the oil, novice, I shall fill the oil tube." Thereupon the novice said: "There is no oil, Venerable sir."[4] In this tale what the novice said is true in both cases: there is no oil since there is not enough to fill the tube yet there is no utter absence of oil since some remains at the base of the bowl. Similarly, in this attainment perception cannot be said to be fully present since it is so subtle that it cannot

1. PP., p. 366. Vibh., p. 274.
2. PP., p. 366. Vism., p. 280.
3. PP., p. 367. Vism., p. 280.
4. PP., pp. 367-68. Vism., p. 281.

perform the decisive function of perceiving; yet it cannot be said to be absent since it remains in residual form.

With this fourth formless *jhāna* the mind has reached the highest possible level of development in the direction of serenity. Consciousness has attained to the most intense degree of concentration, becoming so subtle and refined that it can no longer be described in terms of existence or non-existence. Yet even this attainment, as we will see, is still a mundane state which, from the Buddhist perspective, must finally give way to insight that alone leads to true liberation.

General Remarks on the *Āruppas*

Although the immaterial *jhānas*, unlike the fine material *jhānas*, are not given numerical names, they do follow a fixed sequence and must be attained in the order in which they are presented. That is, the yogin who wishes to achieve the immaterial *jhānas* must begin with the base of boundless space and then proceed step by step up to the base of neither perception nor non-perception. In this respect the accomplishment of the formless attainments corresponds to that of the lower four *jhānas*. However, an important difference separates the modes of progress in the two cases. In the case of the fine material *jhānas*, the ascent from one *jhāna* to another involves a surmounting of *jhāna* factors. To rise from the first *jhāna* to the second the yogin must eliminate applied thought and sustained thought, to rise from the second to the third he must overcome rapture, and to rise from the third to the fourth he must replace pleasant with neutral feeling. Thus progress involves a reduction and refinement of the *jhāna* factors, from the initial five to the culmination in mental one-pointedness and neutral feeling.

Once the fourth *jhāna* is reached the *jhāna* factors remain constant. In the higher ascent to the immaterial attainments there is no further elimination of *jhāna* factors. For this reason the formless *jhānas*, when classified from the perspective of their factorial constitution as is done in the Abhidhamma, are considered as modalities of the fourth *jhāna*.[1] All these *āruppas* are two-factored *jhānas*, constituted by mental one-pointedness and equanimous feeling.

1. See Dhs., p. 68.

Rather than being determined by a surmounting of factors, the order of the *āruppas* is determined by a surmounting of objects. Whereas for the lower *jhānas* the object can remain constant but the factors must be changed, for the immaterial *jhānas* the factors remain constant while the objects change. As we saw, the base of boundless space eliminates the *kasiṇa* object of the fourth *jhāna*, the base of boundless consciousness surmounts the object of the base of boundless space, the base of nothingness surmounts the object of the base of boundless consciousness, and the base of neither perception nor non-perception surmounts the object of the base of nothingness.

Because the objects become progressively more subtle at each level the *jhāna* factors of equanimous feeling and one-pointedness, while remaining constant in nature throughout, become correspondingly more refined in quality. Buddhaghosa illustrates this with two similes. The first compares the four formless *jhānas* to the floors of a four-storied palace with progressively finer objects of sense pleasure on each floor. There is no difference between the floors in regard to their nature as palace-floors, but only in regard to the objects of enjoyment found on them. The second simile compares the four formless *jhānas* to four pieces of cloth of the same measurements, yet made of thick, thin, thinner, and very thin thread respectively, all spun by the same person. Though there is no difference in their nature as pieces of cloth or in their measurements, yet they differ in thier softness to the touch, fineness, and costliness.[1]

Whereas the four lower *jhānas* can each take a variety of objects—the ten *kasiṇas*, the in-and-out breath, etc.—and do not stand in any integral relation to these objects, the four immaterial *jhānas* each take a single object inseparably related to the attainment itself. These objects also relate to each other by way of successive dependence. Buddhaghosa illustrates this with another one of his picturesque analogies. A man arrived at a dirty place where a tent was set up, and being disgusted with the dirt, he hung on to the tent. Another man came along and leant upon the man hanging on to the tent. A third arrived, and thinking both were insecure, stood outside the tent. A fourth came, found the third man more securely placed, and leant upon

1. PP., pp. 369-70. Vism., p. 282.

him. The commentator connects the similes with the four *āruppas* thus:

> The space from which the kasina has been removed is like the tent in the dirty place. The [consciousness of the] base consisting of boundless space, which makes space its object owing to disgust with the sign of the fine-material, is like the man who hangs on to the tent owing to disgust with the dirt. The [consciousness of the] base consisting of boundless consciousness, the occurrence of which is contingent upon [the consciousness of] the base consisting of boundless space whose object is space, is like the man who leans upon the man who hangs on to the tent. The [consciousness of the] base consisting of nothingness, which instead of making the [consciousness of the] base consisting of boundless space its object has the non-existence of that as its object, is like the man who, after considering the insecurity of those two does not lean upon the one hanging on to the tent, but stands outside. The [consciousness of the] base consisting of neither perception nor non-perception, the occurrence of which is contingent upon [the consciousness of] the base consisting of nothingness, which stands in a place outside, in other words, in the non-existence of [the past] consciousness, is like the man who stands leaning upon the last-named, having considered the insecurity of the one hanging on to the tent and the one leaning upon him, and fancying that the one standing outside is well placed.[1]

Although the yogin who aspires to reach the base of neither perception nor non-perception has seen the flaws in the base of nothingness, it is necessary for him to take this base as his object since there is no other object sufficiently subtle to serve as a foundation for reaching the highest formless attainment. This is similar to the case of men who remain loyal to a despotic king because they depend on him for their livelihood.

Although these four immaterial *jhānas* are separately described in the suttas, they are not mentioned as often as the four fine material *jhānas*. The reason for this omission can be understood to be their implicit inclusion in the fourth *jhāna*, made on the

1. PP., pp. 370-71. Vism., p. 283.

basis of their similarity of factors. Therefore, in places where the practices beyond the *jhānas* are discussed, the fourth *jhāna* alone is mentioned as their prerequisite since the *āruppas* are understood to be incorporated within it.

The Modes of Direct Knowledge

In the suttas the meditator who has attained and mastered the fourth *jhāna* is sometimes shown as proceeding to attain certain kinds of supernormal knowledge. These modes of higher knowledge are presented in different sets of varying number in the texts. Some suttas mention three, called the "threefold knowledge" (*tevijjā*): [1] the knowledge of recollecting previous lives (*pubbenivāsānussatiñāna*), [2] the knowledge of the passing away and rebirth of beings (*cutūpapātañāṇa*), and [3] the knowledge of the destruction of the cankers (*āsavakkhayañāṇa*).[1] Some suttas mention five kinds of direct knowledge (*pañcābhiññā*): [1] the knowledge of the modes of supernormal power (*iddhividhañāṇa*), [2] the divine ear-element (*dibbasotadhātuñāṇa*), (3) the knowledge of others' minds (*cetopariyañāṇa*), [4] the knowledge of recollecting previous lives, and [5] the knowledge of the passing away and rebirth of beings.[2] Other suttas expand this list to six (*chalabhiññā*) by adding the knowledge of the destruction of the cankers (*āsavakkhayañāṇa*).[3] In this case the first five are called mundane modes of direct knowledge (*lokiya abhiññā*), the sixth the supramundane direct knowledge (*lokuttara abhiññā*). Still other suttas present a set of eight modes of higher knowledge. This set, which does not have a special name, consists of the above six *abhiññās* augmented by knowledge and vision (*ñāṇadassana*) and the knowledge of the mind-made body (*manomayiddhiñāṇa*).[4] We will discuss these modes of higher knowledge in turn, taking the six *abhiññās* as the basis for our account and then adding explanations of the others. But first a few remarks are called for on the preliminaries for the modes of direct knowledge.

1. AN. 1 : 163-65.
2. SN. 2 : 216.
3. DN. 3 : 281.
4. DN. 1 : 76-77.

The Prerequisites for Direct Knowledge

In order to develop the five mundane *abhiññās*, as well as the knowledge of the mind-created body, it is necessary to have gained proficiency in the eight meditative attainments comprising the four fine material *jhānas* and the four *āruppas*. Although the suttas often show the exercise of the *abhiññās* taking place immediately after the fourth *jhāna*, without mentioning the formless attainments, the commentaries state that the latter also have to be understood as their prerequisites. The reason they are not mentioned is that they are implicitly included by the fourth *jhāna*, which alone serves as the immediate basis for the exercise of the *abhiññās*. The mundane *jhānas* and the exercises based on them, however, are not requirements for the sixth, supramundane *abhiññā*. This latter is the outcome of wisdom rather than of absorption, as we will see below.

For the meditator to achieve the *abhiññās* he should accomplish the eight attainments in each of the eight *kasiṇas*, the four elemental *kasiṇas* (earth, water, fire, and air) and the four color *kasiṇas* (blue, yellow, red, and white). Then he should acquire complete control of his mind in the following fourteen ways.[1]

[1] The meditator must attain *jhāna* in the eight *kasiṇas* in the direct order given in the texts, i.e. from the earth *kasiṇa* through to the white *kasiṇa*, doing so even up to a thousand times in each one until he is fully adept at it. [2] Having mastered the direct order, the yogin should attain *jhāna* in the *kasiṇas* in reverse order, moving from the white *kasiṇa* back to the earth *kasiṇa*. [3] He should next attain *jhāna* again and again in forward and reverse order from the earth *kasiṇa* to the white *kasiṇa* and then back again.

[4] The yogin should attain each of the attainments in direct order from the first *jhāna* up to the base of neither perception nor non-perception. [5] Then he should master the *jhānas* in reverse order, from the eighth down to the first. And next [6] he should move through the *jhānas* in both direct and reverse order.

[7] The meditator should skip alternate *jhānas* while retaining the same *kasiṇa*. That is, with the earth *kasiṇa* as object he should attain the first *jhāna*, third *jhāna*, base of boundless space, and

1. PP., pp. 410-11. Vism., pp. 314-15.

base of nothingness, then repeat the same for the water *kasiṇa*, etc. [8] Then he should skip alternate *kasiṇas* without skipping *jhānas*; he attains the first *jhāna* in the earth, fire, blue, and red *kasiṇas*, then repeats the same for each of the other *jhānas*. [9] The meditator next proceeds to skipping *jhānas* and *kasiṇas* together. He should attain the first *jhāna* in the earth *kasiṇa*, the third in the fire *kasiṇa*, the base of boundless space by removing the blue *kasiṇa*, and the base of nothingness arrived at through the red *kasiṇa*.

[10] The next state, called "transposition of factors", involves attaining the first *jhāna* up to the fourth *āruppa* all in the same *kasiṇa*. [11] He then attains the first *jhāna* in each of the *kasiṇas* from the earth *kasiṇa* through the white *kasiṇa*, a stage called "transposition of objects.' [12] He next masters combined "transposition of factors and objects," changing the *jhānas* and objects in matched correspondance to each other, that is, attaining the first *jhāna* in the earth *kasiṇa*, the second in the water *kasiṇa*, the third in the fire *kasiṇa*, and so forth up to the base of neither perception nor non-perception arrived at from the white *kasiṇa*.

[13] The next step, "definition of factors," means defining each of the *jhānas* from the first to the eighth by way of its constituent factors, the first as five-factored, the second as three-factored, etc. [14] The last step, "definition of object," means defining only the object, as "This is the earth *kasiṇa*," etc. up to "This is the white *kasiṇa*."

After mastering these fourteen modes the meditator should develop the four bases of accomplishment—zeal (*chanda*), consciousness (*citta*), energy (*viriya*), and inquiry (*vimaṁsā*)—cultivating them to a high level of intensity. Having fulfilled all the preliminary conditions, the meditator must direct his mind to the kind of supernormal knowledge he wishes to attain. The *abhiññās* do not come as automatic by-products of *jhāna* but require a prior resolution and determinate effort on the part of the yogin. As the Buddha says, when the meditator's mind is concentrated and purified "he directs, he inclines his mind to the kinds of supernormal power."[1]

1. "Iddhividhāya cittaṁ abhinīharati abhininnāmeti." DN. 1:77-78.

The Six *Abhiññās*

[1] *Knowledge of the modes of super-normal power (iddhividhañāṇa)*

The Pali word *iddhi*, which we translate as "supernormal power," literally means success or accomplishment. The main sense suggested by the word is an ability to perform feats which go against the normal course of natural events. For this reason the *iddhis* have sometimes been interpreted as supernatural or miraculous powers, but from the Buddhist standpoint these powers do not derive from any supernatural source but from a psychic potency based upon a superior understanding of the inner dynamics of nature. Thus they operate completely within the framework of the law of cause and effect and the "miracles" for which they are responsible remain entirely natural.

The kinds of supernormal power exercised by a meditator are described in the texts in the following stock passage:

> When his concentrated mind is thus purified, bright, unblemished, rid of defilement, and has become malleable, wieldy, steady, and attained to imperturbability, he directs, he inclines his mind to the kinds of supernormal power. He wields the various kinds of supernormal power. Having been one, he becomes many; having been many, he becomes one. He appears and vanishes. He goes unhindered through walls, through enclosures, through mountains, as though in open space. He dives in and out of the earth as though in water. He goes on unbroken water as though on earth. Seated cross-legged he travels in space like a winged bird. With his hand he touches and strokes the moon and sun so mighty and powerful. He wields bodily mastery even as far as the Brahma world.[1]

In this passage eight supernormal powers are expounded. We will examine them briefly one by one.

[1] The first supernormal power is becoming many after having been one or becoming one after having been many.[2] This means the ability to create many forms of oneself and then

1. PP., pp. 409, 420. Vism., pp. 315, 323. DN. 1: 77.
2. In Pali: "Eko pi hutvā bahudhā hoti, bahudhā pi hutvā eko hoti."

to dissolve those many forms and return to the condition of having a single body. To exercise this power the meditator should enter the fourth *jhāna* as a basis for direct knowledge and emerge from it. Then he must resolve on the number of forms of himself he wishes to create. He again attains the fourth *jhāna*, emerges, and resolves. Simultaneously with the resolving consciousness he becomes the number of forms he decided upon—a hundred, a thousand, etc., as he wishes. Presumably in most cases the ability to create an increasing number of forms must be gradually acquired. Unless a specific determination is made otherwise, the many created forms will appear just like the original and perform the same actions he performs. But by means of a prior resolution, the yogin can display his many forms with different appearances and cause them to perform different actions. To become one again he should repeat the original procedure, resolving to become one. But if he originally resolved to appear as many for a limited time, the many forms will disappear automatically when the time lapses.[1]

[2] The second power is causing appearance and disappearance.[2] "Causing appearance" means making a dark area appear light, making what is hidden become visible, or making oneself or others become visible even when at a distance. "Causing disappearance" means making a bright area appear dark, making what is manifest become invisible, or making oneself or others become invisible even when within range of sight. The procedure is the same as in the case of the previous power except that the resolution is changed.

[3] To exercise the power of going through walls, enclosures, and mountains as though through space[3] the yogin should attain the fourth *jhāna* in the space *kasiṇa*. Then he does the preliminary work by adverting to the wall, enclosure or mountain, etc. and resolving upon it as space. As a result of his resolution it becomes space and he passes through it unhindered.

[4] In order to acquire the ability to dive in and out of the ground as if it were water[4] the yogin must have obtained the water *kasiṇa* attainment. He enters into the fourth *jhāna* on the

1. PP., pp. 420-27. Vism., pp. 323-28.
2. In Pali: Āvībhāvatirobhāvaṁ.
3. In Pali: Tiro-kuḍḍaṁ tiro-pākāraṁ tiro-pabbataṁ.
4. In Pali: Paṭhaviyā pi ummujja nimmujjaṁ karoti seyyātha pi udake.

water *kasiṇa* and emerges. Then he adverts to a portion of ground and resolves upon it thus "Let there be water." The earth becomes water and he can dive in it, bathe in it, drink it, etc. If he resolves only this much the earth becomes water for him alone, but if he makes a determination it can become water for others as well.

[5] The yogin who wishes to walk on water without sinking as though it were earth[1] should be skilled in the earth *kasiṇa*. He enters the fourth *jhāna* on the earth *kasiṇa*, emerges, and resolves "Let the water become earth." He repeats the procedure, and with the resolution the water in the determined area becomes earth. Then he can walk on it without falling in.

[6] To travel through space like a bird[2] the yogin obtains the earth *kasiṇa* and emerges. He determines upon space as being earth, thinking "Let there be earth." For him space becomes solid like the earth and he can walk, stand, sit, or lie down there just as men normally can do on the ground.

[7] The next power, touching and stroking the sun and moon with one's hand,[3] does not require a special *kasiṇa* but is accomplished simply through the fourth *jhāna* that is made a basis for direct knowledge. The meditator can either go to the sun and moon and touch them, or make them come into hand's reach by a mental resolution, doing so by enlarging his hand. But though he does all this, for others the sun and moon remain the same, their radiance and movement being unaffected.

[8] The last of the powers is exercising bodily mastery as far as the Brahma-world.[4] Having attained the basic *jhāna*, the meditator who wants to go to the Brahma-world can resolve upon it as near and it becomes as he wishes. He can make the near become distant, the many become few, and the few become many. He can see the Brahma's form with his divine sight, hear the Brahma's voice with his divine ear, and know the Brahma's mind with his power of thought reading. He can travel to the Brahma-world with a visible or invisible body and perform many feats of psychic power in the presence of Brahma.[5]

1. In Pali: Udake pi abhijjamāno gacchati seyyathā pi paṭhaviyaṁ.
2. In Pali: Ākāse pi pallaṅkena kamati seyyathā pi pakkhī sakuṇo.
3. In Pali: Ime pi candima-suriyā evaṁ mahiddhike evaṁ mahānubhāve pāṇinā parimasati parimajjati.
4. In Pali: Yāva Brahma-lokā pi kāyena va saṁvatteti.
5. See Pts., pp. 387-388. Vism., pp. 331-332.

The Three Wonders

The possession of *iddhi* is regarded as a desirable quality in a bhikkhu which contributes to the completeness of his spiritual perfection. However, exhibiting supernormal powers to gain adherents, win offerings, or obtain popularity has been prohibited by the Buddha. In the Vinaya the display of supernormal feats or psychic powers is classified as an offense of wrong doing (*āpatti-dukkaṭa*).[1] Nevertheless, while the Buddha rebuked Piṇḍola Bhāradvāja for exhibiting his power to obtain a sandalwood bowl, he expressed approval of Moggallāna's exercise of psychic powers.[2] The reason for this difference is that the former made an indiscreet public exhibition of his power while the latter used them judiciously. The Buddha approved of the exhibition of psychic power only when it helps eliminate the defilements in peoples' minds and makes them free from obsessions.

Sometimes the word *iddhi* appears in combination with another word *pāṭihāriya*, which means literally "prevention" or "warding off" but assumes the sense of "wonder" or "marvel"; the compound *iddhi-pāṭihāriya* thus signifies the "wonder of supernormal powers." The term appears in the suttas in a triad of "wonders" comprising the following : [1] the wonder of supernormal powers (*iddhipāṭihāriya*), [2] the wonder of manifestation or thought-reading (*ādesanāpāṭihāriya*), and [3] the wonder of education (*anusāsanipāṭihāriya*).[3] The first is explained simply by the stock passage on the supernormal powers. The wonder of manifestation involves telling people what their mental states are on the basis of thought-reading, interpretation, or messages received from other beings, human or non-human. The wonder of education is the ability to guide others in their spiritual development, telling them : "You should think these thoughts, you should not think those thoughts; you should attend in this way, not in that way; you should abandon this; you should enter and abide thus." Of these three wonders, the Buddha disapproved of using the first two to convert people to his teaching. He said that there are certain magical sciences (*vijjā*) which can enable a person to perform supernormal feats or practice thought reading and thus

1. Vinp. 2:112.
2. SN. 4:269.
3. DN. 1:212-15. Pts., pp. 401-404.

these wonders cannot be taken as indicators of real spiritual accomplishment. The wonder to which he gave unqualified approval was the wonder of education, which alone leads to liberation from suffering.

The Paṭisambhidāmagga, elaborating this idea, states that the wonderful methods which promote renunciation, non-hatred, mental luminosity, composure of mind, determination of righteousness, wisdom, bliss, the attainment of the *jhānas*, etc., up to the path of arahatship are called the true *iddhi* as they bring real accomplishment and success. The methods that destroy sensual desire, ill will, sloth and torpor, restlessness and remorse, doubt, ignorance, clinging, the hindrances and defilements are called the real *pāṭihāriya* for the reason that they prevent one from falling back into *saṁsāra*.[1] Thus for early Buddhism the practice of the noble path rather than performance of miracles constitutes the truly wonderful accomplishment.

[2] *The second abhiññā : the divine ear-element (dibbasotadhātu)*

The divine ear-element is the ability to hear the sounds of deities as well as of human beings, and to hear sounds that are far off, even in another world system, as well as sounds that are extremely near, such as the sounds of the creatures living in one's own body. The texts describe the divine ear-element as follows:

> He directs, he inclines, his mind to the divine ear-element. With the divine ear-element, which is purified and surpasses the human, he hears both kinds of sounds, the divine and the human, those that are far as well as near.[2]

Technically, the divine ear-element refers to a particular capacity for knowledge, called an "ear-element" for the reason that it exercises the function of the normal ear, namely, acting as a basis for the hearing of sounds. This element is said to be "divine" because it is similar to the ear-element of the deities, which is free from imperfections and capable of receiving far-off sounds.

To obtain the divine ear-element the meditator should attain the basic *jhāna* for direct-knowledge and then emerge from it.

1. Pts., pp. 401-404.
2. PP., p. 446. DN. 1: 79.

Keeping his mind at the level of preliminary work concentration, he should advert first to gross sounds within the normal range of hearing, then gradually to more and more subtle sounds until he can hear the faintest sounds that can only be heard with the most careful attention. He should concentrate on each of the ten directions, attending to the precise "signs" or qualities of the sounds being heard.

When he concentrates his mind on these sounds with an earnest desire to gain the divine ear-element, in time a mind-door adverting consciousness will arise taking one of these sounds for its object. This will be followed by three or four impulsions (*javana*) of the preliminary or access stage, and a fourth or fifth of the absorption level belonging to the fourth *jhāna*. The faculty of knowledge arisen in association with this absorption consciousness is called the divine ear-element.

If the yogin wishes to hear distant sounds he should begin by delimiting a small area, master the ability to hear the sounds in that area, and then extend the range of his hearing outward by degrees. As his ability improves he can hear distinctly all the sounds on earth and in the other planes of existence within a world system and even further. Moreover, if he wants to, he can define each sound separately, even when it is merged with other sounds.

[3] *The third abhiññā : the knowledge of others' minds (cetopariya ñāṇa, paracittavijānana)*

The third *abhiññā* is the knowledge of others' minds, the ability to penetrate with one's own mind the mental states of others. The Buddha describes this *abhiññā* as follows:

> With his mind thus concentrated...he applies and directs his mind to the knowledge of the state of others' minds. Discriminating with his mind he understands the state of others' minds: that of a mind with passion he understands that it is with passion, of one free from passion that it is free from passion...with hatred ...free from hatred...with delusion... free from delusion...that which is composed...distracted... grown great (having attained to the *rūpa* and the *arūpa jhānas*) ...not grown great...mean...lofty...concentrated...not con-

centrated...emancipated...not emancipated. Thus he knows the state of others' minds.[1]

According to the explanation in the *Visuddhimagga*, a meditator who aspires to this knowledge must first have attained the divine eye, the faculty of supernormal vision (to be explained below). He should use the light-*kasiṇa* to extend light, radiating it into the physical hearts of the people whose minds he wishes to understand. With his divine eye he should then examine the color of the heart, which provides a key for interpreting the state of mind. According to Buddhaghosa, when a joyous state of mind is present the blood is red like banyan fruit, when a state accompanied by grief is present the blood is black like rose-apple fruit, and when a state accompanied by serenity is present the blood is clear like a sesamum oil.[2] Once the meditator gains familiarity with reading minds on the basis of the blood color, he can learn to penetrate the minds of others directly, without having to rely on a physical basis for making inferences. It should be pointed out, however, that a meditator possessing this faculty of knowledge still cannot penetrate the minds of those on a higher level of attainment than his own. Thus a worldling with mundane direct knowledge cannot penetrate the mind of an ariyan and know how the latter is free from certain defilements. Similarly, a stream-enterer cannot penetrate the mind of a once-returner, a once-returner the mind of a non-returner, a non-returner the mind of an arahant, or an arahant the mind of a pacceka-buddha or fully enlightened Buddha. The converse, however, is possible: one on a higher plane, if he has the faculty of penetrating others' minds, can know the minds of those on a lower plane.[3]

[4] *The fourth abhiññā : the knowledge of recollecting previous lives (pubbenivāsānussatiñāṇa)*

The knowledge of recollecting previous lives is explained in the suttas as follows :

1. Vajiranāna, *Buddhist Meditation*, pp. 445-46 DN. 1:79-80.
2. PP., p. 449. Vism., pp. 344-45. It should be noted, though, that Buddhaghosa does not mention the correspondence between blood-color and states of mind accompanied by greed, hatred, delusion, and their opposites, as given in the sutta.
3. PP., p. 473. Vism., p. 364.

With his mind thus concentrated...he applies and directs his mind to the knowledge of recollecting previous existences. He recollects various kinds of former lives, such as one birth, two, three, four, five, ten, twenty, thirty, forty, fifty, a hundred, a thousand, a hundred thousand births, many cycles of evolution of the universe, of dissolution, and of evolution and dissolution. 'In that one I had such a name, clan, caste, such sustenance, experiencing such pleasure and pain, and having such an end of life. Passing away thence I was reborn in such a place. There too I had such a name, clan...and such an end of life. Passing away thence I was reborn here'. Thus he remembers various kinds of his former lives with their modes and details.[1]

A meditator who wishes to cultivate this knowledge should attain the fourth *jhāna* as a basis for direct knowledge and then emerge from it. Having emerged he should start recalling his most recent activities in as precise detail as possible. If he cannot recollect something he should attain the basic *jhāna*, emerge, and advert. The experience of the *jhāna* clears away the obstructions to memory so that the apparently lost events become as evident as when a lamp is lit. Beginning with moments, he should go back in increasingly larger units—days, months, years, and so on—until he arrives at the moment of rebirth in the present existence. At this point he should advert to the mind and body at the moment of death in his preceding existence. If he cannot recall his past life at once due to the separation between lives he should not give up but should attain the basic *jhāna*, emerge, and advert again and again if necessary.

When his ability has matured there will arise in him a mind-door adverting consciousness making its object the mind-body compound existing at the death-moment of his previous life. This will be followed by four or five impulsions with the same object, the last of which is an absorption consciousness of the fourth *jhāna*. The knowledge associated with that consciousness is the knowledge of recollecting previous lives. Then beginning with the recollection of a single past life, the meditator should repeat the procedure with more and more past lives, until he can

1. Vajirañāna, *Buddhist Meditation.*, pp. 447-48. DN. 1:81.

recall in detail his past experiences in entire aeons on end.[1] The Buddha compares this knowledge to the memory of a man who travels from village to village: while staying in one village he can recall the number of villages he has already visited, what he did in each village, and all the details of his experience in each village.[2]

[5] *The fifth abhiññā : the divine eye (dibbacakkhu)—the knowledge of the passing away and rebirth of beings (cutūpapātañāṇa)*

The text describing this *abhiññā* reads:

With his mind thus concentrated...he applies and directs his mind to the knowledge of the passing away and rebirth of beings. With his divine vision, purified and surpassing human sight, he sees beings passing away and being reborn again, low or high, of good or bad appearance, in happy or miserable existences, according to their karma. He fully realizes that those beings who are revilers of the noble ones, who are of false views, who acquire the karma of their false views, at the dissolution of the body after death have been reborn in a miserable existence, in hell. But those beings who are given to good conduct in deed, word and thought, who are not revilers of the noble ones, who are of right views, who acquire the karma of their right views, at the dissolution of the body after death have been reborn in a happy existence, in the world of heaven.[3]

The knowledge of the passing away and rebirth of beings is acquired by means of the divine eye, a supernormal faculty of vision called "divine" because it is similar to the vision of the deities in its ability to perceive objects at remote distances and to see objects hidden behind walls, etc. This vision is also said to be "purified" because by bringing both death and rebirth into range, it contributes to the purification of understanding. One who sees only passing away but not rebirth generally inclines to the annihilationist view that a being is extinguished at death; one who sees only birth but not the previous passing away gene-

1. PP., pp. 453-55. Vism., pp. 347-49.
2. DN. 1:81-82.
3. Vajirañāṇa, *Buddhist Meditation*, p. 451. DN. 1:82.

rally inclines to the view that a new being arises. But one who sees both can acquire the purified view of rebirth according to *kamma*, thus abandoning these defiled views. The *Visuddhimagga* points out that one with the divine eye cannot see death and rebirth at the precise moments of their occurrence, due to the brevity and extreme subtlety of these events. What he sees are beings on the verge of death who will now die, and then those who have taken rebirth and have just reappeared.

The commentaries recommend three *kasiṇas* as the object for developing this knowledge—the fire *kasiṇa*, white *kasiṇa*, or light *kasiṇa*; of the three, the light *kasiṇa* is said to be the most effective. After emerging from the basic *jhāna*, the meditator should focus on one of these *kasiṇas*, stopping at the level of access concentration. He should not enter absorption since if he does he will not be able to perform the preliminary work for the direct-knowledge. At the level of access the meditator should extend the *kasiṇa* image over a predetermined area, so that its light illuminates the area and visible forms within its space come into range of his vision. If the light disappears he should again enter the basic *jhāna*, emerge, and pervade the area with light. As time goes on he develops the ability to pervade any area with light and remain watching the visible forms there for a whole day. When visible forms that are not perceptible to the ordinary fleshly eye—such as objects inside the body, objects hidden behind walls, objects in other planes of existence or in other world systems—come into the focus of the meditator's eye of knowledge and are seen directly, then the divine eye has arisen. To make this divine eye the instrument for perceiving the passing away and rebirth of beings, the meditator should apply his divine vision to this object until it comes into view.

The divine eye, or knowledge of passing away and re-arising, has two accessory kinds of knowledge, namely, knowledge of the future (*anāgataṁsa ñāṇa*), and knowledge of faring according to *kamma* (*yathākammūpagañāṇa*).[1] The former is the ability to foresee where a being will be reborn in the future and to foresee the course of future events. The latter is the ability to discern the *kamma* of the past that brought a being to a particular destiny in the present. Though these two types of knowledge are made

1. PP., pp. 471, 477-78. Vism., pp. 363, 367-68.

possible by the divine eye, they differ from the knowledge of the passing away and rebirth of beings in that this last has the present as its province while the other two have as their provinces the future and the past respectively. By counting these modes of direct knowledge separately the number of mundane *abhiññās* possible for a meditator is totaled at seven. But when they are included within the divine eye the number is given as five.

[6] *The sixth abhiññā : the knowledge of the destruction of the cankers (āsavakkhayañāṇa)*

The sixth direct-knowledge available to a meditator is the knowledge of the destruction of the cankers. The "cankers" are called in Pali *āsavas*, meaning literally that which flows out; thus the word is sometimes translated "outflows." The term signifies certain fundamental defilements which "flow out" from the mind, sustaining the process of *saṁsāra*. In the earliest texts the *āsavas* are usually given as three in number: the canker of sensual desire (*kāmāsava*), the canker of (craving for) existence (*bhavāsava*), and the canker of ignorance (*avijjāsava*). Other texts, particularly those of the Abhidhammapiṭaka, add a fourth, the canker of wrong views (*diṭṭhāsava*).

The meditator's attainment of the destruction of the cankers is described in the suttas in the following passage:

> With his mind thus concentrated...he applies, he directs his mind to the knowledge of the destruction of the cankers. He knows suffering as it is; he knows the origin of suffering as it is; he knows the cessation of suffering as it is; he knows the path leading to the cessation of suffering as it is. He knows the cankers as they are; he knows the origin of the cankers as it is; he knows the cessation of the cankers as it is; he knows the path leading to the cessation of cankers as it is. The mind of him who knows thus is liberated from the canker of sensual desire, from the canker of existence, and from the canker of ignorance. In him who is liberated the knowledge arises that he is liberated. He understands: 'Rebirth is destroyed; the noble life has been lived; what was to be done has been done; nothing else remains to be done henceforth'.[1]

1. DN. 1:83-84.

According to the commentary the "knowledge of the destruction of the cankers" is the faculty of knowledge belonging to the path of arahatship, the last of the four stages of enlightenment.[1] As the stock description makes clear, the content of this knowledge is the Four Noble Truths. By knowing and seeing for himself with direct perception the Four Noble Truths in their full depth and range, the meditator eradicates the mental corruptions and attains complete emancipation. As this realization results from insight, we will discuss it more fully in the next chapter, in connection with the supramundane paths.

For the present two observations should be made concerning the sixth *abhiññā*. First, we should note that though the texts often show the knowledge of the destruction of the cankers as following the fourth *jhāna*, the latter is not indispensable for its attainment. The realization of the Four Noble Truths can arise with any *jhāna* as its basis, and it is even recognized that some meditators can achieve the liberating knowledge without any previous experience in the mundane *jhānas*, solely by the power of their faculty of wisdom. What is required in all cases for the attainment of the noble paths is the development of insight, which can be either based upon some prior attainment in *jhānic* concentration or proceed in a "dry" manner based solely upon the momentary concentration connected with mindful observation of phenomena. In this respect the sixth *abhiññā* differs from the other five, which all presuppose proficiency in the eight attainments belonging to absorption-concentration.

For this reason the sixth *abhiññā* differs from the other five in a second respect, namely, that it is regarded as an acquisition exclusive to the Buddha's dispensation. The other five *abhiññās* are all mundane, being based solely upon the development of concentration. Since the methods of developing concentration are available in non-Buddhist disciplines, those who follow these disciplines and achieve sufficient power of concentration can also acquire the mundane *abhiññās*. However, the knowledge of the destruction of the cankers is a supramundane attainment which arises out of insight into the nature of phenomena. Hence it can only be gained by Buddhas, paccekabuddhas, and arahant disciples. In the case of the Buddhas and paccekabuddhas it

1. DN.A. 1:201.

arises out of their own self-evolved wisdom (*sayambhuñāṇa*); in the case of disciples it arises by practicing insight meditation in accordance with the instructions received from a Buddha or from teachers who transmit his dispensation.

Because of these differences between the sixth *abhiññā* and the others, the *abhiññās* are collected together into two groups, overlapping, but distinct. On the one hand there is the five *abhiññās*, comprising the five kinds of mundane direct-knowledge; on the other there is the six *abhiññās*, comprising the five mundane forms of direct-knowledge together with the knowledge of the destruction of the cankers. While the mundane *abhiññās* are regarded as ornaments of a yogin within the Buddha's dispensation, the sixth *abhiññā* is regarded as its vital essence, the supreme goal of the entire practice of meditation.

Other Kinds of Supernormal Knowledge

In addition to the six *abhiññās*, certain suttas mention two other kinds of superior knowledge following the fourth *jhāna*. These are called "knowledge and vision" (*ñāṇadassana*) and "the knowledge of the mind-created body" (*manomaya iddhi ñāṇa*). In the texts they immediately precede the six *abhiññās*, though the eight are not collected together into a single group with a collective name.[1]

> The textual description of "knowledge and vision" is as follows: With his mind thus concentrated...he applies and directs his mind to knowledge and vision. He understands: 'This body of mine is material, composed of the four primary elements. It originates from mother and father, is sustained by rice and gruel, subject to impermanence, erosion, abrasion, dissolution, and disintegration. And this consciousness of mine is dependent on it and bound up with it'.[2]

According to the commentary, "knowledge and vision" in this passage signifies insight-knowledge (*vipassanāñāṇa*).[3] After emerging from the fourth *jhāna*, the yogin directs his attention to his

1. DN. 1:76-77. MN. 2:17-18.
2. DN. 1: 76.
3. DN.A. 1:197.

body and mind. He first discerns the body, and sees it as material, compounded, dependently arisen, impermanent, subject to destruction. He then directs his attention to the mind, and sees the mind occurring in dependence on the body, sharing its conditioned, impermanent, and insubstantial nature. This knowledge of insight, brought to its apex, issues in the knowledge of the destruction of the cankers.

The second auxiliary type of higher knowledge is the knowledge of the mind-made body. The textual description reads:

> With his mind thus concentrated...,he creates from this body another body which has material form, is mind-made, having all its major and minor parts, not deficient in any sense organ.[1]

A meditator wishing to create the mind-made body should emerge from the basic fourth *jhāna*, advert to his own body, and resolve that it be hollow. When it appears to him as hollow, he should do the preliminary work and then resolve "Let there be another body inside it." Another body then appears within his original body which he can draw out "like a reed from its sheath, like a sword from its scabbard, like a snake from its slough."[2]

The Paṭisambhidāmagga describes one other supernormal power of the *iddhi* type not explicitly mentioned in the suttas, though implied by certain incidents. This is the supernormal power of transformation (*vikubbana iddhi*)—the ability to transform the appearance of one's own body or to display illusory forms.[3]

To attain this power the meditator should first resolve to appear in a particular form, such as the form of a boy, a deity, an animal, etc. Then he should enter and emerge from the basic fourth *jhāna* and advert to his appearance in the form chosen. Again he should enter the *jhāna*, emerge, and resolve, "Let me be a boy, etc. of such and such a type." Simultaneously with his resolution he appears as a boy or as anything else he chooses. However, it is not necessary for the meditator to effect the transformation on his own body. He can simply resolve upon showing some form, such as an elephant, a horse, etc., and that form will become manifest before himself and others.

1. DN. 1:77.
2. PP., p. 444. Vism., p. 342.
3. PP., p. 444. Vism., p. 342. Pts., p. 388.

The Jhānas and Rebirth

According to Buddhist doctrine all sentient beings in whom ignorance and craving remain present are subject to rebirth. As long as there is a desire to go on existing in some form the process of existence will continue. The specific factor which determines the place and conditions of rebirth is *kamma*. *Kamma* is volitional action—deeds, words, and thoughts expressive of deliberate intention, either unwholesome (*akusala*) or wholesome (*kusala*). Unwholesome *kammas* are actions rooted in greed, hatred, and delusion, wholesome *kammas* actions rooted in non-greed, non-hatred, and non-delusion. Each *kamma* or intentional action that a person performs becomes accumulated in his mental continuum, where it remains as a force capable of producing results (*vipāka*) in the future. These results correspond to the ethical quality of the action: wholesome *kammas* bring happiness and success, unwholesome *kammas* bring suffering and failure. In relation to the rebirth process, wholesome *kammas* issue in a good rebirth, unwholesome *kammas* in a bad one.

As a kind of wholesome *kamma*, *jhāna* plays a key role in the process of rebirth. Of the many *kammas* a person performs in the course of his lifetime, one *kamma* comes to the surface at the time of death to determine his state of rebirth. The *kammas* that take on this decisive role are ranked into grades of precedence. Priority is given to morally weighty *kamma*, extremely powerful virtuous or evil deeds. Weighty virtuous deeds are the attainment of the *jhānas*; weighty evil deeds include patricide, matricide, killing an arahat, wounding a Buddha, and causing schism in the Sangha. Next in order come morally significant deeds performed near the time of death, then habitual actions, and lastly, miscellaneous stored up *kammas*.[1] Those *kammas* which do not actually generate rebirth can still produce their results in the course of a person's life, either supporting, countering, or annihilating the effects of the rebirth-generative *kamma*.

According to Buddhist cosmology, there are many planes of existence where beings take rebirth through their *kamma*. These planes are grouped into three general spheres: the sense sphere (*kāmāvacarabhūmi*), which is the field of rebirth for evil *kammas*

1. Narada, *Manual*, pp. 259-62.

and for non-*jhānic* meritorious *kammas*; the fine material sphere (*rūpāvacarabhūmi*), which is the field of rebirth for the fine material *jhānas*; and the immaterial sphere (*arūpāvacarabhūmi*), which is the field of rebirth for the *āruppas*.

If an unwholesome *kamma* becomes determinative of rebirth, it will produce rebirth in one of four planes: [1] the woeful state (*niraya*), [2] the animal kingdom (*tiracchānayoni*), [3] the sphere of "hungry ghosts" (*pettivisaya*), and [4] the host of titans (*asurakāya*). These four states are collectively called the plane of misery (*apāyabhūmi*), the bad destinations (*duggati*), and the downfall (*vinipāta*). If a wholesome *kamma* of a sub-*jhānic* type determines rebirth, it will produce rebirth in either the human world (*manussaloka*) or in one of the six sense sphere heavenly worlds, namely: [1] the realm of the four great kings (*cātummahārājikadevaloka*), [2] the realm of the thirty-three gods (*tāvatiṁsa*), [3] the realm of Yama gods (*yama*), [4] the realm of delight (*tusita*), [5] the realm of gods who rejoice in their own creations (*nimmāṇarati*), and [6] the realm of gods who lord over the creations of others (*paranimmitavasavatti*). These seven realms, the human world and the six heavenly worlds, together make up the sense sphere plane of happiness (*kāmāvacara sugatibhūmi*).

Above the sense sphere realms are the fine material realms (*rūpāvacarabhūmi*). Rebirth into these realms is gained through the attainment of the four fine material *jhānas*, providing the *jhāna* is still retained at the time of death. The sixteen realms in this plane are hierarchically ordered in correlation with the four *jhānas*. Those who have practiced the first *jhāna* to a minor degree are reborn in the realm of the retinue of Brahmā (*brahmapārisajja*), those who have practiced it to a moderate degree are reborn in the realm of the ministers of Brahmā (*brahmapurohita*), and those who have practiced it to a superior degree are reborn in the realm of the great Brahmā (*mahābrahma*). Similarly, practicing the second *jhāna* to a minor degree brings rebirth in the realm of minor luster (*parittābha*), to a moderate in the realm of infinite luster (*appamāṇābha*), and to a superior degree in the realm of radiant luster (*ābhassara*). Again, practicing the third *jhāna* to a minor degree brings rebirth in the realm of minor aura (*parittasubha*), to a moderate degree in the realm of infinite aura (*appamāṇasubha*), and to a superior degree in the realm of steady aura (*subhakiṇha*).

Corresponding to the fourth *jhāna* there are seven realms: the realm of great reward (*vehapphala*), the realm of non-percipient beings (*asaññasatta*), and the five pure abodes (*suddhāvāsa*). With this *jhāna* the previous pattern is not observed. It seems that all beings who practice the fourth *jhāna* of the mundane level without reaching any supramundane attainment are reborn in the realm of great reward. There is no differentiation by way of inferior, moderate, or superior grades of development. The realm of non-percipient beings is reached by those who, after attaining the fourth *jhāna*, then use the power of their meditation to take rebirth with only material bodies ; they do not acquire consciousness again until they pass away from this realm. The five pure abodes—called the durable (*aviha*), the serene (*atappa*), the beautiful (*sudassi*), the clear-sighted (*sudassa*), and the highest realm (*akaniṭṭha*)—are open only to non-returners (*anāgāmis*), noble disciples at the penultimate stage of liberation who have eradicated the fetters binding them to the sense sphere and thence automatically take rebirth in higher realms. From here they attain arahatship and reach final deliverance.

Beyond the fine material sphere lie the immaterial realms (*arūpāvacarabhūmi*). These are four in number—the base of boundless space, the base of boundless consciousness, the base of nothingness, and the base of neither perception nor non-perception. As should be evident, these are the realms of rebirth for those who, without having broken the fetters that bind them to *saṁsāra*, achieve and master one or another of the four immaterial *jhānas*. Those yogins who have mastery over an *āruppa* attainment at the time of death take rebirth in the appropriate plane, where they abide until the *kammic* force of the *jhāna* is exhausted. Then they pass away, to take rebirth in some other realm as determined by their accumulated *kamma*.[1]

1. For a schematic diagram of the planes of Buddhist cosmology and their connection with *kamma*, see Appendix 5. A good synopsis of the cosmological picture can be found in Narada, *Manual*, pp. 233-55.

CHAPTER VII

THE WAY OF WISDOM

The goal of the Buddhist path, complete and permanent liberation from suffering, is to be achieved by practicing the three stages of the path—moral discipline (*sila*), concentration (*samādhi*), and wisdom (*pannā*). The mundane *jhānas*, comprising the four fine material *jhānas* and four *āruppas*, pertain to the stage of concentration which they fulfil to an eminent degree. However, taken by themselves, the *jhānas* suffer from two liabilities. Firstly, due to carelessness or complacency, they can be lost. And secondly, their attainment does not suffice to ensure complete deliverance from suffering. The reason the mundane *jhānas* cannot by themselves bring final liberation from suffering is because they are incapable of cutting off its source. The Buddha teaches that the fundamental cause of suffering, the driving power behind the cycle of rebirths, is the defilements (*kilesa*) with their three unwholesome roots—greed, hatred, and delusion. Concentration of the absorptive level, no matter how deeply it might be developed, only induces a suppression of the defilements, not their radical extirpation. It cannot dismantle the latent seeds of the defilements, and thus cannot abandon them at the root. Thence bare mundane *jhāna*, even when sustained, does not by itself terminate the cycle of rebirths. To the contrary it can even help perpetuate the round. For each fine material and immaterial *jhāna* attained, if held to with an attitude of clinging, brings about a rebirth in that particular plane of existence corresponding to its own *kammic* potency, which can then be followed by a rebirth in some lower realm.

What is required to achieve complete deliverance from the cycle of rebirths is the eradication of the defilements. Since the most basic defilement is delusion (*moha*), also called ignorance (*avijjā*), the key to liberation lies in the eradication of ignorance by developing its direct opposite, namely wisdom (*paññā*). In this chapter we will examine the nature of wisdom and the methods by which it is developed. Since wisdom presupposes a certain proficiency in concentration it is inevitable that *jhāna* comes to claim a place in its development. This place, however, is not fixed and invariable, but as we will see allows for differences depending on the individual meditator's disposition.

Fundamental to the discussion in this chapter and the next is a distinction between two terms crucial to Theravāda philosophical exposition. These two terms are "mundane" (*lokiya*) and "supramundane" (*lokuttara*). The term "mundane" applies to all phenomena comprised in the world (*loka*) of the five aggregates of clinging (*pañcupādānakkhandhā*)—material form, feeling, perception, mental formations, and consciousness. It covers subtle states of consciousness as well as material and emotional states, virtue as well as evil, meditative attainments as well as sensual engrossments. The term "supramundane", in contrast, applies exclusively to that which transcends the world of the clinging-aggregates. It covers nine terms, the nine *lokuttarā dhammā*: *nibbāna*, the four noble paths (*magga*) leading to *nibbāna*, and their corresponding four fruits (*phala*) which experience the bliss of *nibbāna*. It is hoped that the discussion to follow will make the meanings of these terms clear.

The Nature of Wisdom

The *Visuddhimagga* presents an analytical exposition of wisdom dealt with under six headings: [1] the definition of wisdom, [2] the sense in which it is called wisdom, [3] its characteristic, function, manifestation, and proximate cause, [4] its classification, [5] its method of development, and [6] its benefits.[1] A brief consideration of these principles should help bring the nature of wisdom to light.

[1] Wisdom, according to Buddhaghosa, is defined as insight knowledge associated with wholesome states of consciousness.[2]

[2] Wisdom (*paññā*) is so called in the sense that it is an act of understanding (*pajānana*), a mode of knowing (*jānana*) distinct from and superior to the modes of perceiving (*sañjānana*) and cognizing (*vijānana*). What distinguishes wisdom from these other forms of cognition is its ability to comprehend the charac-

1. PP., pp. 479-89. Vism., pp. 369-75.
2. PP., p. 479. "Kusalacittasampayuttaṁ vipassanāñāṇaṁ paññā." Vism., p. 369.

teristics of impermanence, suffering and selflessness and to bring about the manifestation of the supramundane path.

[3] Wisdom has the specific characteristic of penetrating the true nature of phenomena. It penetrates the particular and general features of things through direct, unmediated cognition. Its function is "to abolish the darkness of delusion which conceals the individual essences of states" and its manifestation is "non-delusion." Since the Buddha says that one whose mind is concentrated knows and sees things as they are, the proximate cause of wisdom is concentration.[1]

[4] The wisdom instrumental in attaining liberation is divided into two principal types : insight-knowledge (*vipassanā-ñāṇa*) and the knowledge pertaining to the supramundane paths (*magga-ñāṇa*). The first is the direct penetration of the three characteristics of conditioned phenomena—impermanence (*aniccatā*), suffering (*dukkhatā*) and selflessness (*anattatā*). It takes as its objective sphere the five aggregates (*pañcakkhandhā*) —material form, feeling, perception, mental formations, and consciousness.[2] Because insight-knowledge takes the world (*loka*) of conditioned formations (*saṅkhāra*) as its object it is regarded as a mundane (*lokiya*) form of wisdom. Insight-knowledge does not itself directly eradicate the defilements. It serves to prepare the way for the second type of wisdom, the wisdom of the supramundane paths, which emerges when insight has been brought to its climax. The wisdom of the path, occurring in the four distinct stages (to be discussed below), simultaneously realizes *nibbāna*, fathoms the four Noble Truths, and cuts off the difilements. This wisdom is called "supramundane" (*lokuttara*) because it rises up (*uttarati*) from the world (*loka*) of the five aggregates to realize the state transcendent to the world, *nibbāna*.

[5] The Buddhist yogin, striving for deliverance, begins the development of wisdom by first securely establishing its roots—purified moral discipline and concentration. He then learns and masters the basic material upon which wisdom is to work—the

1. "Dhammānaṁ sabhāvapaṭivedhalakkhaṇā paññā. Dhammānaṁ sabhāvapaṭicchādaka-mohāndhakāraviddhaṁsanarasā; asammohapaccupaṭṭhānā; samāhito yathābhūtaṁ jānāti passati ti [AN. 5:3] vacanato pana samādhi tassa padaṭṭhānam." Vism. p. 370.

2. In Pali: *Rūpakkhanda, vedanākkhandha, saññākkhandha, saṅkhārak-khandha, viññānakkhandha.*

aggregates, elements, sense bases, dependent arising, the Four Noble Truths, etc. He commences the actual practice of wisdom by cultivating insight into the impermanence, suffering, and selflessness of the five aggregates. When this insight reaches its apex it issues in supramundane wisdom, the right view factor of the Noble Eightfold Path. The wisdom of the path turns from conditioned formations to the unconditioned *nibbāna*, destroying thereby the latent defilements at their root.

[6] The removal of the defilements, the experiencing of *nibbāna* and the achievement of the states of holiness culminating in arahatship—these, according to Buddhaghosa, are the benefits in developing wisdom.[1]

The Two Vehicles

The Theravāda tradition recognizes two alternative approaches to the development of wisdom, between which yogins are free to choose according to their aptitude and propensity. These two approaches are the vehicle of serenity (*samathayāna*) and the vehicle of insight (*vipassanāyāna*). The meditators who follow them are called, respectively, the *samathayānika*, "one who makes serenity his vehicle," and the *vipassanāyānika*, "one who makes insight his vehicle." Since both vehicles, despite their names, are approaches to developing insight, to prevent misunderstanding the latter type of meditator is sometimes called a *suddhavipassanāyānika*, "one who makes bare insight his vehicle," or a *sukkhavipassaka*, "a dry insight worker." Though all three terms appear initially in the commentaries rather than in the suttas, the recognition of the two vehicles seems implicit in a number of canonical passages.

The *samathayānika* is a meditator who first attains access concentration or one of the eight mundane *jhānas*, then emerges and uses his attainment as a basis for cultivating insight until he arrives at the supramundane path. The experience of the path in any of its four stages always occurs at a level of *jhānic* intensity and thus necessarily includes supramundane *jhāna* under the heading of right concentration (*sammāsamādhi*), the eighth factor of the Noble Eightfold Path. In contrast to the *samathayānika*, the

1. See Vism., Chapter XXIII.

vipassanāyānika does not attain mundane *jhāna* prior to practicing insight-contemplation, or if he does, does not use it as an instrument for cultivating insight. Instead, without entering and emerging from *jhāna*, he proceeds directly to insight-contemplation on the mental and material phenomena that appear in the six spheres of sense experience—the five outer senses and thought. By means of this bare insight he reaches the noble path, which as in the former case again necessarily includes supramundane *jhāna*.

The kingpost of the *vipassanāyānika's* approach is the practice of mindfulness (*sati*), the bare non-discursive observation of the changing phenomena of mind and body. The Buddha expounds the practice of mindfulness in terms of four contemplations—the contemplation of body (*kāya*), feelings (*vedanā*), states of mind (*citta*), and mind-objects (*dhamma*). These four contemplations, the four "foundations of mindfulness" (*satipaṭṭhāna*), bring to the focus of the observational field the diverse kinds of mental and material phenomena with their universal marks of impermanence, suffering, and selflessness. The *samathayānika*, too, at the time he emerges from *jhāna* and begins insight-contemplation, has to practice the four foundations of mindfulness, as these have been called by the Buddha "the only way that leads to the purification of beings, to the overcoming of sorrow and lamentation, to the ending of pain and grief, to the achievement of the right path and the realization of *nibbāna*."[1]

The classical source for the distinction between the two vehicles of serenity and insight is the *Visuddhimagga*, where it is explained that when a meditator begins the development of wisdom

> ...if, firstly, his vehicle is serenity, [he] should emerge from any fine material or immaterial jhana except the base consisting of neither perception nor non-perception, and he should discern, according to characteristic, function, etc., the jhana factors consisting of applied thought, etc. and the states associated with them.[2]

Other commentarial passages allow access concentration (*upacāra-samādhi*) to suffice for the vehicle of serenity. The last *āruppa* is

1. DN. 2: 290.
2. PP., pp. 679-80. Vism., p. 503.

excluded because its factors are too subtle to be discerned by a beginning meditator. The meditator whose vehicle is pure insight, on the other hand, is advised to begin by discerning material and mental phenomena directly, without utilizing a *jhāna* for this purpose. This second type of meditator is sometimes referred to by another name, "dry insight worker", applied because his insight lacks moistening with the waters of *jhāna*.[1]

Although, as we mentioned earlier, the three terms—*samathayānika*, *vipassanāyānika*, and *sukkhavipassaka*—are terms of commentarial coinage, the distinction of vehicles and practitioners seems to draw directly from the Pali Canon. The Buddha generally includes the four *jhānas* in complete expositions of his system of training, placing them before the development of insight and the attainment of the path. A number of suttas, however, give evidence for alternative approaches to the practice. In the Aṅguttara Nikāya the Buddha states :

> There is, monks, one person who gains internal serenity of mind but does not gain the higher wisdom of insight into phenomena;...one person who gains the higher wisdom of insight into phenomena but does not gain internal serenity of mind;...one person who gains neither;...and one person who gains both....[2]

He urges the first, established on his serenity of mind, to strive to gain the wisdom of insight into phenomena, and the second, established on his wisdom of insight into phenomena, to strive to gain serenity of mind. The commentary explains "serenity of mind" as mental concentration of absorption (*appanācittasamādhi*) and the "higher wisdom of insight into phenomena" as the insight-knowledge discerning formations (*saṅkhārapariggahavipassanāñāṇa*), i.e. insight into the five aggregates.[3] The fact that individuals are capable of one attainment in the absence of the other provides a starting point for a differentiation of vehicles adapted to their differing capacities. In the end, however, all meditators have to enter upon the development of insight in order to reach the liberating path.

1. See Vism. T. 2:474.
2. AN. 2:92-93.
3. AN.A. 2:325.

An even clearer enunciation of alternative vehicles to the goal is presented in a sutta spoken by the Venerable Ānanda. On one occasion Ānanda declared to a group of monks that there are some monks who develop insight preceded by serenity (*samathapubbaṅgamaṁ vipassanaṁ*) and some who develop serenity preceded by insight (*vipassanāpubbaṅgamaṁ samathaṁ*). Both approaches, in his account, issue in the supramundane path :

> Herein, friends, a monk develops insight preceded by serenity. As he develops insight preceded by serenity the path arises. He follows that path, develops it and cultivates it. As he follows, develops, and cultivates the path the fetters are abandoned, the latent tendencies are destroyed. Or again, friends, a monk develops serenity preceded by insight. As he develops serenity preceded by insight the path arises. He follows that path, develops and cultivates it. As he does so the fetters are abandoned, the latent tendencies are destroyed.[1]

The commentarial exegesis of this passage (found in the Majjhima Nikāya commentary) explains the procedure for developing insight preceded by serenity thus :

> Here, someone first produces access concentration or absorption concentration; this is serenity. He contemplates with insight that serenity and its concomitant phenomena as impermanent, etc.; this is insight. Thus first comes serenity, afterwards insight.[2]

The procedure for developing serenity preceded by insight is described as follows :

> Here, someone contemplates with insight the five aggregates of clinging as impermanent, etc. without having produced the aforesaid kinds of serenity (access and absorption); this is insight. With the completion of insight there arises in him mental one-pointedness having as object the renunciation of the phenomena produced therein; this is serenity. Thus first comes insight, afterwards serenity.[3]

1. AN. 2:157.
2. MN.A. 1:112.
3. *Ibid.*, 113.

In case it should be suspected that the second type of meditator still attains mundane *jhāna* after developing insight, the subcommentary to the passage points out: "the mental one-pointedness he gains is right concentration of the supramundane path (*maggasammāsamādhi*) and its object, called 'renunciation' (*vavassagga*), is *nibbāna*."[1] The Aṅguttara sub-commentary explicitly identifies the second meditator with the *vipassanāyānika*: " 'He develops serenity preceded by insight' : this is said with reference to the *vipassanāyānika*."[2]

Thus the *samathayānika* attains in order first access concentration or mundane *jhāna* and then insight-knowledge, by means of which he reaches the supramundane path containing wisdom under the heading of right view (*sammādiṭṭhi*) and supramundane *jhāna* under the heading of right concentration (*sammāsamādhi*). The *vipassanāyānika*, in contrast, skips over mundane *jhāna* and goes directly into insight-contemplation. When he reaches the end of the progression of insight-knowledge he arrives at the supramundane path which, as in the previous case, brings together wisdom with supramundane *jhāna*. This *jhāna* counts as his accomplishment of serenity.

The Functions of Jhāna

For a meditator following the vehicle of serenity the attainment of *jhāna* fulfills two functions: first, it produces a basis of mental purity and inner collectedness needed for undertaking the work of insight-contemplation ; and second, it serves as an object to be examined with insight in order to discern the three characteristics of impermanence, suffering, and selflessness. *Jhāna* accomplishes the first function by providing a powerful instrument for overcoming the five hindrances. As we saw, the Buddha declares the five hindrances to be corruptions of the mind and weakeners of wisdom which prevent a man from seeing things as they are.[3] For wisdom to arise the mind must first be concentrated well, and to be concentrated well it must be freed from the hindrances. This task is accomplished by the attainment of

1. MN.T. 1:204.
2. AN.T. 2:344.
3. See Chapter III pp. 28-29.

jhāna: access concentration causes the hindrances to subside, the first and following *jhānas* drive them further and further away. Cleared of the hindrances the mind becomes "pliant and supple, having radiant lucidity and firmness, and will concentrate well upon the eradication of the taints."[1]

In their capacity for producing concentration the *jhānas* are called the basis (*pāda*) for insight, and that particular *jhāna* a yogin enters and emerges from before commencing his practice of insight is designated his *pādakajjhāna*, the basic or foundational *jhāna*. Insight cannot be practiced while absorbed in *jhāna*, since insight-meditation requires investigation and observation, which are impossible when the mind is immersed in one-pointed absorption. But after emerging from the *jhāna* the mind is cleared of the hindrances, and the stillness and clarity that then result conduce to precise, penetrating insight.

The *jhānas* also enter into the *samathayānika's* practice in a second capacity; that is, as objects for scrutinization by insight. The practice of insight consists essentially in the examination of mental and physical phenomena to discover their marks of impermanence, suffering, and selflessness. The *jhānas* a yogin has attained and emerged from provide him with a readily available and strikingly clear object in which to seek out the three characteristics. After emerging from a *jhāna* the meditator will proceed to examine the *jhānic* consciousness, analyzing it into its components, defining them in their precise particularity, and discerning the way they exemplify the three universal marks. This process is called *sammasanañāṇa*, "comprehension-knowledge," and the *jhāna* subjected to such a treatment is termed the *sammasitajjhāna*, "the comprehended *jhāna*."[2] Though the basic *jhāna* and the comprehended *jhāna* will often be the same, the two do not necessarily coincide. A yogin cannot practice coonmprehensi on a *jhāna* higher than he is capable of attaining, but a yogin who uses a higher *jhāna* as his *pādakajjhāna* can still practice insight-comprehension on a lower *jhāna* he has previously attained and mastered. This admitted difference in nature between the *pādaka* and *sammasitajjhānas* leads to discrepant theories about the supramundane concentration of the noble path, as we will see below.[3]

1. Ibid. p. 41.
2. PP., pp. 706-709. Vism., pp. 521-22.
3. See below pp. 182-83.

Whereas the sequence of training undertaken by the *samathayānika* meditator is unproblematic, a difficulty seems to crop up in the case of the *vipassanāyānika's* approach. This difficulty lies in accounting for the concentration he uses to provide a basis for insight. Concentration is needed in order to see and know things as they are, but without access or *jhāna*, what concentration can he use ? The solution to this problem is found in a type of concentration distinct from the access and absorption concentrations pertaining to the vehicle of serenity. This type of mental unification is called "momentary concentration" (*khaṇika samādhi*). Despite its name, momentary concentration does not signify a single moment of concentration amidst a current of distracted thoughts. Rather, it denotes a dynamic concentration which flows from object to object in the ever-changing flux of phenomena, retaining a constant degree of intensity and collectedness sufficient to purify the mind of the hindrances. Momentary concentration arises in the *samathayānika* yogin simultaneously with his post-*jhānic* attainment of insight, but for the *vipassanāyānika* it develops naturally and spontaneously in the course of his insight practice without his having to fix the mind upon a single exclusive object. Thus the follower of the vehicle of insight does not omit concentration altogether from his training, but develops it in a different manner from the practitioner of serenity. Skipping over the *jhānas*, he goes directly into contemplation on the five aggregates and by observing them constantly from moment to moment acquires momentary concentration as an accompaniment of his investigations. This momentary concentration fulfills the same function as the basic *jhāna* of the serenity-vehicle, providing the foundation of mental clarity needed for insight to emerge.

The importance of momentary concentration in the vehicle of insight is testified to by the classical Theravāda exegetical literature, the commentaries and subcommentaries. The *Visuddhimagga*, in its discussion of mindfulness of breathing, states that "at the actual time of insight momentary unification of the mind arises through the penetration of the characteristics (of impermanence, and so on)."[1] Its commentary, the *Paramatthamañjūsā*, defines the phrase "momentary unification of the mind" (*kha-*

1. PP., pp. 311-12. Vism., p. 239.

ṇika-cittekaggatā) as concentration lasting only for a moment, stating: "For that too, when it occurs uninterruptedly on its object in a single mode and is not overcome by opposition, fixes the mind immovably, as if in absorption."[1] The same work contains several other references to momentary concentration. Commenting on Buddhaghosa's remarks that sometimes the path to purification is taught by insight alone, the *Mahā Ṭīkā* points out that this remark is meant to exclude not all concentration, but only "that concentration with distinction," i.e. access and absorption. It should not be taken to imply that there is no concentration in the case of the insight-meditator, "for no insight comes about without momentary concentration."[2] And momentary concentration is the type of concentration appropriate to one whose vehicle is insight:

> ...supramundane concentration and insight are impossible without mundane concentration and insight to precede them; for without the access and absorption concentration in one whose vehicle is serenity, or without the momentary concentration in one whose vehicle is insight, and without the Gateways to Liberation..., the supramundane can never in either case be reached.[3]

The commentary to the Majjhima Nikāya, in a passage quoted fully above (p. 149), states that "someone contemplates with insight the five aggregates of clinging as impermanent, etc. without having produced the aforesaid kinds of serenity." Its subcommentary, clarifying this statement, explains: "The qualification 'without having serenity' is meant to exclude access concentration, not momentary concentration, for no insight is possible without momentary concentration."[4]

In contrast to *jhānic* concentration, momentary concentration is a fluid type of mental collectedness consisting in the uninterrupted continuity of the mind engaged in noticing the passing succession of objects as though fixing it in absorption, holding the

1. PP., pp. 311-12 Fn. 63. Vism. T. 1:342.
2. PP., p. 2 Fn. 3. "Na hi khaṇikasamādhiṁ vinā vipassanā sambhavati." Vism. T. 1:11.
3. PP., p. 3 Fn. 4. Vism. T. 1:15. For the three gateways to liberation, see below pp. 216-17.
4. MN.T. 1:204.

hindrances at bay and building up the power of mental purification. For this reason momentary concentration can be understood as implicitly included in access concentration in the standard definitions of purification of mind as consisting in access and absorption.

The Seven Purifications

The path to deliverance, usually expounded in terms of the three trainings in morality, concentration and wisdom, is sometimes divided further into seven stages called the seven purifications (*sattavisuddhi*). The canonical basis for this system is the Rathavinīta Sutta (MN. No. 24) and the Paṭisambhidāmagga. The scheme claims special prominence in the Theravāda commentarial tradition since it forms the framework for the *Visuddhimagga*. As such it comes to the forefront in every discussion of the progressive stages of Buddhist meditation.

According to this scheme in order to attain full liberation the meditator has to pass through seven kinds of purification. The seven are : [1] purification of morality, [2] purification of mind, [3] purification of view, [4] purification by the overcoming of doubt, [5] purification by knowledge and vision of the right and wrong paths, [6] purification by knowledge and vision of the way, and [7] purification by knowledge and vision.[1] The *Abhidhammattha Saṅgaha* recognizes several other sets of terms essential to the development of wisdom—the three characteristics of phenomena, the three contemplations, the ten kinds of insight knowledge, the three liberations, and the three doors to liberation;[2] but since these all come in the scope of the seven purifications we can take the latter as the basis for our discussion, mentioning the others when they become relevant.

[1] Purification of Morality

The purification of morality, identical with the training in the higher moral discipline (*adhisīlasikkhā*), consists in the fourfold

1. In Pali: [1] sīla visuddhi, [2] citta visuddhi, [3] diṭṭhi visuddhi, [4] kaṅkhāvitaraṇa visuddhi, [5] maggāmaggañāṇadassana visuddhi, [6] paṭipadāñāṇadassana visuddhi, and [7] ñāṇadassana visuddhi.
2. Nārada, *Manual.*, 408-409, 411-12.

purification of morality already discussed, i.e. restraint according to the rules of the Pātimokkha, restraint of the senses, purity of livelihood, and purity in the use of requisites.[1] This is the foundation for the growth of insight just as much as for the development of serenity.

[2] Purification of Mind

Purification of mind coincides with the training in concentration (*samādhi*) or in the higher consciousness (*adhicittasikkhā*). It is defined as the eight attainments of absorption together with access concentration. The *samathayānika* yogin accomplishes purification of mind by achieving access or full absorption in one or several *jhānas*, thereby suppressing the five hindrances. The *vipassanāyānika* disciple, as we noted, achieves purification of mind by means of momentary concentration, which as it overcomes the hindrances can be subsumed under access concentration.

[3] Purification of view

The remaining five purifications pertain to the training in wisdom. The first four belong to the mundane portion of the path, the wisdom of insight (*vipassanā-ñāṇa*); the last belongs to the supramundane portion, the wisdom of the noble path (*magga-ñāṇa*).

Purification of view aims obtaining a correct perspective on the nature of individual existence. Since it is the wrong grasp of existence, crystallized in the view of a substantial self, that keeps the unenlightened chained to *saṁsāra*, to reach liberation this delusive view has to be dissolved. The means of dissolving it is the purified view comprehending the so-called individual as a compound of evanescent phenomena without any inner core of substance or selfhood. To achieve purification of view the meditator has to bring these phenomena into focus, define them in terms of their salient characteristics, and then use this knowledge to remove the erroneous view of a self-subsistent ego.

The *samathayānika* and *vipassanāyānika* approach this purification from different angles, though the end result is the same for both. The former, after emerging from any fine material or immaterial *jhāna* except the last (which is too subtle for analysis),

1. See above, Ch. II, pp. 17-19.

discerns its *jhāna* factors and their concomitants in the light of their specific characteristics, functions, manifestations, and proximate causes. He then defines all these states as "mentality" (*nāma*). He next discerns the physical basis for these mental phenomena, the matter of the heart (*hadayarūpa*),[1] as well as the remaining primary and secondary kinds of material phenomena. These he groups together under the heading of "materiality" (*rūpa*). He thus perceives the living being as a composite of mentality and materiality, *nāmarūpa*, without and over-ruling self hidden within or behind it.

The *vipassanāyānika* begins to purify his view by analyzing the body into the four primary elements—solidity, fluidity, heat, and oscillation. After defining these in terms of their characteristics, he repeats the procedure for the other material phenomena, defining them all as materiality. He then turns to the states of consciousness and their principal concomitants, defining them and grouping them under the heading of "mentality." Thus, like the first kind of yogin, he eventually arrives at the realization that the living being is merely a compound of mutually supporting mental and physical phenomena apart from which there is no separate entity to be identified as a "self," "being," or "person."

The process of analysis can be undertaken using as basis the five aggregates, the twelve sense bases (the six sense faculties including mind and their six respective objects), the eighteen elements (six objects, six faculties, and six consciousness), or any other mode of classification. In the end all are defined in terms of mentality and materiality, resulting in the removal of the view of a self-identical ego.

[4] Purification by Overcoming Doubt

Once the disciple has overcome the false view of a self by discerning the living being as a compound of material and mental phenomena, he next sets out to overcome doubts concerning this compound by investigating the causes and conditions for menta-

1. The ancient Indian physiology, accepted by the Buddhist commentarial tradition, identified the heart with the seat of consciousness. In the canonical texts no such identification is made. Reference is only made to "that matter in dependence on which mind and mind-consciousness occur." See Nārada, *Manual.*, pp. 292-93.

lity-materiality. He understands that the mind-body combination is neither causeless nor created by any single cause but arises due to a multiplicity of causes and conditions. He first seeks out the causes and conditions for the body and discovers that the body is brought into being by four causes operating from the past—ignorance, craving, clinging, and *kamma*—and sustained in the present by nutriment. Then turning to mentality, he finds that all mental phenomena come into being in dependence on conditions, such as sense organs, sense objects, and conascent mental factors, as well as through the defilements and *kamma* accumulated in the past. When he sees that the present occurrence of mentality-materiality is due to causes and conditions, he infers that the same principle applied to its occurrence in the past and will apply to its occurrence in the future. In this way he overcomes all doubt and uncertainty regarding the conditioned origination of mind and matter in the three periods of time.

By discerning the conditional basis for the mental-material compound, the yogin arrives at the realization that the course of existence is merely a succession of active *kammic* processes and passive resultant processes. The aggregates occurring in the past ceased immediately after arising but gave rise to aggregates occurring in the present. The aggregates occurring now will cease in the present and give rise to aggregates occurring in the future. There is nothing permanent passing through this succession. It is merely a sequence of phenomena acting and experiencing without an agent over and above the actions or a subject over and above the experiences.

[5] Purification by Knowledge and Vision into the Right and Wrong Paths

Before the next purification can arise several intermediate steps are necessary. Firstly, after dispelling his doubts by the knowledge of conditionality, the disciple undertakes the form of insight called "comprehension by groups" (*kalāpasammasana*), which involves collecting all phenomena into distinct categories and ascribing to them the three characteristics. Thus the disciple contemplates all material form, feeling, perception, mental formations, and consciousness as impermanent, all as suffering, and all as not self, each being a separate comprehension.[1] This

1. See Pts. p. 51.

same method of comprehension can be applied not only to the five aggregates but to any categorical scheme for classifying the constituents of experience—the six sense doors, the six objects, the six kinds of consciousness, six contacts, six feelings, six perceptions, six volitions, the twelve sense bases, the eighteen elements, etc. The four *jhānas*, four divine abidings (*brahmavihāras*), and four immaterial attainments are also included. Since the text advises a beginner to develop comprehension by contemplating those states that are readily discernible by him, a *samathayānika* yogin will generally choose as his object of comprehension a *jhāna* he has achieved and mastered; this becomes his *sammasitajjhāna*, as we explained above.

Whatever objects he selects as material for comprehension, the disciple must understand the precise way they embody the three characteristics. Firstly, they are all impermanent in the sense that they are subject to destruction (*khayaṭṭhena*). Nothing that comes into being is able to last forever, but whatever arises is bound to eventually pass away. Secondly, they are all suffering in the sense of being fearful (*bhayaṭṭhena*). Since all composite phenomena are impermanent they cannot provide any lasting contentment or security, but when held to with clinging are a potential source of suffering to be regarded as harmful and fearful. And thirdly, they are all selfless in the sense of being coreless (*asāraṭṭhena*). Composite phenomena, being compounded by conditions, lack any inner essence that can be conceived as a self, inner agent or subject, and thus are empty of a core.[1]

When the meditator succeeds in comprehending the various groups in terms of the three characteristics, he acquires comprehension-knowledge, *sammasanañāṇa*. This marks the actual beginning of insight. According to the *Abhidhammattha Saṅgaha* comprehension-knowledge is the first of the ten kinds of insight-knowledge through which a *vipassanā*-practitioner has to pass.[2]

From comprehension-knowledge the disciple passes on to knowledge of contemplation of rise and fall (*udayabbayanupassanāñāṇa*). This knowledge, defined simply as "understanding of contemplating present states' change,"[3] is gained by contemplat-

1. PP., pp. 709-710. Vism., p. 523.
2. Nārada, Manual., pp. 409, 411.
3. PP., p. 734. Pts., pp. 53-54.

ing the presently existent five aggregates as characterized by rise and fall. In brief, it arises by seeing the rise of the aggregates in their characteristic of generation, birth, or arising, and their fall in their characteristic of change, destruction or dissolution. In greater detail, it involves perceiving the arising of each aggregate through its specific conditions and its cessation through the cessation of these conditions. Focussing in more closely on the present process, the meditator realizes that present phenomena, not having been, are brought into being, and that having been they immediately vanish. Formations appear to him as instantaneous, coming into being and passing away with inconceivable rapidity, perpetually renewed.

When he gains this initial understanding of rise and fall the meditator has arrived at tender insight (*taruṇavipassanā*). At this point, as a result of his successful practice, ten unprecedented experiences are likely to arise in him. Because they can impede his progress, these are called the ten imperfections of insight (*vipassanūpakkilesa*). The ten are: illumination, knowledge, rapture, tranquility, happiness, resolution, exertion, mindfulness, equanimity, and attachment.[1] If he is not cautious the unwary meditator can misinterpret these occurrences and think that he has reached one of the stages of enlightenment. Therefore novice yogins are advised not to allow themselves to be deterred by such occurrences but to recognize them for what they are: by-products of insight which can become impediments if wrongly adhered to. The skilled meditator contemplates them as bare phenomena—impermanent, suffering, and selfless. He distinguishes the right path from the wrong, realizing that these ten states are not the path but distractions; insight-knowledge free from imperfections is the path. The knowledge that is established in him by making this distinction is the purification by knowledge and vision into the right and wrong paths.

[6] Purification by Knowledge and Vision of the Way

Having relinquished attachment to the ten imperfections of insight and correctly distinguished the true path from the false, the

1. PP., pp. 739 ff. "Obhāsa, ñāṇa, pīti, passaddhi, sukha, adhimokkha, paggaha, upaṭṭhāna, upekkhā, nikanti,." Vism., pp. 544-45.

disciple now enters upon a steady progression of insights which leads him through increasingly deeper levels of understanding right up to the threshold of the supramundane path. These insights, nine in number, begin with mature knowledge of rise and fall and culminate in conformity knowledge (*anulomañāṇa*), the pinnacle of mundane insight. Together with the previously accomplished comprehension-knowledge (*sammasanañāṇa*), these nine insights complete the ten kinds of insight-knowledge mentioned in the *Abhidhammattha Saṅgaha.*

Knowledge of contemplation of rise and fall (*udayabbayānupassanā-ñāṇa*)

After distinguishing the right path from the wrong the meditator resumes the contemplation of rise and fall. Though he had previously cultivated this knowledge in part, his contemplation was disabled by the imperfections of insight and could not clearly observe the three characteristics. But now that the imperfections have been removed contemplation becomes extremely sharp, causing the three characteristics to stand out in bold relief. By attending to the rise and fall of formations the yogin sees the mark of impermanence—formations changing constantly at every moment, produced and stopped with inconceivable rapadity. As impermanence becomes more conspicuous suffering begins to stand out in its fundamental form, as continuous oppression by rise and fall. The yogin then realizes that whatever changes and causes suffering is insusceptible to the exercise of mastery, hence incapable of being identified as a self or the belongings of a self; this brings the understanding of the mark of selflessness into view. Having uncovered the three characteristics, the meditator sees that the so-called being is nothing but a becoming, a flux of evanescent, painful, impersonal happenings which does not remain the same for two consecutive moments.

Knowledge of contemplation of dissolution (*bhaṅgānupassanā-ñāṇa*)

As the meditator persists in his contemplation of rise and fall, it becomes increasingly apparent that conditioned formations undergo three phases of becoming: a phase of arising (*uppāda*), a phase of presence (*ṭhiti*), and a phase of dissolution (*bhaṅga*). When he can discern these phases clearly, the yogin no longer extends his mindfulness to their arising or presence, but focusses exclusively upon the final phase—their momentary cessation, dissolution, or breaking up. He then sees how formation sbreak up all the time "like fragile pottery being smashed, like fine dust being dispersed, like sesamum seeds being roasted."[1] Applying his direct knowledge of present dissolution to the past and future, he draws the inference that all past formations dissolved and all future ones will dissolve. Since dissolution is the culminating point of impermanence, the most salient aspect of suffering, and the strongest negation of selfhood, the three marks stand forth more distinctly than ever before. The whole field of formations thus becomes evident to contemplation as impermanent, suffering, and selfless. With the insight that formations break up constantly without a pause, and that this ceaseless process of momentary dissolution holds sway over the three periods of time, the meditator arrives at knowledge of contemplation of dissolution.

Knowledge of appearance as terror
(bhayatūpaṭṭhāna-ñāṇa)

As he repeats and cultivates his insight into the destruction, fall, and breakup of formations,

> formations classed according to all kinds of becoming, generation, destiny, station, or abode of beings, appear to him in the form of a great terror, as lions, tigers, leopards,...appear to a timid man who wants to live in peace.[2]

When he sees how past formations have ceased, present ones are ceasing, and future ones will cease, there arises in him knowledge of appearance as terror, born of the understanding that whatever is bound for destruction cannot be relied upon and is therefore fearful.

Knowledge of contemplation of danger
(ādīnavānupassanā-ñāṇa)

Through the knowledge of appearance as terror the meditator finds that there is no shelter, protection, or refuge in any kind of becoming. He sees that there is not a single formation he can pin

1. PP., p. 752. Vism., p. 553.
2. PP., p. 753. Vism., pp. 554-55.

his hopes on: all hold nothing but danger. Then "the three kinds of becoming appear like charcoal pits full of glowing coals,... and all formations appear as a huge mass of dangers destitute of satisfaction or substance."[1] The meditator discerns the potential danger in all existence just as a timid man sees the danger in a delightful forest thicket infested with wild beasts. This is the knowledge of contemplation of danger.

Knowledge of contemplation of dispassion
(nibbidānupassanā-ñāṇa)

Seeing the danger in all compounded things them editator becomes dispassionate towards them. He finds no delight in any state of worldly existence but turns away from them all. Even before he came to this knowledge the meditator had reduced his gross attachments but now, having seen the danger in formations, he gains even greater dispassion towards them on account of their impermanent, fearful, and insecure nature. It should be noted that according to the Paṭisambhidā-magga these last three insights—knowledge of terror, of danger, and of dispassion—represent phases of one kind of insight-knowledge apprehending its object in three different ways.[2]

Knowledge of desire for deliverance
(muñcitukamyatā-ñāṇa)

When the meditator becomes dispassionate towards the formations in all the kinds of becoming his mind no longer cleaves to them. The desire then arises in him to get rid of formations, to be released and liberated from them all. The knowledge that arises in association with this desire is knowledge of desire for deliverance.

Knowledge of contemplation of reflection
(paṭisaṅkhānupassanā-ñāṇa)

In order to be released from the whole field of conditioned phenomena the meditator returns to the contemplation of formations, examining them again and again in terms of impermanence, suffering and selflessness. Looking at them from a variety of

1. PP., p. 755. Vism., p. 556.
2. Pts., p. 259.

angles in the light of the three characteristics, he sees formations as impermanent because they are non-continuous, temporary, limited by rise and fall, disintegrating, perishable, subject to change, etc.; as suffering because they are continuously oppressed, hard to bear, the basis of pain, a disease, a tumor, a dart, a calamity, an affliction, etc.; as not self because they are alien, empty, vain, void, ownerless, without an overlord, with none to wield power over them, etc.[1] This extended understanding of the three characteristics is the knowledge of contemplation of reflection.

Knowledge of equanimity about formations
(saṅkhārupekkhā-ñāṇa)

To deepen his understanding of selflessness the meditator contemplates voidness (*suññatā*) in various ways. He sees that all compounds are empty of self or of anything belonging to a self, that nothing can be identified as "I" or as the property of an "I", as an "other" or as the property of an "other". Perceiving the voidness of selfhood in formations, the meditator abandons both terror and attachment. He develops instead a sense of detached equanimity. With the arising of this knowledge his mind retreats, retracts, and recoils from all the planes of becoming and no longer goes out to them "just as a fowl's feather or a shred of sinew thrown on a fire retreats, retracts, and recoils, and does not spread out."[2] At this stage, if he should perceive *nibbāna*, the goal, he will reject formations and resolve upon *nibbāna*. But if he does not see *nibbāna* the meditator will continue in the knowledge of equanimity about formations until his contemplation acquires further maturity.

When his knowledge ripens and the move to the supramundane path becomes imminent, insight settles down in one of the three contemplations—on impermanence, suffering, or selflessness, as determined by the meditator's disposition. Because they lead directly to the liberating experience of the noble path, these contemplations, at the pinnacle of insight, are called the three gateways to liberation (*tīni vimokkhamukhāni*). The contemplation of impermanence becomes the gateway to the signless liberation

1. PP., p. 760. Vism., p. 559.
2. PP., p. 766. Vism., p. 564.

(*animitta vimokkha*) for it directs the mind to *nibbāna* as the signless element; the contemplation of suffering becomes the gateway to the desireless liberation (*appaṇihitavimokkha*) for it directs the mind to *nibbāna* as the desireless element; and the contemplation of non-self becomes the gateway to the void liberation (*suññata-vimokkha*) for it directs the mind to *nibbāna* as the void element.

The liberation to which these contemplations are gateways is the supramundane path. Though one in essence the path gains three names according to the aspect of *nibbāna* it focusses upon, as Buddhaghosa explains:

> And here the signless liberation should be understood as the noble path that has occurred by making nibbāna its object through the signless aspect. For that path is signless owing to the signless element having arisen, and it is a liberation owing to deliverance from defilements. In the same way the path that has occurred by making nibbāna its object through the desireless aspect is desireless. And the path that has occurred by making nibbāna its object through the void aspect is void.[1]

The factor that determines which particular "gateway" will be entered and which liberation attained is the spiritual faculty predominant in the meditator's mental makeup. One with strong faith (*saddhā*) tends to settle down in contemplation of impermanence, one with strong concentration (*samādhi*) in the contemplation of suffering, and one with strong wisdom (*paññā*) in the contemplation of selflessness; thereby they each attain the path of liberation corresponding to their specific contemplation. As it is said in the Paṭisambhidāmagga:

> When one who has great resolution brings [formations] to mind as impermanent, he acquires the signless liberation. When one who has great tranquillity brings [them] to mind as painful, he acquires the desireless liberation. When one who has great wisdom brings [them] to mind as not-self, he acquires the void liberation.[2]

Insight-knowledge that has reached its climax and is about to issue in the supramundane path is also known by another name,

1. PP., p. 768. Vism., p. 565.
2. PP., p. 768. Pts., p. 254.

"insight leading to emergence" (*vuṭṭhānagāmini-vipassanā*).[1] This name covers three kinds of knowledge: fully matured equanimity about formations and the two that follow it—conformity knowledge (*anuloma-ñāṇa*) and change-of-lineage knowledge (*gotrabhū-ñāṇa*). The word "emergence" (*vuṭṭhāna*) signifies the supramundane path, which is called thus because externally it rises up from formations to *nibbāna* and internally it rises up from defilements and defiled conditions to a state of complete purity. Since these last three kinds of mundane knowledge lead immediately to the path they are collectively named insight leading to emergence.

Conformity knowledge (*anuloma-ñāṇa*)

As the meditator cultivates equanimity about formations his faculties grow stronger and sharper. Then, at a certain point, the realization dawns that the path is about to arise. A thought-process of equanimity-knowledge occurs comprehending formations through one of the three characteristics—as either impermanent, or suffering, or selfless; the mind then sinks into the life-continuum (*bhavaṅga*). Following the life-continuum there arises in the stream of consciousness a mind-door adverting (*manodvārāvajjana*) apprehending formations as impermanent, or suffering, or selfless, in accordance with the previous process of equanimity-knowledge. Immediately after the adverting two or three impulsions occur making formations their object in terms of the same characteristic. The three are individually called "preliminary work" (*parikamma*), "access" (*upacāra*), and "conformity' (*anuloma*), but they are most commonly collected under the group name "conformity." In very quick-witted meditators the moment of preliminary work is passed over and only the two moments of access and conformity occur. Conformity knowledge receives its name because it conforms to the functions of truth in the eight kinds of insight-knowledge preceding it and in the thirty-seven states partaking of enlightenment to follow. It is the last moment of insight-knowledge before the change over to the supramundane path supervenes.

1. PP., pp. 772-75. Vism., pp. 567-69.

[7] Purification by Knowledge and Vision

Change-of-lineage

The last purification, purification by knowledge and vision, consists of the knowledge of the four supramundane paths—the path of stream-entry, the path of the once-returner, the path of the non-returner, and the path of arahatship. However, immediately after conformity knowledge and before the moment of the first path, there occurs one thought-moment called change-of-lineage knowledge (*gotrabhūñāṇa*). This knowledge has the function of adverting to the path. Because it occupies an intermediate position it belongs neither to purification by knowledge and vision of the way nor to purification by knowledge and vision, but is regarded as unassignable. It receives the name "change-of-lineage" because by reaching this stage of knowledge the meditator passes out of the "lineage of the worldling" (*puthujjhana-gotta*) and enters the "lineage of the noble ones" (*ariyagotta*).[1] In bringing about such a radical transformation change-of-lineage is clearly a most important and crucial moment of spiritual development.

The three kinds of conformity knowledge—preliminary work, access, and conformity proper—dispel the "murk of defilements" that conceals the Four Noble Truths. Each of the three clears away a degree of delusion, permitting the truths to become more and more manifest. However, though conformity-knowledge dispels the delusion that conceals the truths, it cannot penetrate them. For the truths to be penetrated *nibbāna* must be realized as object. Change-of-lineage knowledge, which arises right after conformity, is the first state of consciousness to make *nibbāna* its object. It is the initial advertance to *nibbāna,* and the proximate, immediate and decisive-support condition for the arising of the first path.

The first path and fruit

Change-of-lineage knowledge perceives *nibbāna* but cannot destroy the defilements. The eradication of defilements is the work of the four supramundane paths (*lokuttaramagga*). Each path attainment is a momentary experience apprehending *nib-*

1. PP., p. 785. Vism., p. 577.

bāna, understanding the Four Noble Truths, and cutting off certain defilements. The first path, as Buddhaghosa explains, arises in immediate succession to change-of-lineage:

> ...After, as it were, giving a sign to the path to come into being it [change-of-lineage] ceases. And without pausing after the sign given by that change-of-lineage knowledge the path follows upon it in uninterrupted continuity, and as it comes into being it pierces and explodes the mass of greed, the mass of hatred, and the mass of delusion, never pierced and exploded before.[1]

The first path is called the path of stream entry (*sotāpattimagga*) since the disciple who has reached this path has entered the stream of the Dhamma (*dhammasota*), the Noble Eightfold Path, which will take him to *nibbāna* as surely as the waters in a stream will be carried to the ocean.[2] On entering this path he has passed beyond the level of a worldling and become a noble one, an *ariyan*, who has seen and understood the Dhamma for himself.

When the path-knowledge arises it breaks through the mass of greed, hatred, and delusion, the root-defilements which drive living beings from birth to birth in beginningless *saṁsāra*. Each supramundane path has the special function of eradicating defilements. The defilements cut off by the successive paths are classified into a set of ten "fetters" (*saṁyojana*), so called because they keep beings chained to the round of existence. The ten fetters, which all arise out of the three unwholesome roots, are: [1] wrong views of personality, [2] doubt, [3] clinging to rites and rituals, [4] sensual desire, [5] ill will, [6] lust for fine material existence, [7] lust for immaterial existence, [8] conceit, [9] restlessness, and [10] ignorance.[3] The ten are divided into two groups: the first five are called the fetters pertaining to the lower worlds (*orambhāgiyāni saṁyojanāni*) because they keep beings tied to the sensuous realms; the last five are called the fetters pertaining to the higher worlds (*uddhambhāgiyāni saṁyojanāni*) because they remain operative even in the fine material and immaterial

1. PP., pp. 787-88. Vism., p. 579.
2. SN. 5:347.
3. In Pali: [1] sakkāyadiṭṭhi, [2] vicikicchā, [3] sīlabbataparāmāsa, [4] kāmacchanda, [5] vyāpāda, [6] rūparāgā, [7] arūparāga, [8] māna, [9] uddhacca, and [10] avijjā.

realms.[1] Some of these fetters—doubt, sensual desire, ill will, and restlessness—are identical with the five hindrances abandoned by *jhāna*. But whereas mundane *jhāna* only suppresses them, leaving the latent tendencies untouched, the supramundane paths cut them off at the root. With the attainment of the fourth path the last and subtlest of the fetters are eradicated. Thus the arahat, the fully liberated one, is described as "one who has eliminated the fetters of existence" (*parikkhīṇabhava-saṁyojana*).[2]

The path of stream-entry eradicates the first three fetters—the fetters of false views of personality, doubt, and clinging to rites and rituals. The first is the view that the five aggregates can be identified with a self or can be seen as containing, contained in, or belonging to a self.[3] The more theoretical forms of this view are attenuated by insight-knowledge into impermanence suffering, and selflessness, but the subtle latent holding to such views can only be destroyed by path-knowledge. "Doubt" is uncertainty with regard to the Buddha, Dhamma, Saṅgha, and the training; it is eliminated when the disciple sees for himself the truth of the Dhamma.[4] "Clinging to rites and rituals" is the belief that liberation from suffering can be obtained merely by observing rites and rituals. Having followed the path to its climax, the disciple understands that the Noble Eightfold Path is the one way to the end of suffering, and so can no more fall back on rites and rituals. The path of stream entry not only cuts off these fetters but also eliminates greed for sense pleasures and resentment that would be strong enough to lead to states of loss, i.e. to rebirth in the four lower realms of the hells, tormented spirits, animals, and titans.[5] For this reason the stream-enterer is released from the possibility of an unfortunate rebirth.

The path of stream-entry is always followed by another occasion of supramundane experience called the fruit of stream entry (*sotāpattiphala*). Fruition follows the path necessarily and immediately, succeeding it without a gap. It occurs as the result of the path, sharing its object, *nibbāna*, and its world-transcending character. But whereas the path performs the active function of

1. AN. 5:17.
2. MN. 1:4.
3. MN. 1:300.
4. MN. 1:101.
5. Dhs., p. 208.

cutting off defilements, the fruit simply enjoys the bliss and peace that result from the path's completion of its function. Also, whereas the path is limited to only a single moment of consciousness, fruition covers either two or three moments. In the case of a quick-witted meditator who passes over the moment of preliminary work the cognitive process of the path contains only two moments of conformity knowledge. Thus in his thought-process, immediately after the path has arisen and ceased, three moments of fruition occur. In the case of an ordinary meditator there will be three moments of conformity knowledge and thus, after the path, only two moments of fruition.

The three moments of conformity knowledge and the moment of change-of-lineage are wholesome states of consciousness pertaining to the sense sphere (*kāmāvacarakusalacitta*). The path consciousness and the fruition that follows it are supramundane states of consciousness (*lokuttara citta*), the former wholesome (*kusala*) and the latter resultant (*vipāka*). The path and fruit necessarily occur at the level of one of the *jhānas*—from the first to the fourth *jhāna* in the fourfold scheme, from the first to the fifth in the fivefold scheme. They partake of the character of *jhāna* because they contain the *jhāna*-factors endowed with an intensity of absorption corresponding to that of the fine material sphere *jhānas*. But unlike the mundane *jhānas* these *jhānas* of the path and fruit are supramundane, having an altogethe differ-ent object and function than their counterparts, as we will see in the next chapter.

The following diagram illustrates the thought-process of the path and fruit of stream-entry in the case of a normal meditator with three moments of conformity preceding the path and two moments of fruition succeeding it :

A															B	
...	...	...	...	...	...	...	...	...	...	...	...	...	...	...	...	...
1	2	3	4	5	6	7	8	9	10	11	12	13	14	15	16	17
bh	l	ch	d	p	u	a	g	m	ph	ph	bh	bh	bh	bh	bh	bh

Here line *A* represents the four thought-moments preceding the path process. This comprises the past *bhavaṅga* or life-continuum (*bh*), its vibration (*l*), its cutting off (*ch*), and the mind's advertance to formations as impermanent, suffering, or selfless through the mind-door (*d*). Line *B* represents the lapsing of the mind back into the passive life-continuum after the fruition phase is over. *P* represents the moment of preliminary work (*parikamma*), *u* the moment of access (*upacāra*), *a* the moment of conformity (*anuloma*), and *g* the moment of change-of-lineage (*gotrabhū*) where the ordinary stream of consciousness belonging to the sensual plane changes over to the lineage of the noble path. The following *m* represents the noble path consciousness (*maggacitta*), which is necessarily limited to a single thought-moment. After this there are two *ph's* representing the fruit of stream-entry, then the mind relapses into the life-continuum, represented by *bh* repeated six times. The groups of three dots in each *citta* represent the birth (*uppāda*), duration (*ṭhiti*), and dissolution (*bhaṅga*) of each thought moment.[1]

After the attainment of fruition the stream-enterer reviews the path, fruition, and *nibbāna*. He will generally also review the defilements he has destroyed by the path and the defilements remaining to be destroyed by the higher paths; this, however, is not invariably fixed and is sometimes omitted by some meditators.[2] The ariyan disciples who have passed through the next two fruitions will likewise review their attainments in the same way. Thus for each there will be at a minimum three and at a maximum five items to be reviewed. For the arahat, however, there will be a maximum of four since he has no more defilements to be eliminated. In this way there are a maximum of nineteen kinds of reviewing (*paccavekkhana*) followingt he supramundane attainments.

The disciple at the moment of the path of stream-entry is called "one standing on the path of stream-entry" or the first noble person; from the moment of fruition up to the attainment of the next path he is called a stream-enterer (*sotāpanna*), reckoned as the second noble person. Though conventionally the person standing on the path and the one abiding in the fruit can be described as one and the same individual at two different moments, the philosophical perspective requires another kind of descriptive device. From the standpoint of ultimate truth, accor-

1. Adopted from Nārada, *Manual.*, pp. 214-19. Vism., pp. 111-12. *Compendium*, pp. 54-55.

2. Nārada, *Manual.*, p. 410. Vism., p. 581.

ding to Buddhism, an individual endures as such for only one thought-moment. Therefore, in classifying the types of noble persons, the Buddha drew upon the distinction between the thought-moments of path and fruition as the basis for a distinction between two types of noble persons. This bifurcation applies to each of the four stages of deliverance: for each, the individual at the path-moment is reckoned as one type of noble person, the same individual from the moment of fruition on as another type of noble person.

The texts extoll the stream-enterer as acquiring incalculable benefits as a result of his attainment. He has closed off the doors to rebirth in the woeful states of existence and can declare of himself:

> Destroyed for me is rebirth in the hells, in the animal kingdom, in the spirit realm, in the planes of misery, the bad destinations, the downfall. I am a stream-enterer, no longer subject to decline, assured of and destined for full enlightenment.[1]

He can be certain that he is released from five kinds of fear and hostility: the fear and hostility that come from taking life, from stealing, from sexual misconduct, from false speech, and from taking intoxicants. He is endowed with the four factors of stream-entry (*sotāpattiyaṅgāni*): unwavering confidence in the Buddha, the Dhamma, and the Sangha, and unblemished moral discipline. He has penetrated and seen the truth with correct understanding.[2] By so penetrating the truth he has limited his future births to a maximum of seven in the happy realms of the human and heaven worlds, drying up the great ocean of suffering that laid beyond this. Thus the Buddha says that for the stream-enterer who has seen the Dhamma the amount of suffering that remains is like a pinch of dust on the finger nail, while the suffering that has been exhausted is like the dust on the mighty earth.[3]

1. SN. 2:68.
2. *Ibid.* 69-70
3. Stream-enterers are divided into three kinds: assuming that they will not go further in that same lifetime, one with sluggish faculties will be reborn seven times in the happy destinations; one with medium faculties will be reborn an intermediary number of times; and one with keen faculties will be reborn once more in the human world and there make an end of suffering. (See PP., pp. 833-34. Vism., pp. 611-12.)

The second path and fruit

A disciple who has attained to stream-entry is not debarred from progressing to higher stages of deliverance in that same life. He can advance all the way to arahatship if he has sufficient supporting conditions and puts forth the necessary effort. Therefore the yogin abiding at the stage of stream-entry is advised to strive for the next higher path, the path of the once-returner (*sakadāgāmimagga*), either in the same session or at a later time. He should stir up the spiritual faculties, the powers, and the factors of enlightenment, and with this equipment contemplate the whole range of formations included in the five aggregates in the light of impermanence, suffering, and selflessness. As before he again passes through the progressive series of insights beginning with knowledge of rise and fall and culminating in knowledge of equanimity about formations. If his faculties have not yet reached sufficient maturity his contemplation will remain in equanimity about formations. But if and when his faculties mature, he passes through the moments of conformity knowledge and change-of-lineage knowledge and attains to the second noble path, the path of the once-returner.[1]

Unlike the other noble paths, the second path does not eradicate any fetters completely. However, it attenuates sensual desire and ill-will to such a degree that they no longer occur strongly or frequently but remain only as weak residues. The three unwholesome roots are weakened along with the other fetters derived from them. Following the path-consciousness in immediate succession come two or three moments of the fruit of the once-returner (*sakadāgāmiphala*), the inevitable consequence of the path. After fruition reviewing knowledge occurs, as described. The meditator at the moment of the path is known as the third noble person, from the moment of the fruit on as a once-returner (*sakadāgāmi*), the fourth noble person. He is called a "once-

1. The thought-moment immediately preceding the three higher paths only receives the name "change-of-lineage" figuratively, due to its similarity to the moment preceding the path of stream-entry. The yogi actually crossed over to the noble one's lineage (*ariyagotta*) earlier, with the moment before the first path. Hence the moment immediately preceding the three higher paths is technically known by another name, *vodāna*, meaning "cleansing", so called "because it purifies from certain defilements and because it makes absolute purification (i.e. *nibbāna*) its object." Vism. T. 2:487-88.

returner" because, if he does not go further in this life, he is bound to make an end of suffering after returning to this world one more time. The standard sutta description reads: "With the destruction of the (first) three fetters and the attenuation of greed, hate, and delusion, the monk becomes a once returner, one who puts an end to suffering after returning to this world only one more time."[1]

The third path and fruit

As before, the ardent meditator resumes contemplation on the impermanence, suffering, and selflessness of the aggregates, striving to attain the third stage of deliverance, the stage of a non-returner (*anāgāmi*). When his faculties mature he passes through the preliminary insights and reaches the third path, the path of the non-returner (*anāgāmimagga*). This path destroys sensual desire and ill will, the two fetters weakened by the second path. Immediately after the third path its fruition occurs, after which he reviews his position as before. At the moment of the path the yogin is known as one standing on the path of a non-returner, the fifth noble person, from the moment of fruition on as a non-returner, the sixth noble person. He is called a non-returner because he no longer returns to the sensuous realm. If he does not penetrate further he is reborn spontaneously in some higher realm, generally in the pure abodes (*suddhāvāsa*) of the fine material sphere, and there reaches final *nibbāna*: "With the destruction of the five lower fetters, the monk is reborn spontaneously (in a higher world) and there attains *nibbāna*, without returning from that world."[2]

The fourth path and fruit

Again, either in the same session or at some future time, the meditator sharpens his faculties, powers, and enlightenment factors, contemplating the three characteristics of formations. He ascends through the series of insights up to equanimity about formations. When his faculties mature there arise in him conformity and change-of-lineage, followed by the fourth and final path, the path of arahatship (*arahattamagga*). This path eradi-

1. AN. 2:238.
2. *Ibid.*

cates the remaining five fetters—desire for existence in the fine material realm, desire for existence in the immaterial realm, conceit, restlessness, and ignorance. The path is followed immediately by its fruition, the fruit of arahatship (*arahattaphala*), after which reviewing knowledge occurs. The text reads: "With the destruction of the cankers he here and now enters and dwells in the cankerless liberation of mind, liberation by wisdom, realizing it for himself with direct knowledge."[1]

At the moment of the path the yogin is reckoned as one standing on the path of arahatship, the seventh noble person; at the moment of fruition he becomes an arahat, the eighth noble person. At this point he has completed the development of the path and reached the goal of full liberation.

> He is one of the Great Ones with cankers destroyed, he bears his last body, he has laid down the burden, reached his goal and destroyed the fetter of becoming, he is rightly liberated with [final] knowledge and worthy of the highest offerings of the world with its deities.[2]

The eight individuals, from the person standing on the path of stream-entry to the arahat, make up the ariyan Sangha, the community of noble persons forming the third refuge and third jewel of Buddhist veneration. As the Buddha says:

> Bhikkhus, there are these eight persons worthy of offerings and hospitality, of gifts and homage, an incomparable field of merit to the world.
> The stream-enterer, he who has entered the path to the realization of the fruit of stream-entry, the once-returner, he who has entered the path to the realization of the fruit of once-returner, the non-returner, he who has entered the path to the realization of the fruit of non-returner, the arahat, and he who has entered the path to arahatship.[3]

1. AN. 2:238.
2. PP., p. 792. Vism., p. 582.
3. AN. 4:292-93.

Chapter VIII

JHĀNA AND THE NOBLE ATTAINMENTS

In the last chapter it was mentioned that the supramundane paths and fruits always occur as occasions of *jhāna*. In the present chapter we will make these supramundane *jhānas* the objects of our examination, exploring them in relation to their mundane counterparts and to the cognitive processes to which they belong. We will then consider two special achievements in the meditative field accessible only to particular types of noble persons—the attainment of fruition (*phalasamāpatti*) and the attainment of cessation (*nirodhasamāpatti*). This will be followed by an overview of the Theravāda Buddhist typology of noble persons, presented in order to determine their relation to the mundane accomplishment of *jhāna*. This overview will enable us to assess, in the last section of this chapter, the place of *jhāna* in the life of the arahat, the spiritually perfected man in Theravāda Buddhism.

Supramundane Jhāna

The supramundane paths and fruits, as we saw, necessarily arise as states of *jhānic* consciousness. They occur as states of *jhāna* because they contain within themselves the *jhāna*-factors elevated to an intensity corresponding to that of the factors in the mundane *jhānas*. Since they possess the *jhāna*-factors these states are able to fix upon their object with the force of full absorption. Thence, taking the absorptive force of the *jhāna* factors as the criterion, the paths and fruits may be reckoned as belonging to either the first, second, third or fourth *jhāna* of the fourfold scheme, or to the first, second, third, fourth or fifth *jhāna* of the fivefold scheme.

The basis for the recognition of a supramundane type of *jhāna* goes back to the suttas, especially to the section of "The Great Discourse on the Foundations of Mindfulness" (DN. No. 22) where the Buddha defines right concentration of the Noble Eightfold Path by the standard formula for the four *jhāna*. However, it is in the Abhidhamma system that the connection between the *jhānas*, paths, and fruits comes to be worked out with great intricacy of detail. The Dhammasaṅgaṇi, in its section on states of consciousness, expounds each of the path and fruition states of consciousness as occasions, first, of one or another of the four *jhānas* in the tetradic scheme, and then again as occasions of one or another of the five *jhānas* in the pentadic scheme.[1] Standard Abhidhammic exposition, as formalized in the synoptical manuals of Abhidhamma, employs the fivefold scheme and brings each of the paths and fruits into connection with each of the five *jhānas*. In this way the eight types of supramundane consciousness—the path and fruition consciousness of stream-entry, the once-returner, the non-returner, and arahatship—proliferate to forty types of supramundane consciousness, since any path or fruit can occur at the level of any of the five *jhānas*. It should be noted, however, that there are no paths and fruits conjoined with the immaterial attainments, the reason being that supramundane *jhāna* is presented solely from the standpoint of its factorial constitution, which for the immaterial attainments and the fifth *jhāna* is identical—equanimity and one-pointedness.

The fullest treatment of the supramundane *jhānas* in the authoritative Pali literature can be found in the Dhammasaṅgaṇi's exposition of the supramundane states of consciousness, read in conjunction with the commentary on these passages in the *Aṭṭhasālinī*. The Dhammasaṅgaṇi opens its analysis of the first wholesome supramundane consciousness with the words:

> On the occasion when one develops supramundane *jhāna* which is emancipating, leading to the demolition (of existence), for the abandonment of views, for reaching the first plane, secluded from sense pleasures......one enters and dwells in the first *jhāna*.[2]

It then goes on to enumerate the various wholesome mental pheomena present on the occasion of that consciousness, defining each of these by their standard synonyms. We will consider the most significant auxiliary constituents of the supramundane

1. Dhs., pp. 74-86.
2. "Yasmiṁ samaye lokuttaraṁ jhānaṁ bhāveti niyyānikaṁ apacayagāmiṁ diṭṭhigatānaṁ pahānāya pathamāya bhūmiyā pattiyā vivicceva kāmehi ..paṭhamaṁ jhānaṁ upasampajja viharati." Dhs., p. 72.

jhānas shortly, but first it is instructive to look at the introductory phrase itself in the light of its commentarial elucidation.

The *Aṭṭhasālinī* explains the word *lokuttara*, which we have been translating "supramundane," as meaning "it crosses over the world, it transcends the world, it stands having surmounted and overcome the world."[1] It glosses the phrases "one develops *jhāna*" thus: "One develops, produces, cultivates absorption *jhāna* lasting for a single thought-moment." This gloss shows us two things about the consciousness of the path: first that it occurs as a *jhāna* at the level of full absorption (*appanā*), and second that this absorption of the path lasts for only a single thought-moment (*ekacittakkhaṇika*). The word "emancipating" (*niyyānika*) is explained to mean that this *jhāna* goes out (*niyyāti*) from the world, from the round of existence, the phrase "leading to demolition" (*apacayagāmi*) that it demolishes and dismantles the process of rebirth.

This last phrase points to a striking difference between mundane and supramundane *jhāna*. The Dhammasaṅgaṇi's exposition of the former begins: "On the occasion when one develops *the path for rebirth in the fine material sphere*...one enters and dwells in the first jhāna" [my italics]. Thus, with this statement, mundane *jhāna* is shown to sustain the round of rebirths; it is a wholesome *kamma* leading to renewed existence. But the supramundane *jhāna* of the path does not promote the continuation of the round. To the contrary it brings about the round's dismantling and demolition, as the *Aṭṭhasālinī* shows with an illustrative simile :

> The wholesome states of the three planes are said to lead to accumulation because they build up and increase death and rebirth in the round. But not this. Just as when one man has built up a wall eighteen feet high another might take a club and go along demolishing it, so this goes along demolishing and dismantling the deaths and rebirths built up by the wholesome *kammas* of the three planes by bringing about a deficiency in their conditions. Thus it leads to demolition.[2]

1. "Yasmiṁ samaye rūpūpapattiyā maggaṁ bhāveti vivicceva kāmehi ..paṭhamaṁ jhānaṁ upasampajja viharati." Dhs., p. 44.
2. Dhs. A., p. 259.

The *jhāna* is said to be cultivated "for the abandoning of views." This phrase signifies the function of the first path, which is to eradicate the fetters. The supramundane *jhāna* of the first path cuts off the fetter of personality view and all speculative views derived from it. The *Aṭṭhasālinī* points out that here we should understand that it abandons not only wrong views but other unwholesome states as well, namely doubt, clinging to rites and rituals, and greed, hatred, and delusion strong enough to lead to the plane of misery. The phrase "for reaching the first plane" the commentary explicates as meaning for attaining the fruit of stream entry.

Immediately after this passage the Dhammasaṅgaṇi lists the constituent phenomena found in the supramundane *jhāna*, followed by their definitions. The elaborate and complex expository method of the canonical Abhidhamma work has been streamlined in the *Abhidhammattha Saṅgaha*. By avoiding repetitions of the same factor under different headings the manual assigns thirty-eight mental factors (*cetasikas*) to the first *jhāna* state of consciousness, whether of any of the four paths and fruits. These are the seven factors common to all states of consciousness, the six general variables, the nineteen universal beautiful factors, wisdom, and three abstinences—right speech, right action, and right livelihood. Two immeasurables—compassion and sympathetic joy—are always excluded from the paths and fruits.[1]

We saw earlier (pp. 94-95) that the *Abhidhammattha Saṅgaha* attributes thirty-five possible mental factors to the first mundane *jhāna*. This invites a comparison between the composition of the two states. Firstly it will be noticed that compassion and sympathetic joy can be present in mundane *jhāna* but not in the supramundane. The reason is that those mental factors have sentient beings for object, while the paths and fruits objectify *nibbāna*.[2] Secondly we should note that the three abstinences (*viratittaya*) are present in the supramundane *jhānas* but not in the mundane.

1. Nārada, *Manual.*, pp. 127-29. NB: The higher *jhānas* have respectively thirty-seven, thirty-six, and thirty-five components as applied thought, sustained thought, and rapture are abandoned at these levels.

2. The other two immeasurables—loving kindness and equanimity—are particular modes of the mental factors "non-hatred" and "specific neutrality." Since their parent factors do not necessarily have sentient beings for object they can be present even with other objects and are, in fact, universal concomitants of wholesome states of consciousness.

This is because in mundane consciousness an abstinence is only present on an occasion when one is deliberately exercising restraint of speech, body, or livelihood. In mundane *jhāna* no such restraint is being applied; it is only applied in wholesome sense sphere consciousness when one is resisting the impulse towards moral transgression. Even then only one abstinence can occur at a time, and only with respect to one violation covered by the abstinence—for right speech abstaining from lying, slander, harsh speech, *or* idle chatter; for right action abstaining from killing, stealing, *or* sexual misconduct; for right livelihood abstaining from one *or* another form of wrong livelihood. But in the supramundane *jhānas* the three abstinences occur simultaneously, and they occur with respect to all the violations covered by the abstinence. In the paths they have the function not merely of inhibiting immoral actions, but of destroying the tendencies for these transgressions to occur. For this reason the Dhammasaṅgaṇi describes each abstinence as *setughāta*, "breaking the bridge," which the commentary explains as meaning that the abstinence uproots the condition for misconduct of speech, action or livelihood.[1]

In the Dhammasaṅgaṇi's enumeration of states, the factor of wisdom enters into the supramundane *jhānas* as three new faculties spread out over the four paths and fruits. These three are the faculty of "I shall know the unknown" (*anaññātaññassāmitindriya*), the faculty of final knowledge (*aññindriya*), and the faculty of the completion of final knowledge (*aññātavindriya*).[2] The first is present in the first path, the second in the six intermediate states from the first fruition through the fourth path, and the third in the fourth fruition, the fruit of arahatship. The faculty of "I shall know the unknown" is the wisdom-faculty of one standing on the path of stream-entry, the "unknown" being, according to the commentary, the deathless state of *nibbāna* or the Four Noble Truths, neither of which has been known before in beginningless *saṁsāra*.[3] The faculty of final knowledge is the faculty of wisdom in those at the intermediate stages of progress, while the faculty of the completion

1. Dhs. A., p. 264.
2. Dhs., pp. 77, 91, 138.
3. Dhs. A., p. 261.

of final knowledge is the fully matured wisdom of the arahat. None of these faculties is present as such in mundane *jhāna*.

A good number of constituent factors present in mundane *jhāna* are repeated again in the analysis of supramundane *jhāna*, but to these the Dhammasaṅgaṇi adds two qualifying phrases not given in the definitions of their mundane counterparts. These are the phrases "path factor" (*maggaṅga*) and "enlightenment factor" (*bojjhaṅga*). The former attaches to all those states which, under one or another of their different names, enter into the Noble Eightfold Path as right view, right intention, right speech, right action, right livelihood, right effort, right mindfulness and right concentration.[1] Though five of these states—right view, right intention, right effort, right mindfulness, and right concentration—are present in mundane *jhāna*, they are not present as path factors for on those occasions they do not pertain to the noble path leading directly to the cessation of suffering.

The phrase "enlightenment factor" attaches to the states belonging to the seven factors of enlightenment: mindfulness, investigation of phenomena, energy, rapture, tranquility, concentration, and equanimity. This collection is called "enlightenment" or "awakening" (*bodhi*) because, when it arises at the moment of the supramundane paths, it enables the noble disciple to awaken from the sleep of the defilements. Its components can be present in the mundane *jhānas* but not as enlightenment factors. They function as enlightenment factors only in the supramundane *jhānas* of the noble paths and fruits, for only then do they contribute immediately to the attainment of enlightenment.

Besides these, several other differences between mundane and supramundane *jhāna* may be briefly noted. Firstly, with regard to their object, the mundane *jhānas* have a conceptual entity (*paññatti*) as object; for the *kasiṇas*, impurities, mindfulness of breathing, etc. the object is the counterpart sign, for the divine abodes

1. It should be noted that in the paths and fruits occurring at the level of the second through fifth *jhānas*, only seven path factors are present. This is because right intention (*sammāsaṁkappa*) is a form of *vitakka*, which subsides with the attainment of the second *jhāna*. Similarly, in the paths and fruits of the fourth and fifth *jhānic* levels only six enlightenment factors are present, rapture having been abandoned with the attainment of the fourth *jhāna* of the fivefold system.

(*brahmavihāra*) it is sentient beings. In contrast, for the supramundane *jhāna* of the paths and fruits the object is exclusively *nibbāna*, a truly existent state (*sabhāvadhamma*).

With regard to their predominant tone, in mundane *jhāna* the element of serenity prevails. Though the factor of wisdom enters into the mundane *jhānas* it does not do so with any special prominence. In contrast, the supramundane *jhāna* of the paths and fruits brings serenity and insight into balance. Wisdom is present as right view (*sammadiṭṭhi*) and serenity as right concentration (*sammāsamādhi*). Both function together in perfect harmony, neither one exceeding the other.[1]

This difference in prevailing tone leads into a difference in function or activity between the two kinds of *jhāna*. Both the mundane and supramundane are *jhānas* in the sense of closely attending (*upanijjhāna*) but in the case of mundane *jhāna* this close attention issues merely in an absorption into the object, an absorption that can only suppress the defilements temporarily. In the supramundane *jhāna*, particularly of the four paths, the coupling of close attention with wisdom brings the exercise of four functions at a single moment. These four functions each apply to one of the Four Noble Truths, representing the particular way that noble truth is penetrated at the time the paths arise comprehending the truths. The four functions are full understanding (*pariññā*), abandonment (*pahāna*), realization (*sacchikiriya*), and development (*bhāvanā*). The path penetrates the first noble truth by fully understanding suffering; it penetrates the second noble truth by abandoning craving, the origin of suffering; it penetrates the third noble truth by realizing *nibbāna*, the cessation of suffering; and it penetrates the fourth noble truth by developing the Noble Eightfold Path, the way to the end of suffering. The *Visuddhimagga* quotes a passage from the ancients to clear away doubts that one experience can perform four functions simultaneously:

> For this is said by the Ancients 'just as a lamp performs four functions simultaneously in a single moment—it burns the wick, dispels darkness, makes light appear, and uses up the oil—so too, path knowledge penetrates to the four truths simultaneously in a single moment—it penetrates to suffering by

1. See Pts., p. 288.

penetrating to it with full-understanding, penetrates to origination by penetrating to it with abandoning, penetrates to the path by penetrating to it with developing and penetrates to cessation by penetrating to it with realizing. What is meant? By making cessation its object it reaches, sees and pierces the four truths'.[1]

Filling in the simile, Buddhaghosa explains that as the lamp burns the wick the path knowledge understands suffering; as the lamp dispels darkness the path abandons craving; as the lamp makes light appear the path develops the factors of the Noble Eightfold Path; and as the lamp consumes the oil, the path realizes *nibbāna*, which destroys the defilements. Though this fourfold function is peculiar to the path-consciousness and is not fully shared by fruition, the latter still exercises a decisively cognitive function in that it is said to "closely attend to the real characteristic, the truth of cessation."[2]

The Jhānic Level of the Path and Fruit

When the paths and fruits are assigned to the level of the four or five *jhānas*, the question arises as to what factor determines their particular level of *jhānic* intensity. In other words, why do the path and fruit arise for one yogin at the level of the first *jhāna*, for another at the level of the second *jhāna*, and so forth? The *Visuddhimagga* and the *Aṭṭhasālinī* deal with this issue in terms of the question as to what governs the difference in the number of the noble path's enlightenment factors (*bojjhaṅga*), path factors (*maggaṅga*) and *jhāna* factors (*jhānaṅga*). The texts present three theories concerning the determinant of the *jhānic* level of the path.[3] These theories were apparently formulated by ancient commentators and handed down in succession through their lineages of pupils. The first, ascribed to the Elder Tipiṭaka Cūḷa Nāga, holds that it is the basic *jhāna* (*pādakajjhāna*), i.e. the *jhāna* used as a basis for the insight leading to emergence in immediate proximity to the path, that governs the difference in the *jhānic*

1. PP., pp. 808. Vism., p. 593.
2. "Phalaṁ pana nirodhasaccaṁ tathalakkhanaṁ upanijjhāyati." Dhs.A. p. 211.
3. PP., pp. 778-80. Vism., pp. 572-73. Dhs.A., pp. 271-74.

level of the path. A second theory, ascribed to the Elder Mahā Datta of Moravāpi, says that the difference is governed by the aggregates made the objects of insight (*vipassanāya ārammaṇabhūtā khandhā*) on the occasion of insight leading to emergence. A third theory, ascribed to the Elder Tipiṭaka Cūḷa Abhaya, holds that it is the personal inclination (*puggalajjhāsaya*) of the meditator that governs the difference.

According to the first theory, the path arisen in a dry insight meditator who lacks *jhāna*, and the path arisen in one who possesses a *jhāna* attainment but does not use it as a basis for insight, and the path arisen by comprehending formations after emerging from the first *jhāna*, are all paths of the first *jhāna* only. They all have eight path factors, seven enlightenment factors, and five *jhāna* factors. When the path is produced after emerging from the second, third, fourth, and fifth *jhānas*, and using these as the basis for insight, then the path pertains to the level of the *jhāna* used as a basis—the second, third, fourth or fifth. The path will have respectively, four, three, two, and again two *jhāna* factors. However, these paths will possess only seven path factors, since "right intention" (*sammāsaṁkappa*), as a mode of applied thought (*vitakka*), has been eliminated in the second and higher *jhānas*. Those paths associated with the fourth and fifth *jhānas* will also lack the enlightenment factor of rapture (*pītisambojjhaṅga*), and thus have only six enlightenment factors. For a meditator using an immaterial *jhāna* as basis the path will be a fifth *jhāna* path.

Thus in this first theory, when formations are comprehended by insight after emerging from a basic *jhāna*, then it is the *jhāna* attainment emerged from at the point nearest to the path, i.e. just before insight leading to emergence is reached, that makes the path similar in nature to itself.

According to the second theory the path that arises is similar in nature to the states which are being comprehended with insight at the time insight leading to emergence occurs. Thus if the meditator, after emerging from a meditative attainment, is comprehending with insight sense sphere phenomena or the constituents of the first *jhāna*, then the path produced will occur at the level of the first *jhāna*. On this theory, then, it is the comprehended *jhāna* (*sammasitajjhāna*) that determines the *jhānic* quality of the path. The one qualification that must be added is that a yogin cannot contemplate with insight a *jhāna* higher than he is capable of attaining.

According to the third theory, the path occurs at the level of whichever *jhāna* the meditator wishes—either at the level of the *jhāna* he has used as the basis for insight or at the level of that *jhāna* he has made the object of insight-comprehension. In other words, the *jhānic* quality of the path accords with his personal inclination. However, mere wish alone is not sufficient. For the path to occur at the *jhānic* level wished for, the mundane *jhāna* must have been either made the basis for insight or used as the object of insight-comprehension.

The difference between the three theories can be understood through a simple example.[1] If a meditator reaches the supramundane path by contemplating with insight the first *jhāna* after emerging from the fifth *jhāna*, then according to the first theory his path will belong to the fifth *jhāna*, while according to the second theory it will belong to the first *jhāna*. Thus these two theories are incompatible when a difference obtains between basic *jhāna* and comprehended *jhāna*. But according to the third theory, the path becomes of whichever *jhāna* the meditator wishes, either the first or the fifth. Thus this doctrine does not necessarily clash with the other two.

Buddhaghosa himself does not make a decision among these three theories. He only points out that in all three doctrines, beneath their disagreements, there is the recognition that the insight leading to emergence determines the *jhānic* character of the path. For this insight is the proximate and principal cause for the arising of the path, so whether it be the insight leading to emergence near the basic *jhāna* or that occurring through the contemplated *jhāna* or that fixed by the meditator's wish, it is in all cases this final phase of insight that gives definition to the supramundane path, fixing its path factors and *jhāna* factors.[2] Since fruition that occurs immediately after the path has an identical constitution to the path, its own supramundane *jhāna* is determined by the path. Thus a first *jhāna* path produces a first *jhāna* fruit, and so on for the remaining *jhānas*.

1. Dhs.A., p. 274. *Expositor*, 2:310.
2. PP., pp. 778-79. Vism., p. 573.

Two Attainments of the Noble Ones

The Theravāda tradition recognizes two special meditative attainments which are open only to particular types of noble persons. These two are the attainment of fruition (*phalasamāpatti*) and the attainment of cessation (*nirodhasamāpatti*). The former is a *jhāna* proper of the supramundane class; the latter, though not a *jhāna*, still demands complete mastery over the mundane *jhānas* as a prerequisite for its achievement. We will now consider each of these attainments in turn.

The Attainment of fruition

The fruition consciousness (*phalacitta*) is a supramundane state of consciousness classed as a resultant (*vipāka*) because it is produced by the corresponding path consciousness. Like the path consciousness, which it resembles almost exactly in content, fruition is a *jhāna* operating at the *jhānic* level of the path. Fruition consciousness occurs in two ways. Its initial occurrence, which we have already discussed, takes place in the cognitive series of the path, when it arises in immediate succession to the path consciousness. On that occasion it persists for two or three thought-moments experiencing the bliss of liberation, and then subsides, followed by the life-continuum. But fruition consciousness can occur in another way too. This second mode of occurrence takes the form of a special meditative attainment called the attainment of fruition (*phalasamāpatti*). It is accessible only to the noble persons of the four stages of deliverance, and comes in four grades corresponding to the four stages: the fruition attainment of stream-entry, the fruition attainment of the once-returner, the fruition attainment of the non-returner, and the fruition attainment of arahatship.

Like the fruition consciousness occurring in immediate succession to the path, the attainment of fruition is a supramundane *jhāna* having *nibbāna* for its object. But whereas fruition in the cognitive series of the path lasts only for two or three thought-moments, the fruition attainment entered subsequently by a noble person can last for as long as the meditator determines; it can continue as a series of states of fruition consciousness following one another in uninterrupted succession for hours or even days on end. Thus fruition attainment provides the ariyans with a special resort to which they can turn in order to experience for themselves the bliss of *nibbāna* here and now.

The *Visuddhimagga* discusses fruition attainment under a number of headings. It first defines the attainment of fruition as consisting in the "absorption of the noble fruition in cessation," which the *Mahā Ṭīkā* glosses as meaning that fruition attainment is "the occurrence of the noble fruition-*jhāna* in the mode of absorption with *nibbāna* as its object."[1] This definition discloses two important facts about the attainment of fruition: that it is a *jhāna* and that this *jhāna* has *nibbāna* as its object. Though fruition consciousness, on occasions of fruition attainment, is not preceded by a path—each path being unique and unrepeatable—its *jhānic* level always continues to correspond to that of the path from which it originally issued. Thus a yogin who attained a first *jhāna* path will subsequently enter only a first *jhāna* fruition attainment, one who had a second *jhāna* path will always attain a second *jhāna* fruition, etc.

Fruition attainment is beyond the range of worldlings but is available to all noble ones. Each noble person attains that fruition corresponding to his own level of liberation: the stream-enterer attains the fruition of stream-entry, the once-returner the fruition of a once-returner, and so forth. Those who have reached a higher path do not attain a lower fruition while those on a lower level do not attain a higher fruition.

The ariyans resort to this attainment for the purpose of experiencing *nibbānic* bliss here and now. They enter it by turning the mind away from all mundane objects and focus singit exclusively upon *nibbāna*. To attain fruition the noble disciple should go into solitary retreat, make a prior determination to enter fruition, and then develop insight on formations, going through the series of insights beginning with knowledge of rise and fall. Insight progresses as far as conformity, followed by change-of-lineage knowledge with formations as its object; then "immediately next to it consciousness becomes absorbed in cessation with the attainment of fruition."[2] Since the prior determination was made

1. PP., p. 820. "Yā ariyaphalassa nirodhe appanā." Vism., p. 602. "Ariyassa phalajhānassa nibbāne ārammaṇabhūte appanākārena pavatti." Vism. T. 2:515.

2. PP., p. 822. Vism., p. 603. N.B.: Whereas change-of-lineage

for fruition, not for a higher path, insight only issues in fruition attainment and not in a higher path. The attainment of the latter requires a separate and different guiding aspiration before developing insight.

Fruition attainment is made to last by a prior volition determining the time of the attainment: for it is by determining it thus 'I shall emerge at such a time' that it lasts until that time comes. Emergence comes when the mind turns away from *nibbāna* and takes as its object some sign of formations. Immediately after fruition attainment ends the mind lapses into the life-continuum (*bhavaṅga*). Fruition attainment also occurs momentarily in the process of emerging from the attainment of cessation.

Fruition attainment acquires three names according to the dominant mode of insight in the course of insight-contemplation immediately preceding absorption. If the dominant insight is the contemplation of impermanence, the fruition reached is called the signless liberation (*animittavimokkha*); if the contemplation of suffering dominates fruition is called the desireless liberation (*appaṇihitavimokkha*); and if the contemplation of selflessness dominates fruition is called the void liberation (*suññatavimokkha*). But in a looser sense all three names can be applied to any fruition. For any fruition has as object *nibbāna*—the signless, desireless, and void element; and again any fruition has a nature which is void of lust, hatred, and delusion, lacks the signs of lust, hatred, and delusion and is without desires rooted in lust, hatred, and delusion.[1]

The Attainment Of Cessation

A second attainment in the meditative field restricted to yogins of ariyan stature is the attainment of cessation, *nirodhamāsapatti*, also called the cessation of perception and feeling (*saññāvedayitanirodha*). The distinguishing feature of this attainment is the

---

preceding the path has *nibbāna* for its object, change-of-lineage preceding fruition attainment objectifies formations. The reason is given in the *Visuddhimagga Mahā Ṭīkā*: "Why does change-of-lineage not have *nibbāna* as its object here as it does when it precedes the path? Because states belonging to fruition are not associated with an outlet [as in the case of the path]. For this is said 'What states are an outlet? The four unincluded paths'." Vism.T. 2:518.

1. Nārada, *Manual.*, pp. 422-23. MN. 1:298.

cessation of all mental activity in its entirety, for which reason the *Visuddhimagga* defines it as "the non-occurrence of consciousness and its concomitants owing to their progressive cessation."[1]

The attainment of cessation can be obtained only by non-returners and arahats who possess the eight mundane attainments, i.e. the four *jhānas* and the four *āruppas*. Worldlings, stream-enterers, and once-returners—even those possessing all eight attainments—cannot obtain it, nor can it be obtained by non-returners and arahats who lack mastery over the eight attainments. The reason stream-enterers and once-returners cannot attain it is that they lack the necessary qualifications. To attain cessation requires full possession of the two powers of serenity and insight. Because those below the level of a non-returner have not fully abandoned sensual desire, their power of serenity is not perfected, and without the perfecting of the power of serenity there is no attainment of cessation. Cessation can also only be reached in "five constituent becoming," i.e. in realms where all five aggregates are found. It cannot be reached in the immaterial realms since it must be preceded by the four fine material *jhānas*, which are lacking in those realms.

Non-returners and arahats with the required qualifications attain to cessation because, being wearied by the occurrence and dissolution of formations, they think: "Let us dwell in bliss by being without consciousness here and now and reaching the cessation that is *nibbāna*."[2] To enter cessation the qualified meditator must strive to bring about the cessation of consciousness belonging to the base of neither perception nor non-perception. This demands the balanced coupling of serenity and insight. One who utilizes serenity alone can reach the base of neither perception nor non-perception but cannot reach cessation. One who utilizes insight alone can enter fruition attainment but not cessation. The attainment of cessation requires the alternative application of both serenity and insight.

A meditator wishing to attain cessation enters the first *jhāna*,

1. PP., pp. 824. "Ya anupubbanirodhavasena cittacetasikānaṁ dhammānaṁ appavatti." Vism., p. 604.

2. PP., p. 828. Vism., p. 607. N.B.: The *Visuddhimagga Mahā Ṭīkā* points out that the phrase "cessation that is *nibbāna*" means that cessation is similar to the *nibbāna* element without residue (*anupādisesa nibbānadhātu*). It should not be taken literally as establishing identity between the two. Vism.T. 2:902.

emerges from it, and contemplates its formations with insight as impermanent, suffering, and selfless. He repeats the same procedure with each meditative attainment up to the base of nothingness, the next to last immaterial *jhāna*. After emerging from the base of nothingness he then must perform four preparatory tasks. First he resolves that any requisites he has with him that belong to others will not be damaged by fire, water, wind, thieves, rats, etc. while he is in cessation. This resolution gives effective protection during the duration of his attainment; his own belongings are protected from damage by the power of the attainment itself. Secondly he resolves that if he is needed by the community of bhikkhus he will emerge from his attainment before a bhikkhu comes to call him. Thirdly he resolves that if the Buddha needs to summon him he should emerge before a bhikkhu is sent to call him. And fourthly he determines that his life span will last at least seven days from the moment he attains cessation.

Having performed these four preparatory tasks, the meditator attains the base of neither perception nor non-perception. Then after one or two turns of consciousness have passed the process of consciousness ceases; he becomes without consciousness, attaining to cessation. The stopping of consciousness takes place automatically, as a result of the meditator's determination to reach cessation. The meditator will remain in cessation for as long as he has predetermined. But if he has not done the four preliminary tasks, after reaching the base of neither perception nor non-perception he will return to the base of nothingness without attaining cessation.[1]

Like the attaining of cessation, emergence from cessation takes place automatically, through the exhaustion of the pre-determined time, unless interrupted earlier by the waiting of the bhikkhus, the summons of the Buddha, or the end of the life-span. Emergence comes about by means of the fruition of non-returning in the case of a non-returner and the fruition of arahatship in the case of an arahat. Immediately upon emerging from cessation, the yogin goes through a series of fruition consciousnesses appropriate to his spiritual level. But for all yogins who emerge from cessation the mind inclines to *nibbāna*. For this reason a non-returner who has come out from cessation can use his attainment

1. PP., pp. 831-32. Vism., p. 610.

as a basis for achieving arahatship. As the Buddha says: "A bhikkhu, completely passing beyond the base of neither perception nor non-perception, enters and dwells in the cessation of perception and feeling. Having seen with wisdom his cankers are destroyed."[1]

The attainment of cessation is the acme of a graduated process of bringing to a stop the formations of body and mind. The bhikkhuni Dhammadinnā explains that there are three types of formations—the bodily formation (*kāyasaṅkhāra*), the verbal formation (*vacīsaṅkhāra*), and the mental formation (*cittasaṅkhāra*). The bodily formation is in-and-out breathing, a physiological process connected with the body; the verbal formation is applied and sustained thought, the mental factors directing verbalization; the mental formation is perception and feeling, cognitive processes connected with the mind. For one who is entering the attainment of cessation, Dhammadinnā states, the verbal formation ceases first (in the second *jhāna*), the bodily formation ceases next (in the fourth *jhāna*), and the mental formation ceases last (with the entrance into cessation).[2]

The question might arise as to the difference between a corpse and a meditator in the attainment of cessation. The Venerable Sāriputta explains:

> When a bhikkhu is dead, friend, has completed his term, his bodily formations have ceased and are quite still, his verbal formations have ceased and are quite still, his mental formations have ceased and are quite still, his life is exhausted, his heat has subsided, and his faculties are broken up. When a bhikkhu has entered upon the cessation of perception and feeling, his bodily formations have ceased and are quite still, his verbal formations have ceased and are quite still, his mental formations have ceased and are quite still, his life is unexhausted, his heat has not subsided, his faculties are quite whole.[3]

Another question which might arise concerns the differences between the base of neither perception nor non-perception, the attainment of fruition, and the attainment of cessation. The

1. MN. 1:175.
2. MN. 1:302. See also SN. 4:217.
3. PP., pp. 832-33. MN. 1:296.

attainment of cessation differs from the first two in that these two are states of consciousness made up of mind and mental factors (*citta-cetasika*) while cessation is not a state of consciousness but the stopping of the mental continuum together with its factors. The fourth *āruppa* is a purely mundane attainment in the sphere of serenity accessible to all meditators with the necessary strength of concentration. Its object is purely mundane—the four aggregates of the third *āruppa*. It does not presuppose any achievements in insight or any attainment of ariyan stature; it is thus held in common by both Buddhist and non-Buddhist meditators. The attainment of fruition, in contrast, is a supramundane state bringing into balance both serenity and insight. Its object is supramundane, *nibbāna*. Each fruition is open only to those ariyans who have reached the corresponding level of deliverance and it is entered by a preliminary course of practice in insight contemplation on the three characteristics. The attainment of cessation, as distinct from both, is neither mundane nor supramundane, neither conditioned nor unconditioned. As the cessation of consciousness it takes no object. It is open solely to non-returners and arahats having the eight attainments and is reached through an alternating course of serenity and insight. Moreover, to enter the attainment of cessation requires the fulfilment of the four preliminary tasks, while such preparations are not needed for the base of neither perception nor non-perception or for the attainment of fruition.

The Seven Types of Noble Persons

All noble persons, as we saw, acquire supramundane *jhāna* along with their attainment of the noble paths and fruits. The noble disciples at each of the four stages of deliverance, moreover, have access to the supramundane *jhāna* of their respective fruition attainments to which they can resort to experience the peace of *nibbāna*. However, it remains problematic to what extent they share in the possession of mundane *jhāna*. To determine an answer to this question it is helpful to consult an early typology of noble disciples described most fully in the Kīṭagiri Sutta (MN. No. 70), reformulated in the Puggalapaññatti of the Abhidhammapitaka, and clarified further in the commentaries. This typology classifies the eight noble persons of the four paths and fruits into seven types: [1] the faith-devotee, [2] the one liberated by faith, [3] the body-witness, [4] the one liberated in both ways, [5] the truth-devotee, [6] the one attained to understanding, and [7] the one liberated by wisdom.[1] A look at the explanation of these seven types will enable us to see the range of *jhānic* attainment reached by the noble disciples, and from there to assess the place of mundane *jhāna* in the early Buddhist picture of the perfected individual.

The seven types divide into three general classes, each class being defined by the predominance of a particular spiritual faculty. The first two types are governed roughly by predominance of faith, the middle two by predominance of concentration, and the last three by predominance of wisdom. To this division, however, certain qualifications will have to be made as we go along.

[1] The faith devotee is explained in the suttas thus:

> Herein, monks, some person has not reached with his own (mental) body those peaceful immaterial deliverances (*santā vimokkhā āruppā*) transcending material form; nor, after seeing with wisdom, have his cankers (*āsavas*) been destroyed. But he has a certain degree of faith in the Tathāgata, a certain degree of devotion to him, and he has these qualities—the faculties of faith, energy, mindfulness, concentration, and wisdom. This person, monks, is called a faith-devotee.[2]

The Puggalapaññatti definition reads:

> What person is faith-devotee? In a person practising for the realization of the fruit of stream-entry the faculty of faith is predominant; he develops the noble path led by faith, with faith as the forerunner. This person is called a faith-devotee. A person practising for the realization of the fruit of stream-entry is a faith-devotee. When established in the fruit he is one liberated by faith.[3]

1. In Pali: [1] saddhānusāri, [2] saddhāvimutta, [3] kāyasakkhi, [4] ubhatobhāgavimutta [5] dhammānusāri [6] diṭṭhippatta, and [7] paññāvimutta.
2. MN. 1:479.
3. Pug. P., p. 182.

Whereas the sutta explanation explicitly mentions the lack of the "peaceful immaterial deliverances", i.e. the four immaterial *jhānas*, the Puggalapaññatti omits this, but mentions his status as a person on the path of stream-entry. Both concur in recognizing the faith-devotee as a disciple with predominance of faith. When the immaterial *jhānas* are excluded from the faith devotee's spiritual equipment, this implies nothing with regard to his achievement of the four lower mundane *jhānas*. It would seem that the faith-devotee can have previously attained any of the four fine material *jhānas* before reaching the path, and can also be a dry-insight worker bereft of mundane *jhāna*. The commentaries add a new element—a connection between the disciple's subject of insight-contemplation and his dominant faculty. Thus for the faith-devotee the subject of insight is impermanence. The Visuddhimagga says: "When a man brings [formations] to mind as impermanent and, having great resolution, acquires the faith faculty, he becomes a faith devotee at the moment of the stream-entry path."[1]

[2] The one liberated by faith is strictly and literally defined as a noble disciple at the six intermediate levels, from the fruit of stream-entry through to the path of arahatship, who lacks the immaterial *jhānas* and has a predominance of the faith faculty. The Buddha explains the one liberated by faith as follows:

> Herein, monks, some person has not reached with his own (mental) body those peaceful immaterial deliverances transcending material form; but having seen with wisdom, some of his cankers have been destroyed, and his faith in the Tathāgata is settled, deeply rooted, well established. This person, monks, is called one liberated by faith.[2]

As in the case of the faith-devotee, the one liberated by faith, while lacking the immaterial *jhānas*, may still be an obtainer of the four mundane *jhānas* as well as a dry insight worker.

The Puggalapaññatti states that the person liberated by faith is one who understands the Four Noble Truths, has seen and verified by means of wisdom the dhammas proclaimed by the Tathāgata, and having seen with wisdom has eliminated some of

1. PP., p. 770. Vism., p. 566.
2. MN. 1:478.

his cankers. However, he has not done so as easily as the *diṭṭhippatta*, the person attained to understanding, whose progress is easier due to his superior wisdom.[1] The fact that the one liberated by faith has destroyed only some of his cankers implies that he has advanced beyond the first path but not yet reached the final fruit, the fruition of arahatship.[2]

[3] The "body witness" is a noble disciple at the six intermediate levels, from the fruit of stream-entry to the path of arahatship, who has a predominance of the faculty of concentration and can obtain the immaterial *jhānas*. The sutta explanation reads:

> And what person, monks, is a body-witness? Herein, monks, some person has reached with his own (mental) body those peaceful immaterial deliverances transcending material form, and having seen with wisdom, some of his cankers have been destroyed. This person, monks, is called a body-witness.[3]

The Puggalapaññatti offers a slight variation on this phrasing: "What person is a body-witness? Here some person has reached with his own mental body the eight deliverances, and having seen with wisdom, some of his cankers are destroyed."[4] For the sutta's "immaterial deliverances" (*āruppā vimokkhā*) the Puggalapaññatti substitutes "the eight deliverances" (*aṭṭhavimokkhā*). These eight deliverances consist of three meditative attainments pertaining to the fine material sphere (inclusive of all four lower *jhānas*), the four immaterial *jhānas*, and the attainment of cessation.[5] But though the Puggalapaññatti makes this reformulation, it should not be thought either that the achievement of all eight deliverances is necessary to become a body-witness or that the achievement of the three lower deliverances is sufficient. What is both requisite and sufficient to receive the designation "body-

1. Pug. P., pp. 184-85.
2. The *Visuddhimagga*, however, says that arahats in whom faith is predominant can also be called "liberated by faith" (PP., p. 770. Vism., p. 566). Its *Ṭīkā* points out that this remark is only intended figuratively, not literally, in the sense that for those arahats arahatship results from being *saddhāvimutta* at the moment of the fourth path. Literally such arahats would be *paññāvimutta*. (Vism.T. 2:468).
3. MN. 1:478.
4. Pug. P., p. 184.
5. DN. 3:159. MN. 2:12. See Vajirañāṇa, *Buddhist Meditation*, pp. 484-86.

witness" is the partial destruction of defilements coupled with the attainment of at least the lowest immaterial *jhāna*. Thus the body-witness becomes fivefold by way of those who obtain any of the four immaterial *jhānas* and the one who also obtains the attainment of cessation.[1]

The *Visuddhimagga* connects the body-witness with suffering as a subject of insight and concentration as a predominant faculty: "When a man brings (formations) to mind as painful and, having great tranquillity, acquires the faculty of concentration, he is called a body-witness in all eight instances,"[2] i.e. from the path of stream-entry through arahatship. Its *Ṭīkā* explains that this extension of the scope of body-witness to persons on the first path and to arahats is figurative in intention and should not be taken as literal. Literally, a body-witness is found only in the intermediate six stages. According to the *Ṭīkā* "one with the eight attainments on the first path would have to be either a faith-devotee or a truth-devotee; the same person at the final fruition would be one liberated in both ways (*ubhatobhāgavimutta*)."[3]

[4] One who is liberated in both ways is an arahat who has completely destroyed the defilements and possesses the immaterial attainments. The commentaries explain the name "liberated in both ways" as meaning "through the immaterial attainment he is liberated from the material body and through the path [of arahatship] he is liberated from the mental body."[4] The sutta defines this type of disciple thus:

> And what person, monks, is liberated in both ways? Herein, monks, someone has reached with his own (mental) body those peaceful immaterial deliverances transcending material form, and having seen with wisdom, his cankers are destroyed. This person, monks, is called liberated in both ways.[5]

1. Vism. T. 2:466.
2. PP., p. 770. Vism., p. 566.
3. Vism. T. 2:466. The position that one with the eight attainments on the first path can be a faith-devotee or a truth-devotee conflicts with the explanation of these types in the Kiṭāgiri Sutta. However, the sevenfold typology of this sutta makes no provision for a disciple of the first path who gains the immaterial *jhānas*.
4. "Arūpasamāpattiyā rūpakāyato vimutto. Maggena nāmakāyato." MN.A. 2:131.
5. MN. 1:477.

The Puggalapaññatti gives basically the same formula, but replaces "immaterial deliverances" with "the eight deliverances."[1] The same principle of interpretation that applied to the body-witness applies here: the attainment of any immaterial *jhāna*, even the lowest, is sufficient to qualify a person as both-ways liberated. As the Mahāṭīkā says: "one who has attained arahatship after gaining even one [immaterial *jhāna*] is liberated in both ways."[2] This type becomes fivefold by way of those who attain arahatship after emerging from one or another of the four *āruppas*, and the one who attains arahatship after emerging from the attainment of cessation.[3]

[5] The "truth-devotee" is a disciple on the first path in whom the faculty of wisdom is predominant. Here "dhamma" has the meaning of wisdom. The Buddha explains the truth-devotee as follows:

> Herein, monks, some person has not reached with his own (mental) body those peaceful immaterial deliverances transcending material form; nor, after seeing with wisdom, have his cankers been destroyed. But the teachings proclaimed by the Tathāgata are accepted by him through mere reflection, and he has these qualities—the faculties of faith, energy, mindfulness, concentration, and wisdom. This person, monks, is called a truth-devotee.[4]

The Puggalapaññatti defines the truth-devotee in the same way as the faith-devotee, except that it substitutes wisdom for faith as the predominant faculty and as the leader and forerunner in the development of the path. It adds that when a truth-devotee is established in the fruit of stream-entry he becomes one attained to understanding (*diṭṭhippatta*).[5] The sutta and Abhidhamma works again differ as to emphasis, the one stressing lack of the immaterial *jhānas*, the other the ariyan stature. The *Visuddhimagga* connects the truth-devotee with the contemplation of selflessness: "When a man brings [formations] to mind as not self and having great wisdom, acquires the faculty of understand-

1. Pug. P., p. 184.
2. Vism.T. 2:466.
3. MN.A. 3:131.
4. MN. 1:479.
5. Pug. P., p. 185.

ing, he becomes a Dhamma-devotee at the moment of the stream-entry path."[1] Presumably, though the four immaterial *jhānas* are denied for the truth-devotee, he may have any of the four fine material *jhānas* or be a bare insight practitioner without any mundane *jhāna*.

[6] The one attained to understanding is a noble disciple at the six intermediate levels who lacks the immaterial *jhānas* and has a predominance of the wisdom faculty. The Buddha explains:

> And what person, monks, is the one attained to understanding? Herein, monks, someone has not reached with his own (mental) body those peaceful immaterial deliverances transcending material form, but having seen with wisdom some of his cankers are destroyed, and the teachings proclaimed by the Tathāgata have been seen and verified by him with wisdom. This person, monks, is called one attained to understanding.[2]

The Puggalapaññatti defines the one attained to understanding as a person who understands the Four Noble Truths, has seen and verified by means of wisdom the *dhammas* proclaimed by the Tathāgata, and having seen with wisdom has eliminated some of his cankers.[3] He is thus the "wisdom counterpart" of the one liberated by faith, but progresses more easily than the latter by virtue of his sharper wisdom.

[7] The one liberated by wisdom is an arahat who does not obtain the immaterial attainments. In the words of the sutta:

> And what person, monks, is the one liberated by wisdom? Herein, monks, someone has not reached with his own (mental) body those peaceful material deliverances transcending material form, but having seen with wisdom his cankers are destroyed. This person, monks, is called one liberated by wisdom.[4]

The Puggalapaññatti's definition merely replaces "immaterial deliverances" with "the eight deliverances."[5] Though such arahats do not reach the immaterial *jhānas* it is quite possible for them to attain the lower *jhānas*. The sutta commentary in fact

1. PP., p. 770. Vism., p. 566.
2. MN. 1:478.
3. Pug. P., p. 185.
4. MN. 1:477-78.
5. Pug. P., p. 185.

states that the one liberated by wisdom is fivefold by way of the dry insight-worker and the four who attain arahatship after emerging from the four *jhānas*.

It should be noted that the one liberated by wisdom is contrasted not with the one liberated by faith, but with the one liberated in both ways. The issue that divides the two types of arahat is the lack or possession of the four immaterial *jhānas* and the attainment of cessation. The person liberated by faith is found at the six intermediate levels of sanctity, not at the level of arahatship. When he obtains arahatship, lacking the immaterial *jhānas*, he becomes one liberated by wisdom even though faith rather than wisdom is his predominant faculty. Similarly a meditator with predominance of concentration but lacking the immaterial attainments also becomes one liberated by wisdom when he attains arahatship. But a yogin who reaches arahatship while possessing the immaterial attainments will still be "one liberated in both ways" even if wisdom rather than concentration claims first place among his spiritual endowments, as was the case with the Venerable Sāriputta.

Jhāna and the Arahat

From the standpoint of their spiritual stature the seven types of noble persons can be divided into three categories. The first, which includes the faith-devotee (*saddhānusāri*) and the truth-devotee (*dhammānusāri*), consists of those on the path of stream-entry, the first of the eight ariyan persons. The second category, comprising the one liberated by faith (*saddhāvimutta*), the body-witness (*kāyasakkhi*), and the one attained to understanding (*diṭṭhippatta*), consists of those on the six intermediate levels, from the stream-enterer to one on the path of arahatship. The third category, comprising the one liberated in both ways (*ubhatobhāgavimutta*) and the one liberated by wisdom (*paññāvimutta*), consists only of arahats.

The *ubhatobhāgavimutta*, "one liberated in both ways," and the *paññāvimutta*, "one liberated by wisdom," thus form the terms of a two fold typology of arahats distinguished on the basis of their accomplishment in *jhāna*. The *ubhatobhāgavimutta* arahat experiences in his own person the "peaceful deliverances" of the immaterial sphere, the *paññāvimutta* arahat lacks this full experience of the immaterial *jhānas*. Each of these two types, according to the commentaries, again becomes fivefold—the *ubhatobhāgavimutta* by way of those who possess the ascending four immaterial *jhānas* and the attainment of cessation, the *paññāvimutta* by way of those who reach arahatship after emerging from the four fine material *jhānas* and the dry insight meditator whose insight lacks the support of mundane *jhāna*.

The possibility of arahatship without possession of a mundane *jhāna* has sometimes been questioned by Theravāda Buddhist scholars, but the weight of the Theravāda tradition leans towards the recognition of such an attainment. We have already mentioned the *suddhavipassanāyānika*, the yogin with bare insight as his vehicle, also called the *sukkhavipassaka*, the dry insight meditator. That this kind of meditator does not already possess a *jhāna* which he just neglects to use as a basis for insight seems implicit from the distinction the *Visuddhimagga* makes in its discussion of the *jhānic* level of the path :

> ...the path arisen in a bare-insight [dry insight] worker, and the path arisen in one who possesses a *jhāna* attainment but who has not made the *jhāna* the basis for insight,...are paths of the first *jhāna* only.[1]

Here, when the dry-insight worker is distinguished from the *jhāna*-attainer who does not use his *jhāna* to develop insight, the clear implication is that the former does not have a basic *jhāna*. If he did there would be no reason to speak of the two as separate cases.

Further evidence for the existence of arahats lacking mundane *jhāna* is provided by the Susīma Sutta together with its commentaries.[2] In this sutta the monk Susīma is perplexed about a group of monks who claim to have reached arahatship yet deny possessing supernormal powers or the peaceful deliverances of the immaterial sphere. To the question how they can be arahats without these attainments they reply: "We are liberated by wisdom" (*paññāvimuttā kho mayaṁ*). Confused by this answer, Susīma goes to the Buddha for clarification. The Buddha declares: "Susīma, first the knowledge of the structure of phenomena arises, after-

1. PP., p. 779. Vism., p. 573.
2. SN. 2:119-23.

wards the knowledge of *nibbāna*." Then he explains the impermanence, suffering, and selflessness of the five aggregates. He shows how contemplation of the three characteristics leads to dispassion, detachment and emancipation, elucidates the law of dependent arising, and convinces Susīma that knowledge of the causal law can issue in liberation without requiring any possession of supernormal powers or the immaterial attainments.

It is true that in the sutta itself a lack of *jhāna* is not ascribed to the group of arahats liberated by wisdom. The text only mentions the absence of the five *abhiññās* and the *āruppas*. But the exegetical sources on the sutta fill in the gap, showing that these arahats reached their goal without mundane *jhāna* of absorption level. The commentary rephrases the monks' reply "'We are liberated by wisdom" to make explicit the fact that they are dry insight meditators: "'We are liberated by wisdom, friend' : we are contemplatives, dry insight workers, liberated by wisdom alone."[1] The commentary explains the knowledge of the structure of phenomena (*dhammaṭṭhitiñāṇa*) as insight knowledge and the knowledge of *nibbāna* (*nibbāne ñāṇa*) as path knowledge. It states that the Buddha gave the long disquisition on insight "for the purpose of showing the arising of knowledge even without concentration."[2] The subcommentary makes the sutta's purport still clearer by explaining the commentary's phrase "even without concentration" as meaning "even without concentration previously accomplished, reaching the characteristic of serenity," adding that "this is said in reference to the *vipassanāyānika*."[3] From all this it follows that these arahats, attaining emancipation by wisdom without prior concentration of the serenity level, lacked mundane *jhāna*. As arahats, however, they would necessarily have reached the supramundane *jhāna* of the paths and fruits, with constant access to the *jhāna* of the attainment of fruition.

1. "Āvuso mayaṁ nijjhānakā sukkhavipassakā paññāmatten'eva vimuttā ti dasseti." SN.A. 2:117. N.B.: The word *nijjhānakā* is ambiguous: the word *nijjhāna* is used in the suttas to mean reflection or contemplation and we here follow that usage by rendering its derivative as "contemplative"; but the purport might also be "lacking *jhāna*," as the prefix *nir* sometimes has a privative as well as augmentative meaning.

2. "Vinā pi samādhiṁ evaṁ ñāṇuppattidassanatthaṁ." *Ibid.*

3. "Samatha lakkhaṇappattaṁ purimasiddhaṁ vinā pi samādhinti vipassanā yānikaṁ sandhāya vuttaṁ." SN.T. 2:125.

In contrast to the *paññāvimutta* arahats, those arahats who are *ubhatobhāgavimutta* enjoy a twofold liberation. Through their mastery over the formless attainments they are liberated from the material body (*rūpakāya*), capable of dwelling in this very life in the meditations corresponding to the immaterial planes of existence; through their attainment of arahatship they are liberated from the mental body (*nāmakāya*), presently free from all defilements and sure of final emancipation from future becoming. *Paññāvimutta* arahats only possess the second of these two liberations.

The double liberation of the *ubhatobhāgavimutta* arahat should not be confused with another double liberation frequently mentioned in the suttas in connection with arahatship. This second pair of liberations, called *cetovimutti paññāvimutti*, "liberation of mind, liberation by wisdom," is shared in common by all arahats. It appears in the stock passage descriptive of arahatship: "With the destruction of the cankers he here and now enters and dwells in the cankerless liberation of mind, liberation by wisdom, having realized it for himself with direct knowledge." That this twofold liberation belongs to *paññāvimutta* arahats as well as to those who are *ubhatobhāgavimutta* is made clear by the Putta Sutta, where the stock passage is used for two types of arahats called the "white lotus recluse" and the "red lotus recluse":

> How, monks, is a person a white lotus recluse (*samaṇapuṇḍarika*)? Here, monks, with the destruction of the cankers a monk here and now enters and dwells in the cankerless liberation of mind, liberation by wisdom, having realized it for himself with direct knowledge. Yet he does not dwell experiencing the eight deliverances with his body. Thus, monks, a person is a white lotus recluse.
>
> And how, monks, is a person a red lotus recluse (*samaṇapaduma*)? Here, monks, with the destruction of the cankers a monk here and now enters and dwells in the cankerless liberation of mind, liberation by wisdom, having realized it for himself with direct knowledge. And he dwells experiencing the eight deliverances with his body. Thus, monks, a person is a red lotus recluse.[1]

1 AN 2:87.

Since the description of these two types coincides with that of *paññāvimutta* and *ubhatobhāgavimutta* the two pairs may be identified, the white lotus recluse with the *paññāvimutta*, the red lotus recluse with the *ubhatobhāgavimutta*. Yet the *paññāvimutta* arahat, while lacking the experience of the eight deliverances, still has both liberation of mind and liberation by wisdom.

Other suttas help fill in the meaning of "liberation of mind" and "liberation by wisdom." The latter term is almost invariably used in reference to arahatship, signifying the arahat's permanent deliverance from ignorance through his full penetration of the Four Noble Truths. The term "liberation of mind" has a more varied application. In some places it signifies the temporary release of the mind from defilements given by attainments in serenity meditation, as when the fourth *jhāna*, the four *Brahmavihāras*, and the base of nothingness are spoken of as forms of liberation of mind.[1] But elsewhere liberation of mind is held up as the final goal of the Buddhist meditative discipline. In this context it is usually qualified by the adjective "unshakeable" (*akuppā*). Thus the "unshakeable liberation of mind" is called the chief of all liberations of mind. After attaining enlightenment the Buddha declares: "Unshakeable is the liberation of my mind." And elsewhere he says: "This is the goal of the holy life, monks, this is its essence, this is its consummation—the unshakeable liberation of the mind."[2]

When liberation of mind and liberation by wisdom are joined together and described as "cankerless" (*anāsava*), they can be taken to indicate two aspects of the arahat's deliverance. *Cetovimutti* or liberation of mind signifies the release of his mind from craving and its associated defilements, *paññāvimutti* or liberation by wisdom the release from ignorance: "With the fading away of lust there is liberation of mind, with the fading away of ignorance there is liberation by wisdom."[3] "As he sees and understands thus his mind is liberated from the canker of sensual desire, from the canker of existence, from the canker of ignorance—"[4]

1. MN. 1:296-98.
2. MN. 1:298, SN. 5:423, MN. 1:197.
3. "...Rāgavirāgā cetovimutti avijjāvirāgā paññāvimutti." AN. 1:61.
4. MN. 1:183-84.

here release from the first two cankers can be understood as liberation of mind, release from the canker of ignorance as liberation by wisdom. In the commentaries "liberation of mind" is identified with the concentration factor in the fruit of arahatship, "liberation by wisdom" with the wisdom factor:

> By the word 'mind' (*ceto*) the concentration concomitant with the fruit of arahatship is meant, by the word 'wisdom' the concomitant wisdom is meant. The concentration there is called 'liberation of mind' because it has liberated the mind from lust, the wisdom is called 'liberation by wisdom' because it has liberated the mind from ignorance.[1]

Since every arahat reaches arahatship through the Noble Eightfold Path, he must have attained supramundane *jhāna* in the form of right concentration, the eighth factor of the path, defined as the four *jhānas*. This *jhāna* remains with him as the concentration of the fruition attainment of arahatship, which occurs at the level of supramundane *jhāna* corresponding to that of his path. Thus he always stands in possession of at least the supramundane *jhāna* of fruition, called the *anāsavaṁ cetovimutti*, "cankerless liberation of mind." However, this consideration does not reflect back on his mundane attainments, requiring that every arahat possesses mundane *jhāna*.

Nevertheless, though early Buddhism acknowledges the possibility of a dry-visioned arahatship, the attitude prevails that *jhānas* are still desirable attributes in an arahat. They are of value not only prior to final attainment, as a foundation for insight, but retain their value even afterwards as well. The value of *jhāna* in the stage of arahatship, when all spiritual training has been completed, is twofold. One concerns the arahat's inner experience, the other his outer significance as a representative of the Buddha's dispensation.

On the side of inner experience the *jhānas* are valued as providing the arahat with a "blissful dwelling here and now" (*diṭṭhadhammasukhavihāra*). The suttas often show arahats attaining to *jhāna* and the Buddha himself declares the four *jhānas* to be figuratively a kind of *nibbāna* in this present life.[2] With respect to levels

1. MN.A. 1:169.
2. See AN. 4:453-54.

and factors there is no difference between the mundane *jhānas* of an arahat and those of a non-arahat. The difference concerns their function. For non-arahats the mundane *jhānas* constitute wholesome *kamma*; they are deeds with a potential to produce results, to precipitate rebirth in a corresponding realm of existence. But in the case of an arahat mundane *jhāna* is no more *kamma*. Since he has eradicated ignorance and craving, the roots of *kamma*, his actions leave no residue; they have no capacity to generate results. For him the *jhānic* consciousness is a mere functional consciousness which comes and goes and once gone disappears without a trace.

The value of the *jhānas* extends beyond the confines of the arahat's personal experience to testify to the spiritual efficacy of the Buddha's dispensation itself. The *jhānas* are regarded as ornamentations of the yogin, testimonies to the accomplishment of the spiritually perfect man and the effectiveness of the teaching he follows. A worthy monk is able to "gain at will, without trouble or difficulty, the four *jhānas* pertaining to the higher consciousness, blissful dwellings here and now." This ability to gain the *hānas* at will is a "quality that makes a monk an elder." When accompanied by several other spiritual accomplishments it is an essential quality of "a recluse who graces recluses" and of a monk who can move unobstructed in the four directions. Having ready access to the four *jhānas* makes an elder dear and agreeable, respected and esteemed by his fellow monks. Facility in gaining the *jhānas* is one of the eight qualities of a completely inspiring monk (*samantapāsādika bhikkhu*) perfect in all respects; it is also one of the eleven foundations of faith (*saddhāpadānāni*). It is significant that in all these lists of qualities the last item is always the attainment of arahatship, "the cankerless liberation of mind, liberation by wisdom," showing that all desirable qualities in a bhikkhu culminate in arahatship.[1]

On one occasion, when a number of chief disciples met together in a lovely Salwood at Gosinga on a beautiful moonlit night, the discussion arose among them as to what type of monk could illumine that Salwood. The Venerable Revata answered that it would be a monk who delights in solitary meditation, who is delighted by solitary meditation, who is intent on mental tran-

1. AN. 2:23, 3:131, 135, 114; 4:314-15, 5:337.

quility. The Venerable Sāriputta replied that it would be a monk who could abide in whatever meditative attainment he wanted in the morning, midday, and evening.[1] Sāriputta himself is extolled for his ability to enter the four *jhānas*, the four *āruppas*, and the attainment of cessation without giving rise to the thought "I am attaining," "I have attained" or "I have emerged." The reason he can avoid such thoughts is that, as an arahat, he has uprooted all "I"-making, "mine"-making, and tendencies to conceit.[2] Elsewhere the Buddha praises Sāriputta for his skill in entering each of the nine attainments, analyzing them into their constituent formations, and contemplating them with a mind unconfined by attraction or repulsion.[3]

The higher the degree of his mastery over the meditative attainments, the higher the esteem in which an arahat monk is held and the more praiseworthy his accomplishment is considered to be. On one occasion the Buddha met with three arahat bhikkhus—the Venerable Anuruddha, Nandiya, and Kimbila—and elicited from them the admission that they were all capable of attaining the four *jhānas*, the four *āruppas*, cessation, and the fruit of arahatship. After this discussion the Buddha declared that if all the people in the world were to recollect these three young men with a mind of confidence, it would lead to their welfare and happiness for a long time to come. He concludes: "See how these three young men are faring for the welfare of the many folk, out of compassion for the world, for the good, welfare and happiness of gods and men."[4]

Though the *paññā-vimutta* and *ubhatobhāgavimutta* arahats are equal with respect to release from suffering, special regard extends to the latter, and the greater his facility in meditation the higher the regard. Thus the Buddha says:

> When a monk has mastered these eight deliverances in direct order, in reverse order, and in both orders, when he can attain to and emerge from any one of them, whenever he chooses, wherever he chooses and for as long as he chooses—when too, with the destruction of the cankers, he enters and abides

1. MN. 1:213-15.
2. SN. 3:235-38.
3. MN. Sutta No. 111.
4. MN. 1:211.

in the cankerless liberation of mind, liberation by wisdom, after realizing it for himself here and now through direct knowledge—then such a monk is called one liberated in both ways. There is no other liberation in both ways higher and more excellent than this liberation in both ways.[1]

The highest respect goes to those monks who possess not only liberation in both ways but the six *abhiññās*, the first five the outcome of the eight attainments of serenity, the sixth, the supramundane *abhiññā* of arahatship, the outcome of insight. The Buddha declares that a monk endowed with the six *abhiññās* is worthy of gifts and hospitality, worthy of offerings and reverential salutations, a supreme field of merit for the world.[2] In the period after the Buddha's *parinibbāna*, the Venerable Ānanda was asked whether the Buddha had designated a successor, to which he replied in the negative. He also denied that the Sangha had selected a single monk to be its leader. However, he said, there were monks in the Order who were regarded with special reverence and esteem, and to whom other monks looked for guidance and support. What qualified a monk to give guidance to others was endowment with ten qualities: moral virtue, learning, contentment, mastery over the four *jhānas*, the five mundane *abhiññās*, and attainment of the cankerless liberation of mind, liberation by wisdom.[3] Perhaps it was because he was extolled by the Buddha for his facility in the meditative attainments and the *abhiññās* that the Venerable Mahākassapa assumed the presidency of the first great Buddhist council held in Rājagaha after the Buddha's passing away.

In the Ambaṭṭha Sutta the Buddha recites a verse praising the man endowed with knowledge and conduct (*vijjācaraṇasampanna*): "The nobleman (*khattiya*) is the best among men for those who look to lineage, but one endowed with knowledge and conduct is best among gods and men."[4] Conduct (*caraṇa*), he explains, includes moral discipline, sense restraint, mindfulness and discernment, contentment, solitary living, the abandonment of the five hindrances, and finally, as the outcome of these practices,

1. DN. 2:71.
2. AN. 3:280-81.
3. MN. 3:11-12.
4. DN. 1:99.

the attainment of the four *jhānas* . Knowledge (*vijjā*) consists in insight-knowledge, the knowledge of the mind-made body, the five mundane *abhiññās*, and the knowledge of the destruction of the cankers. The Buddha concludes his exposition by saying of a bhikkhu who has fulfilled this training:

> This bhikkhu is called 'endowed with knowledge', 'endowed with conduct', 'endowed with knowledge and conduct'. There is no other endowment with knowledge and conduct higher or more excellent than this endowment with knowledge and conduct.[1]

1. *Ibid.* 100.

CONCLUSION

The *jhānas* are an important aspect of training in the contemplative system of Theravāda Buddhism, representing the most eminent form of concentration (*samādhi*). They enter into the discipline as the training in the higher consciousness, into the Noble Eightfold Path as right concentration, and directly or indirectly relate to all the thirty-seven training principles leading to enlightenment. Of the two principal types of Buddhist meditation, serenity meditation (*samathabhāvanā*) and insight meditation (*vipassanābhāvanā*), they fall on the side of serenity, though the mental unification they induce makes them also a helpful instrument for developing insight. The *jhānas* we found can occur at two levels, one mundane (*lokiya*) and the other supramundane (*lokuttara*). As mundane they pertain to the preliminary stages of the path leading up to insight where they can be developed to any of eight degrees, the four fine material *jhānas* and the four immaterial *jhānas* (*āruppas*). As supramundane they pertain to the four paths and fruits, the stages of enlightenment and liberation culminating in *nibbāna*, the end of suffering. The mundane *jhānas* are not absolutely necessary for all practitioners, but the Buddha frequently commends them as a superior form of concentration helpful for producing the mental purification needed as a base for wisdom.

In order to understand the dynamics by which the *jhānas* work to purify the mind we adopted the Theravāda perspective of consciousness as an ever-changing continuum of evanescent mental events each composed of a multiplicity of factors, some of which cause defilement and distraction, others purification and inner unity. The defiling factors, classed as the five hindrances—sensual desire, ill will, sloth and torpor, restlessness and worry, and doubt—must be overcome by a meditator aspiring to liberation. Various methods are prescribed to achieve this, some designed specifically to counter individual hindrances, others such as general mindfulness applicable to all at once. As he persists in his practice of concentration the meditator strengthens five positive mental factors—applied thought, sustained thought, rapture, happiness, and one-pointedness. These, called the *jhāna*-

factors, counter-act the hindrances and unify the mind on its object. When the hindrances are suppressed, a luminous mental replica of the meditation subject named the counterpart sign appears, marking the attainment of "access concentration" where the mind stands at the threshold of absorption. By strengthening the factors still further the meditator can enter full absorption, the initial level of which is the first *jhāna* endowed with the five *jhāna* factors as its principal components.

The meditator must first master and perfect the first *jhāna*, then he can go further in the direction of serenity by attaining the second, third, and fourth *jhānas*. The ascent through these states involves the successive elimination of coarser mental factors. In each case the meditator reflects that the state he has mastered is endangered by its proximity to the stage immediately below and by its own inherent grossness; then he aspires to the higher stage as more serene, peaceful, and sublime. Thus he eliminates applied and sustained thought to reach the second *jhāna*, rapture to reach the third, and happiness to reach the fourth. The factors that remain are the constituting factors of the *jhāna*—rapture, happiness, and one-pointedness for the second, happiness and one-pointedness for the third, and neutral feeling and one-pointedness for the fourth. If the meditator's faculties are not sharp, he may have to overcome applied and sustained thought separately. To account for this possibility the Abhidhamma, with its penchant for precise analysis, includes a scheme of five *jhānas* covering the same range of meditative experience.

After achieving mastery over the four fine material *jhānas*, an ardent meditator can continue to refine his concentration by attaining the four immaterial *jhānas*: the base of boundless space, the base of boundless consciousness, the base of nothingness, and the base of neither perception nor non-perception. Whereas the course of progress through the lower *jhānas* takes place by means of the successive elimination of mental factors, progress through the immaterial *jhānas* occurs through a surmounting of objects. All four immaterial states have the same factorial constitution, identical with that of the fourth *jhāna*, i.e. neutral feeling and one-pointedness. They differ essentially with respect to their objective basis, taking in order successively more subtle objects. The first objectifies the infinity of space, the second the consciousness pertaining to the base of boundless space, the third the non-existent aspect of the same consciousness, and the fourth the mental aggregates belonging to the base of nothingness. This last *āruppa*, the base of neither perception nor non-perception, marks the utmost limit in the unification of consciousness and the highest degree to which serenity can be pursued.

If he so desires, a meditator who has thoroughly mastered the eight attainments can develop certain supernormal modes of knowledge. These, known as the *abhiññās*, are five in number: the knowledge of the modes of supernormal power, the knowledge of the divine ear-element, the knowledge of penetrating others' minds, the knowledge of recollecting previous lives, and the knowledge of the passing away and rearising of beings. These *abhiññās* are all mundane, the products of concentration. Though not essential to the path, they are still embellishments of an accomplished meditator, useful if handled with understanding and applied with compassion. Beyond these lies a sixth *abhiññā*, "the knowledge of the destruction of the cankers," the realization of liberation resulting from insight.

The mundane *jhānas* do not destroy the defilements but only suppress them. The type of purification they produce is thus only temporary, suitable as a basis for insight but incapable by itself of bringing liberation. A meditator who has reached the eight attainments without going further will be reborn according to his level of *jhānic* accomplishment. If he reaches the four lower *jhānas* he will be reborn in the fine material world, if he reaches the immaterial *jhānas* he will be reborn in the immaterial world. In any case he remains in bondage to *saṁsāra* and is not yet free from suffering. Therefore *jhāna* by itself is not sufficient for reaching the ultimate goal.

To obtain liberation from the recurring cycle of rebirths what is required is wisdom, culminating in the supramundane wisdom of the noble paths that eradicates defilements. Since the root-cause of bondage and suffering is ignorance about the true nature of phenomena, wisdom, which uncovers the true nature of phenomena, is the means to freedom. Wisdom comes in two stages: first the wisdom of insight (*vipassanāñāṇa*) which is the direct seeing of the three characteristics of impermanence, suffering, and selflessness in material and mental formations, then the wisdom of the noble paths (*maggañāṇa*) which sees *nibbāna* and penetrates the Four Noble Truths.

The complete course of development culminating in deliverance has been divided into seven stages of purification. The first two—purification of morality and purification of mind—coincide with the training in moral discipline and concentration. The remaining five—purification of view, purification by overcoming doubt, purification by knowledge of the right and wrong paths, purification by knowledge and vision of the way, and purification by knowledge and vision—pertain to the development of wisdom. The wisdom of insight develops especially through the purification by knowledge and vision of the way; it culminates in the wisdom of the supramundane paths, which make up purification by knowledge and vision.

The four paths are designated the path of stream-entry, the path of the once-returner, the path of the non-returner, and the path of arahatship. These paths are occasions of enlightenment experience which penetrate by direct knowledge the Four Noble Truths. They exercise the function of eradicating the defilements or "fetters" that cause bondage to *saṁsāra*, reducing thereby the duration of the round of rebirths. Each successive path eliminates (or attenuates) a subtler layer of defilements, until with the fourth path all the defilements are cut off and the production of future rebirths stopped. The paths lead immediately to their fruits, resultant states of consciousness that enjoy the happiness of *nibbāna* made possible by the work of the paths.

The consideration that mundane *jhāna* does not suffice for attaining liberation but has to be supplemented by wisdom led us to investigate the relation of the *jhānas* to the attainment of the paths and the states of deliverance that result from them. Among Buddhist scholars in Theravāda countries the question has been disputed as to whether or not the *jhānas* are needed for reaching the supramundane paths. The key to resolving this controversy we found to be the distinction, implicit in the suttas and made explicit in the Abhidhamma and commentaries, between mundane and supramundane *jhāna*. Mundane *jhāna* is the most eminent type of concentration, but its attainment is not indispensable for all meditators in order to reach the paths and fruits. The Theravāda tradition divides meditators into two types according to the way they arrive at the supramundane path. One is the *samathayānika*, the practitioner who makes serenity his vehicle, the other is the *vipassanāyānika*, the practitioner who makes bare insight his vehicle. The former first develops serenity to the level of one of the eight attainments or their access, then uses that serenity as his base of concentration in order to develop insight. The latter, also known as the dry insight worker (*sukkha-vipassaka*), proceeds directly to insight-contemplation on conditioned phenomena, producing a mobile momentary concentration as a concomitant of his contemplation without initially developing serenity to the level of *jhānic* intensity.

For the dry insight meditator mundane *jhāna* is dispensable, but for the meditator of the serenity vehicle it plays two vitally important roles: first it provides him with a foundation of calm conducive to developing insight, second it serves as a readily available subject to be investigated with insight in order to see the three characteristics of existence. In the first capacity the *jhāna* is called the basic *jhāna* (*pādakajjhāna*), in the second it is called the comprehended *jhāna* (*sammasitajjhāna*).

For meditators of both vehicles, however, *jhāna* is attained when they reach the supramundane paths and fruits. The paths and fruits, according to the Pali texts, always occur at a level of *jhānic* absorption and thus are considered forms of *jhāna*. Since to reach deliverance all practitioners have to pass through the same paths and fruits regardless of their means of approach, *jhāna* of the supramundane kind enters into the experience of every meditator who arrives at the path. It belongs as much to the path of the one following the vehicle of pure insight as it does to the path of the one following the vehicle of serenity. *Jhāna* of this kind occurs as the right concentration (*sammāsamādhi*) of the Noble Eightfold Path, defined by the Buddha with the formula for the four *jhānas*.

Thus the answer to the question whether *jhāna* is needed to reach *nibbāna* is clear, settled by the recognition of two kinds of *jhāna*: mundane *jhāna* is helpful but not absolutely necessary, supramundane *jhāna* is essential but does not necessarily presuppose the mundane. It results from insight either alone or in combination with mundane *jhāna*.

The supramundane *jhānas* occur in the same degrees as the mundane, the four of the suttanta scheme and the five of the Abhidhamma scheme. Each has the *jhāna* factors appropriate to its particular level of absorption. Nevertheless, we find that certain significant differences separate the two. The mundane *jhānas* merely suppress defilements, the supramundane eradicate them. The mundane remain in the orbit of the round of rebirths, the supramundane dismantle the round. The mundane involve a predominance of serenity, the supramundane a balance of serenity with wisdom. The mundane take an idea or image for object, the supramundane the unconditioned reality, *nibbāna*.

One question that has arisen is what determines the *jhānic* level of the paths and fruits, but the Theravāda tradition has not settled this with unanimity. Some elders hold that it is the basic *jhāna*, some that it is the comprehended *jhāna*, still others that it depends on the meditator's choice. The *jhānic* level of the fruit, however, always conforms to that of the path. Each noble person of the four levels retains access to supramundane *jhāna* as the attainment of fruition (*phalasamāpatti*) appropriate to his level. Thus the four persons are always capable of entering supramundane *jhāna* as a way of experiencing bliss and peace here and now. In addition non-returners and arahats who have mastered the eight attainments can enter a special meditative attainment called cessation (*nirodhasamāpatti*), reached by alternating the mundane *jhānas* with insight up the eight degrees to the point where the mental process stops.

One final problem that remained concerned the relation of the noble persons (*ariyapuggala*) to the mundane accomplishment of *jhāna*. This problem we addressed through an ancient classification of the noble persons into seven types on the basis of their dominant faculties. Those on the path of stream-entry divide into two—the faith-devotee (*saddhānusāri*) and the truth-devotee (*dhammānusāri*)—according to whether they give prominence to faith or wisdom. These become, respectively, the one liberated by faith (*saddhāvimutta*) and the one attained to understanding (*diṭṭhippatta*) in the six intermediate stages; one who gains the immaterial *jhānas* is classified separately as a body-witness (*kāyasakkhi*). Arahats, at the last stage, again divide into two: those who obtain the immaterial attainments are called liberated in both ways (*ubhatobhāgavimutta*), those who do not obtain them are called those liberated by wisdom (*paññāvimutta*). For these latter any of the three faculties—faith, concentration or wisdom—can be dominant. All that keeps them in this class is lack of the immaterial *jhānas*. They may have any of the four *jhānas* or none at all.

Doubt has sometimes been cast on the possibility of arahatship without *jhāna*. But we find that although all arahats possess the *jhāna* of their supramundane fruition, they are not all regarded as having mundane *jhāna*. Theravāda tradition recognizes a class of dry-visioned arahats who reach their goal by pure insight, remaining devoid of mundane *jhāna* even afterwards. Nevertheless, though such a kind of arahatship is possible, the Pali tradition, beginning even with the Buddha himself, regards the ability to gain the four *jhānas* without strain or difficulty as a valuable asset of an arahat, desirable both as a personal accomplishment and as a testimony to the spiritual efficacy of the Buddha's dispensation. A similar high regard extends to the achievement of the five mundane *abhiññās*, while the highest praise goes to *ubhatobhāgavimutta* arahats who have mastered both the eight deliverances and the five *abhiññās*.

The gradations in the veneration given to arahats on the basis of their mundane spiritual achievements implies something about the value-system of Theravāda Buddhism. It suggests that while final liberation may be the ultimate and most important value, it is not the sole value even in the spiritual domain. Alongside it, as embellishments rather than alternatives, stand mastery over the range of the mind and mastery over the sphere of the knowable. The first is accomplished by the attainment of the eight mundane *jhānas*, the second by the attainment of the *abhiññās*. Together, final liberation adorned with this twofold mastery is esteemed as the highest and most desirable way of actualizing the ultimate goal.

APPENDIX 1

The Thirty-seven Constituents of Enlightenment (*sattatiṁsa bodhi-pakkhiyadhammā*)

I. The Four Foundations of Mindfulness (*cattaro satipaṭṭhānā*)

1. Contemplation of the body as a foundation of mindfulness (*kāyānupassanā satipaṭṭhāna*)
2. Contemplation of feelings as a foundation of mindfulness (*vedanānupassanā satipaṭṭhāna*)
3. Contemplation of states of mind as a foundation of mindfulness (*cittānupassanā satipaṭṭhāna*)
4. Contemplation of mental objects as a foundation of mindfulness (*dhammānupassanā satipaṭṭhāna*)

II. The Four Right Endeavors (*cattāro sammappadhāna*)

1. The effort to prevent unarisen evil states (*anuppannānaṁ pāpakānaṁ akusalānaṁ dhammānaṁ anuppādāya vāyāma*)
2. The effort to abandon arisen evil states (*uppannānaṁ pāpakānaṁ akusalānaṁ dhammānaṁ pahānāya vāyāma*)
3. The effort to arouse unarisen wholesome states (*anuppannānaṁ kusalānaṁ dhammānaṁ uppādāya vāyāma*)
4. The effort to increase arisen wholesome states (*uppannānaṁ kusalānaṁ dhammānaṁ bhiyyobhāvāya vāyāmati*)

III. The Four Bases of Success (*cattāro iddhipādā*)

1. The base of success consisting in zeal (*chandiddhipāda*)
2. The base of success consisting in energy (*viriyiddhipāda*)
3. The base of success consisting in consciousness (*cittiddhipāda*)
4. The base of success consisting in inquiry (*vīmaṁsiddhipāda*)

IV. The Five Spiritual Faculties (*pañcindriyāni*)

1. The faculty of faith (*saddhindriya*)
2. The faculty of energy (*viriyindriya*)
3. The faculty of mindfulness (*satindriya*)

4. The faculty of concentration (*samādhindriya*)
5. The faculty of wisdom (*paññindriya*)

V. The Five Spiritual Powers (*pañca balāni*)

1. The power of faith (*saddhābala*)
2. The power of energy (*viriyabala*)
3. The power of mindfulness (*satibala*)
4. The power of concentration (*samādhibala*)
5. The power of wisdom (*paññābala*)

VI. The Seven Factors of Enlightenment (*satta bojjhaṅgā*)

1. The mindfulness factor of enlightenment (*satisambojjhaṅga*)
2. The investigation of phenomena factor of enlightenment (*dhammavicaya sambojjhaṅga*)
3. The energy factor of enlightenment (*viriyasambojjhaṅga*)
4. The rapture factor of enlightenment (*pītisambojjhaṅga*)
5. The tranquility factor of enlightenment (*passaddhisambojjhaṅga*)
6. The concentration factor of enlightenment (*samādhisambojjhaṅga*)
7. The equanimity factor of enlightenment (*upekkhāsambojjhaṅga*)

VII. The Noble Eightfold Path (*ariya aṭṭhaṅgikamagga*)

1. Right view (*sammādiṭṭhi*)
2. Right intention (*sammāsaṁkappa*)
3. Right speech (*sammāvācā*)
4. Right action (*sammākammanta*)
5. Right livelihood (*sammā ājīva*)
6. Right effort (*sammāvāyāma*)
7. Right mindfulness (*sammāsati*)
8. Right concentration (*sammāsamādhi*)[1]

1. DN. 2:120. MN. 2:11-12.

APPENDIX 2

FORTY SUBJECTS OF MEDITATION[1]

Subjects (*kammaṭṭhāna*)	6 Temperaments (*chacaritāni*)	3 Concentrations (*tayo bhāvanāyo*)			3 Signs (*tīni nimittāni*)			4 *Jhānas*		
The Totalities (*kasiṇa*):										
Earth kasina (*paṭhavi kasiṇa*)	All	P.	Ac.	Ab.	P.	Le.	Cp.	1st	to	4th[2]
Water kasina (*āpo-kasiṇa*)	,,	,,	,,	,,	,,	,,	,,	,,	,,	,,
Fire kasina (*tejo-kasiṇa*)	,,	,,	,,	,,	,,	,,	,,	,,	,,	,,
Air kasina (*vāyo-kasiṇa*)	,,	,,	,,	,,	,,	,,	,,	,,	,,	,,
Blue kasina (*nīla-kasiṇa*)	Hating	,,	,,	,,	,,	,,	,,	,,	,,	,,
Yellow kasina (*pīta-kasiṇa*)	,,	,,	,,	,,	,,	,,	,,	,,	,,	,,
Red kasina (*lohita-kasiṇa*)	,,	,,	,,	,,	,,	,,	,,	,,	,,	,,
White kasina (*odāta-kasiṇa*)	,,	,,	,,	,,	,,	,,	,,	,,	,,	,,
Light kasina (*āloka-kasiṇa*)	All	,,	,,	,,	,,	,,	,,	,,	,,	,,
Limited space kasina (*ākāsa-kasiṇa*)	,,	,,	,,	,,	,,	,,	,,	,,	,,	,,
Ten Kinds of Foulness (*dasa asubha*):										
The bloated (*uddhumātaka*)	Lustful	,,	,,	,,	,,	,,	,,	,,		
The livid (*vinīlaka*)	,,	,,	,,	,,	,,	,,	,,	,,		
Festering (*vipubbaka*)	,,	,,	,,	,,	,,	,,	,,	,,		
Cut-up (*vicchiddaka*)	,,	,,	,,	u,,	,,	,,	,,	,,		

1. Vism., pp. 89-90.

2. Note: Key to abbreviations at end of this appendix.

ubjects (*kammaṭṭhāna*)	6 Temperaments (*chacaritāni*)	3 Concentrations (*tayo bhāvanāyo*)			3 Signs (*tīni nimittāni*)			4 *Jhānas*
		P.	Ac.	Ab.	P.	Le.	Cp.	
The gnawed (*vikkhāyitaka*)	Lustful	P.	Ac.	Ab.	P.	Le.	Cp.	1st
The scattered (*vikkhittaka*)	,,	,,	,,	,,	,,	,,	,,	,,
The hacked and scattered (*hata-vikkhittaka*)								
The bleeding (*lohitaka*)	,,	,,	,,	,,	,,	,,	,,	,,
The worm-infested (*pulavaka*)	,,	,,	,,	,,	,,	,,	,,	,,
A skeleton (*aṭṭhika*)	,,	,,	,,	,,	,,	,,	,,	,,
Ten Kinds of Recollections (*dasa anussatiyo*):								
Recol. of Buddha (*buddhānussati*)	Faithful	,,	,,	,,	,,	,,	,,	No jhāna
Recol. of Dhamma (*dhammānussati*)	,,	,,	,,	,,	,,	,,	,,	,, ,,
Recol. of Sangha (*saṅghānussati*)	,,	,,	,,	,,	,,	,,	,,	,, ,,
Recol. of virtue (*silānussati*)	,,	,,	,,	,,	,,	,,	,,	,, ,,
Recol. of generosity (*cāgānussati*)	,,	,,	,,	,,	,,	,,	,,	,, ,,
Recol. of deities (*devatānussati*)	,,	,,	,,	,,	,,	,,	,,	,, ,,
Recol. of peace (*upasamānussati*)	Intelligent	,,	,,	,,	,,	,,	,,	,, ,,
Recol. of death (*maraṇānussati*)	,,	,,		,,	,,	,,	,,	,, ,,
Mindfulness of body (*kāyagatāsati*)	Lustful	,,	,,	,,	,,	,,		1st ,,
Mindfulness of breathing (*ānāpānasati*)	Deluded & Speculative	,,	,,	,,	,,	,,		1st to 4th
Four Divine Abidings (*cattāro brahmavihārā*):								
Loving kindness (*mettā*)	Hating	,,	,,	,,	,,	,,		,, ,, 3rd
Compassion (*karuṇā*)	,,	,,	,,	,,	,,	,,		,, ,, ,,

Subjects (*kammaṭṭhāna*)	6 Temperaments (*chacaritāni*)	3 Concentrations (*tayo bhāvanāyo*)	3 Signs (*tīni nimittāni*)	4 *Jhānas*
Gladness (*muditā*)	,,	,, ,, ,,	,, ,,	,, ,, ,,
Equanimity (*upekkhā*)	,,	,, ,, ,,	,, ,,	4th
One Perception (*ekā saññā*) :		P. Ac.		
Perception of repulsiveness in nutriment (*āhāre paṭikkūla-saññā*)	Intelligent	,, ,,	P. Le.	No jhāna
One Definition (*ekavavatthāna*)				
Defining of the four elements (*catudhātuvavaṭṭhāna*)	,,	,, ,,	,, ,,	,, ,,
Four Immaterial States (*cattāro āruppā*):				
The base consisting of boundless space (*ākāsānañcāyatana*)	All	,, ,, ,,	,, ,,	Arūpajjhān
The base consisting of boundless consciousness (*viññāṇancāyatana*)	,,	,, ,, ,,	,, ,,	,,
The base consisting of nothingness (*ākincaññāyatana*)	,,	,, ,, ,,	,, ,,	,,
The base consisting of neither perception nor non-perception (*nevasaññānāsaññāyatana*)	,,	,, ,, ,,	,, ,,	,, [1]

1. Six temperaments: [1] lustful (*rāgacarita*), [2] hating (*dosacarita*),, [3] deluded (*mohacarita*), [4] faithful (*saddhācarita*, [5] intelligent (*buddhicarita*), and [6] speculative (*vitakka-carita*). Three concentrations: [1] preliminary (*parikamma*), [2] access (*upacāra*), and [3] absorption (*appanā*). Three signs: [1] preliminary (*parikamma*), [2] learning (*uggaha*), and [3] counterpart (*paṭibhāga*). P *P*=preliminary; *Ac*=access; *Ab*=absorption, *Le*=learning; *Cp*=counterpart sign.

APPENDIX 3

	The Eight Attainments:[1]	Jhāna Factors:
4 āruppas:	4th āruppa	Neutral feeling and one-pointedness
	3rd āruppa	" " " " "
	2nd āruppa	" " " " "
	1st āruppa	" " " " "
4 fine material jhānas	4th jhāna	neutral feeling and one-pointedness
	3rd jhāna	happiness and one-pointedness
	2nd jhāna	happiness, and one-pointedness
	1st jhāna	rapture,

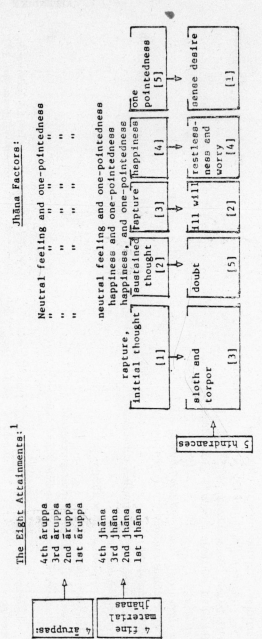

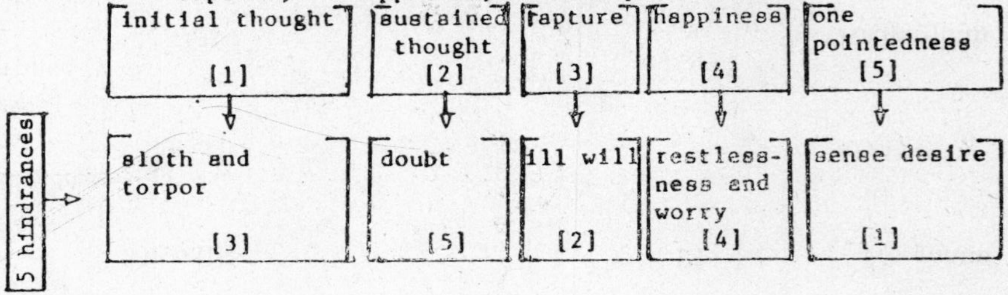

1. Read from the bottom. *Jhāna* factors in Pali: *vitakka, vicāra, pīti, sukha, ekaggatā* and *adukkhamasukhā vedanā*. Five hindrances: *kāmacchanda, byāpada, thīna-middha, uddhacca-kukkucca* and *vicikicchā*. Arrows indicate the hindrances suppressed by each factor of the first *jhāna*. Note that as the meditator reaches higher *jhānas* he eliminates lower *jhāna* factors. The factors of the fourth fine material *jhāna* are same as those of the immaterial *jhānas*.

APPENDIX 4

Kamma and Rebirth[1]

Kinds of kamma			Places of rebirth (bhūmi)	
Immaterial kammas (arūpāvacarajjhāna)	Base of neither perception nor non-perception (nevasaññānāsaññāyatana)	Immaterial spheres (arūpāvacara bhūmi)	31. Plane of neither perception nor non-perception (nevasaññānāsaññā yatana bhūmi)	Immaterial spheres (arūpāvacarabhūmi)
	Base of nothingness (ākiñcaññāyatana)		30. Plane of nothingness (ākiñcaññāyatana bhūmi)	
	Base of infinite consciousness (viññāṇañcāyatana)		29. Plane of infinite consciousness (viññāṇañcāyatana bhūmi)	
	Base of infinite space (ākāsānañcāyatana)		28. Plane of infinite space (ākāsānañcāyatana bhūmi)	
Fine material kammas (rūpāvacarajjhāna)	Fourth jhāna (catutthajjhāna)	Fine material spheres (rūpāvacara bhūmi)	27. The highest realm (akaniṭṭha bhūmi)	4th jh. spheres (C. J. bhūmi); 5 pure abodes (pañca suddhāvāsa)
			26. The clear sighted realm (sudassa bhūmi)	
			25. The beautiful realm (sudassi bhūmi)	
			24. The serene realm (atappa bhūmi)	
			23. The durable realm (aviha bhūmi)	
			22. The realm of non-percipient beings (asaññasatta bhūmi)	
			21. The realm of great reward (vehapphala-bhūmi)	
	Third jhāna (tatiyajjhāna)		20. The realm of steady aura (subhakiṇha-bhūmi)	3rd jh. sphere (t. jh. bhūmi)
			19. The realm of infinite aura (appamāṇa-subha bhūmi)	
			18. The realm of minor aura (parittasubha-bhūmi)	

1. Read from the bottom.

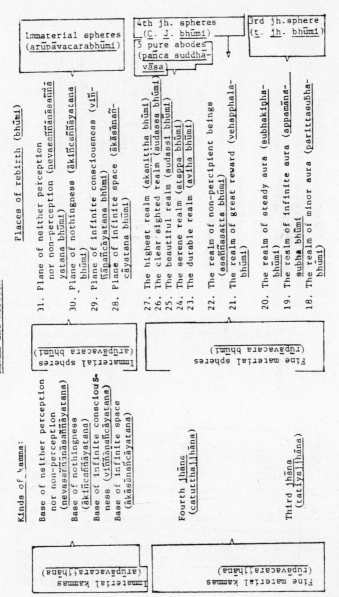

Kinds of kamma:[1]

- Fine material kammas (rūpāvacarajjhāna)
  - Second jhāna (dutiyajjhāna)
  - First jhana (paṭhamajjhāna)
- Sense sphere wholesome kamma (kāmāvacara kusala kamma)
  - Sense sphere wholesome kamma (kāmāvacara kusala kamma)
- Unwholesome kamma (akusalakamma)

Places of rebirth (bhūmi)

Fine material spheres (rūpāvacara bhūmi)

17. The realm of radiant luster (ābhassara bhūmi)
16. The realm of infinite luster (appamānābha bhūmi)
15. The realm of minor luster (parittābha bhūmi)
14. The realm of the great Brahmā (Mahābrahma bhūmi)
13. The realm of the ministers of Brahmā (Brahmapurohita bhūmi)
12. The realm of the retinue of Brahmā (Brahmapārisajja bhūmi)

Seven fortunate sense spheres (sattakāma sugati)

11. The realm of gods who lord over the creation of others (paranimmitavasavatti bhūmi)
10. The realm of gods who rejoice in their own creation (nimmānarati bhūmi)
9. The realm of delight (tusita bhūmi)
8. The realm of Yama gods (Yāma bhūmi)
7. The realm of thirty-three gods (tāvatiṃsa bhūmi)
6. The realm of the four great kings (cātummahārājika bhūmi)
5. Human realm (manussaloka)

4 unfortunate planes (4 apāya bhūmi)

4. The host of titans (asuranikāya)
3. The hungry ghosts (petaloka)
2. The animal kingdom (tiracchānayoni)
1. Woeful states of existence (nirayabhūmi)[2]

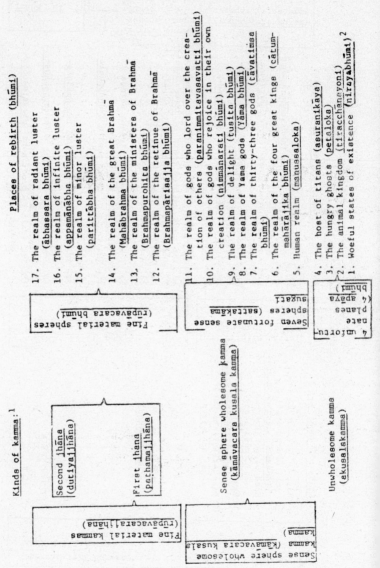

GLOSSARY

Abhijjamāna	unbroken
Abhiññā	direct knowledge
Abyāpajja	free from trouble
Ādesanā	manifestation
Adhicitta	higher consciousness
Adhipaññā	higher wisdom
Adhisīla	higher morality
Ādīnava	danger, unsatisfactoriness
Adukkhamasukha	neither-pain-nor-pleasure
Āhāra	nutriment
Ajjhupekkhana	equanimity
Akallatā	indisposition
Akammaññatā	unwieldiness
Akaniṭṭha	the highest realm
Ākāraparivitakka	reflection on reason
Ākāravatī	rational
Ākāsānañcāyatana	the base of boundless space
Ākiñcaññāyatana	the base of nothingness
Akusala	unwholesome
Amanasikāra	non-attention
Anāgāmi	non-returner
Anāgataṁsañāṇa	knowledge of the future
Anaññātaññassāmitindriya	the faculty of 'I shall know the unknown'
Ananta	unbounded
Ānāpānasati	mindfulness of breathing
Anattā	selfless, non-self
Aṅga	factor
Anicca	impermanent
Animitta	signless
Aññātavindriya	the faculty of the completion of final knowledge
Aññindriya	the faculty of final knowledge
Anubhavana	experiencing
Anuloma	conformity

Anupādisesanibbānadhātu	the nibbāna element without residue
Anupassanā	contemplation
Anupāyamanasikāra	inexpedient reflection, reflection on wrong track
Anupubbasaṅkhāranirodha	the gradual cessation of formation
Anusāsana	education or instruction
Anussati	recollection
Apacayagāmi	leading to demolition
Aparihāniya	invincible
Aparisesa	without remainder
Apāyabhūmi	the plane of misery
Apilāpanatā	not floating away
Appamānābha	the realm of infinite lustre
Appamānasubha	the realm of infinite aura
Appanā	absorption
Appanihita	desireless
Arahat	a perfectly enlightened individual (untranslated)
Ārambhadhātu	element of effort
Ārammaṇa	object
Ariya	noble; a noble one
Āruppa	immaterial state
Arūpāvacarabhūmi	immaterial sphere
Asaṅkhata	unconditioned
Asaṅkheyya	incalculable
Asaññasatta	the realm of non-percipient beings
Asāraka	coreless
Āsava	canker
Āsavakkhayañāṇa	knowledge of the destruction of the cankers
Assāda	gratification
Asubha	foulness
Asurakāya	the host of titans
Atappa	the serene realm
Atītabhavaṅga	past moment of life continuum
Attanodhammatāya	by one's own nature
Aṭṭhakathā	commentaries

Āvajjana	adverting
Aveccappasāda	confidence born of understanding
Āvībhāva	appearance
Aviha	the durable realm
Avijjā	ignorance
Bala	power
Bhaṅga	dissolution
Bhava	existence, becoming
Bhāvanā	development
Bhavaṅga	life continuum
Bhavaṅgupaccheda	cutting off or arrest of the passive consciousness
Bhaya	fear, fearful, terror
Bhūmi	plane, realm
Bojjhaṅga	enlightenment factor
Brahmapārisajja	retinue of Brahmā
Brahmapurohita	ministers of Brahmā
Brahmavihāra	divine abiding
Byāpāda	ill will
Candimā	moon
Caraṇa	conduct
Carita	temperament
Cātummahārājika	the realm of the four great kings
Cetasika	mental factor
Cetopariyañāṇa	the knowledge of others' mind
Cetovimutti	liberation of mind
Chanda	zeal
Citta	mind, consciousness
Cittavīthi	active process of consciousness
Cutūpapātañāṇa	the knowledge of passing away and rebirth of beings
Dassana	vision
Dhamma	[1] doctrine, truth; [2] mental object, phenomena
Dhammacchando	desire for dhamma
Dhammānusāri	truth-devotee
Dhātumanasikāra	reflection on the modes of materiality
Dibbacakkhu	the divine eye

Dibbasotadhātu	the divine ear-element
Dibbavihāra	heavenly dwelling
Diṭṭhadhammanibbāna	nibbana here and now
Diṭṭhi	views, wrong views
Diṭṭhippatta	attained to understanding
Domanassa	grief
Dosa	hatred
Ekaggatā	one-pointedness (of mind)
Ekodibhāva	unification (of mind)
Gantha	bodily ties
Garuka	weighty
Gotrabhū	change-of-lineage
Hadayarūpa	the matter of the heart
Iddhi	wonder or marvel
Iddhividhañāṇa	knowledge of the modes of supernormal powers
Indriya	faculty
Indriyasamattapaṭipādana	balancing the spiritual faculties
Indriyasaṁvara	the restraint of the senses
Jhāna	states of absorption in meditation [untranslated]
Jhānaṅga	jhāna factor
Jhānakkantika	skipping alternate jhānas
Jhāyati	thinks
Kalāpasammasana	comprehension by groups
Kalyāṇamitta	good friend
Kāma	sense pleasure; sensual desire
Kāmacchanda	sensual desire
Kāmapariḷāha	the fever of sensuality
Kāmapariyesanā	the search for sensual gratification
Kamati	travels
Kāmāvacara	sense sphere
Kamma	volitional action [untranslated]
Kāmūpādāna	clinging to sense pleasure
Kasiṇa	a device used as an object of concentration [untranslated]
Kasiṇukkantika	skipping alternate kasina
Kattukamyatā	desire to accomplish some aim
Kāya	body

Kāyasakkhi	body-witness
Kāyaviveka	bodily seclusion
Khandha	aggregates
Khaṇika	momentary
Khaya	destruction
Khuddika	minor
Kilesa	defilement
Kukkucca	worry
Kusala	wholesome
Kusalacittassekaggatā	wholesome one-pointedness of mind
Lakkhaṇa	characteristics
Lakkhaṇūpanijjhāna	the contemplation of the characteristics of phenomena
Lobha	greed
Lokiya	mundane
Lokuttara	supramundane
Magga	path
Mahāpurisavitakka	thoughts of a great man
Māna	conceit
Manodvāra	mind door
Manomayiddhiñāṇa	knowledge of the mind-created body
Manussaloka	the human world
Micchāsamādhi	wrong concentration
Middha	torpor
Moha	delusion
Nāma	mentality
Nāmarūpa	mentality-materiality
Ñāṇa	knowledge
Nevasaññānāsaññāyatana	the base of neither perception nor-non-perception
Nibbāna	[untranslated]
Nibbidā	dispassion
Niggaha	restraining
Nikkamadhātu	element of exertion
Nimittavaḍḍhana	extension of sign
Nimmānarati	rejoicing in one's own creation
Nirāmisasukha	spiritual happiness
Niraya	woeful state

Nirodha	cessation
Nirujjhati	ceases
Nīvaraṇa	hindrance
Niyyānika	emancipating
Ogha	floods
Okkantika	showering
Orambhāgiya	pertaining to the lower worlds
Paccattaṁ	within oneself (within themselves)
Paccavekkhaṇa	reviewing
Paccayaṭṭhāna	objective station
Paccekabuddha	individual or silent Buddha [untranslated]
Paccupaṭṭhāna	manifestation
Pāda	basis
Pādakajjhāna	basic jhāna
Paggaha	exerting the mind
Pahāna	abandonment
Pahānaṅga	factors of abandonment
Pajānana	the act of understanding
Pakkhapātita	partiality
Pakkhī	bird
Palibodha	impediment
Pallaṅka	sitting cross-legged
Pāmojja	gladness
Pañca	five
Pāṇi	hand
Paññā	wisdom
Paññatti	a conceptual entity
Paññāvimutta	liberated by wisdom
Paññāvimutti	liberation by wisdom
Papañca	impediments
Parakkamadhātu	element of striving
Paranimmitavasavatti	the realm of gods who lord over the creations of others
Pariggaha	discerning
Parikammanimitta	preliminary sign
Parikammasamādhi	preliminary concentration
Parikkhāra	requisites
Parimajjati	strokes

Parimasati	touches
Parinibbāna	final nibbāna
Pariññā	full understanding
Parittābha	the realm of minor lustre
Parittasubha	the realm of minor aura
Parivitakka	reflection
Pariyāyena	figuratively
Passaddhi	tranquility
Paṭibhāganimitta	counterpart sign
Paṭigha	aversion
Pāṭihāriya	wonder
Paṭiloma	reverse order
Paṭisaṁvedeti	experiences
Pavivekasukha	happiness born of seclusion from sense pleasures and the hindrances
Pettivisaya	the sphere of tormented spirits or "hungry ghosts"
Phala	fruit, fruition
Pharaṇa	pervading
Phassa	contact
Pīti	rapture
Pubbaṅgama	forerunner
Pubbenivāsānussatiñāṇa	the knowledge of recollecting previous lives
Puggala	individual
Puggalajjhāsaya	inclination of individuals
Purecārika	precursor
Puthujjana	the ordinary man
Rāga	lust
Rasa	function
Rūpa	material form
Rūpāvacara	fine material sphere
Sabbacittasādhāraṇa	universal concomitant of consciousness
Sabhāva	the true nature
Sacchikiriya	realization
Saddhā	faith
Saddhānusārī	faith-devotee
Saddhāpadānāni	foundations of faith

Saddhāvimutta	liberated by faith
Sakadāgāmi	Once-returner
Sakkāyadiṭṭhi	personality-view
Sakuṇa	bird
Samādhi	concentration
Samādhikkhandha	group of concentration
Samannāgataṅgāni	factors of possession
Samantapāsādikā	completely inspiring
Samāpatti	attainment
Samatha	serenity
Samathayānika	one who makes serenity his vehicle
Samatikkama	having surmounted
Saṁkappa	intention
Sammā	right
Sammasana	comprehension
Sammasitajjhāna	comprehended jhāna
Sampahaṅsana	encouraging
Sampajañña	discernment
Sampasādana	confidence
Saṁsāra	the round of repeated becoming
Samucchedappahāna	abandonment by eradication
Saṁvara	restraint
Saṁvatteti	exercises
Saṁyojana	fetter
Sandiṭṭhikanibbāna	immediately visible nibbāna
Sañjānana	the mode of perceiving
Saṅkantika	transposition
Saṅkappa	intention
Saṁkhāra	[1] formation, [2] mental formation, [3] volitional formation
Saññā	perception
Santuṭṭhi	contentment
Sati	mindfulness
Satipaṭṭhāna	foundation of mindfulness
Sayambhūñāṇa	self-evolved wisdom
Setughāta	breaking the bridge
Sikkhā	training
Sīla	morality

Sīlabbataparāmāsa	clinging to rites and rituals
Sobhana	beautiful
Somanassa	joy
Sotāpanna	stream-enterer
Sotāpatti	stream-entry
Subhakiṇha	the realm of steady aura
Suddhāvāsa	the pure abode
Sugatibhūmi	plane of happiness
Sukha	happiness, pleasure, pleasant
Sukkhavipassaka	dry insight worker
Suññatā	voidness
Suriya	sun
Tadaṅganibbāna	a factor of nibbāna
Takkavīthi	reasoning
Tatramajjhattatā	specific neutrality
Tāvatiṁsa	the realm of the thirty-three gods
Tevijja	triple knowledge
Thīna	sloth
Ṭhīti	presence
Ṭīkā	subcommentary
Tiracchānayoni	animal kingdom
Tirobhāva	disappearance
Tirokuḍḍaṁ	through walls
Tiro-pabbataṁ	through mountains
Tiro-pākāraṁ	through enclosures
Tisso sikkhā	three trainings
Tuṇhībhāva	silence
Ubbega	uplifting
Ubhatobhāgavimutta	liberated in both ways
Udaka	water
Udayabbaya	rise and fall
Uddhacca	restlessness
Uddhambhāgiya	pertaining to the higher worlds
Uggahanimitta	learning sign
Ummujja-nimujjaṁ	dive in and out
Upacāra	access
Upacārasamādhi	access concentration
Upādāna	clinging
Upadhiviveka	seclusion from the substance

Upakkilesa	impediment, corruption
Upanijjhāna	contemplation
Upekkhā	equanimity
Uppāda	arising
Uttarati	rises up
Vacisaṅkhāra	activity of speech
Vasitā	mastery
Vatthukāma	objective sense pleasure
Vavassagga	renunciation
Vavatthāpana	definition
Vedanā	feeling
Vedayita	being felt
Veditabba	to be realized
Vicāra	sustained thought
Vicaya	investigation
Vicikicchā	doubt
Vihiṁsā vitakka	thought of harming
Vijānana	mode of cognizing
Vijjā	knowledge
Vijjācaraṇasampanna	endowed with knowledge and conduct
Vikkhambhanaviveka	seclusion by suppression
Vikkhambanappahāna	abandoning by way of suppression
Vikubbana	transformation
Vīmaṁsa	inquiry
Vimokkha (Vimokha)	liberation
Vimokkhamukha	gateway to liberation
Vimutti	emancipation
Vimuttirasa	taste of freedom
Vinipāta	the downfall
Vinīvaraṇacitta	the mind devoid of the hindrances
Viññāṇa	consciousness
Viññāṇañcāyatana	base of boundless consciousness
Viññu	the wise
Vipāka	result
Vipassanā	insight
Vipassanāyānika	one who makes (bare) insight his vehicle

Viriya	energy
Visuddhi	purification
Vitakka	applied thought
Viveka	seclusion
Vuṭṭhāna	emergence
Yāna	vehicle
Yathākammūpagañāṇa	knowledge of faring according to kamma
Yoga	bonds
Yogin	meditator
Yonisomanasikāra	wise consideration

LIST OF ABBREVIATIONS USED

AN.	The Aṅguttara Nikāya
AN.A.	The Aṅguttara Nikāya Aṭṭhakathā (manorathapūraṇi)
AN. T.	The Aṅguttara Nikāya Ṭīkā (Sāratthamañjūsā)
BD.	The Book of the Discipline
BMTP.	Buddhist Meditation in Theory and Practice
Dhp.	The Dhammapada
Dhs.	The Dhammasaṅgani
Dhs.A.	The Dhammasaṅgani Aṭṭhakathā (Aṭṭhasālinī)
DN.	The Dīgha Nikāya
DN.A.	The Dīgha Nikāya Aṭṭhakathā (Sumaṅgala Vilāsini)
DN.T.	The Dīgha Nikāya Ṭīkā
Dial.	Dialogues of the Buddha
GS.	The Book of the Gradual Saying
KS.	The Book of the Kindred Sayings
Milp.	The Milindapañha
MLS.	The Middle Length Sayings
MN.	The Majjhima Nikāya
MN.A.	The Majjhima Nikāya Aṭṭhakathā (Papañcasūdani)
MN.T.	The Majjhima Nikāya Ṭīkā
PI.	Progress of Insight
PP.	Path of Purification
Psy. Ethics.	Buddhist Psychological Ethics
Pts.	The Paṭisambhidāmagga
Pts.A.	The Paṭisambhidāmagga Aṭṭhakathā (Saddhammappakāsinī)
Pug. P.	The Dhātukathā Puggalapaññattipāli
QKM.	The Questions of King Milinda
SN.	The Saṁyutta Nikāya
SN.A.	The Saṁyutta Nikāya Aṭṭhakathā (Sāratthapakāsanī)
SN.T.	The Saṁyutta Nikāya Ṭīkā
Vibh.	The Vibhaṅga

Vimv.T.	The Vimativinodani Ṭīkā (Samantapāsādikā-ṭīkā)
Vinp.	The Vinaya Piṭakaṁ
Vin.A.	The Vinayaṭṭhakathā (Samantapāsādikā)
Vism.	The Visuddhimagga
Vism. T.	The Visuddhimagga Mahā Ṭīkā (Paramattha-mañjūsā)

SELECTED BIBLIOGRAPHY

PRIMARY SOURCES

Because the Burmese Buddhasāsana Samiti editions of the commentaries and subcommentaries sometimes use titles different from those by which the works are generally known, we enclose the standard titles in brackets before giving the titles of the commentaries and subcommentaries used by the Buddhasāsana Samiti.

1. *Pali Texts of the Tipiṭaka*

Vinaya Piṭaka

Oldenberg, Hermann, ed. *The Vinaya Piṭakam : One of the Principal Buddhist Holy Scriptures in the Pali Language.* Pali Text Society [Publication Series], vols. 147-48, 160-62. 5 vols., London: Luzac & Co., 1879-1964.

Sutta Piṭaka

Anderson, Dines and Smith, Helmer, eds., *Sutta-Nipāta,* New ed., Pali Text Society [Publication Series] Vol. 72. 1913; reprint. London: Luzac & Co., 1965.

Feer, M. Léon, ed., *The Saṁyutta-Nikāya of the Sutta-Piṭaka.* [Pts. 1-5: *Sagātha-Vagga, Nidāna-Vagga, Khandha-Vagga, Salāyatana-Vagga,* and *Mahā-Vagga,* edited by M. Léon Feer; pt. 6: Indexes by Mrs. Rhys Davids]. Pali Text Society [Publications], vols. 8, 19, 25, 31, 42, 56. 6 vols. 1884-1904; reprint. London: Luzac & Co., 1960-70.

Mahā Niddesapāḷi. [Pali Text in Burmese script). Rangoon, Burma: Buddhasāsana Samiti, 1960.

Morris, Richard and Hardy, E. eds., *The Aṅguttara-Nikāya.* [Pt. 1: *Ekanipāta, Dukanipāta,* and *Tikanipāta,* edited by Richard Morris. 2d ed., revised by A. K. Warder; pt. 2: *Catukka-Nipāta,* edited by Richard Morris; pt. 3: *Pañcaka-Nipāta and Chakka-Nipāta,* edited by E. Hardy; pt. 4: *Sattaka-Nipāta, Aṭṭhaka-Nipāta, and Navaka-Nipāta,* edited by E. Hardy; pt. 5: *Dasaka-Nipāta and Ekādasaka-Nipāta,* edited by E. Hardy; pt. 6: Indexes by Mable Hunt;

revised and edited by C. A. F. Rhys Davids]. Pali Text Society [Publications], vols. 10, 20, 35, 44, 46, 66. 6 vols. 1880-1910; reprint, London: Luzac & Co., 1956-67.

Paṭisambhidāmaggapāḷi. [Pali Text in Burmese script]. Rangoon, Burma: Buddhasāsana Samiti, 1962.

Rhys Davids, T. W. and Carpenter, J. Estlin, eds. *The Digha Nikāya.* [Vols. 1-2: edited by T. W. Rhys Davids and J. Estlin Carpenter; vol. 3: edited by J. Estlin Carpenter]. Pali Text Society [Publications], vols. 22, 52, 67. 3 vols. 1880-1910; reprint, London: Luzac & Co., 1960-67.

Trenckner, V. and Chalmer, Robert, eds. *The Majjhima-Nikāya.* [Vol. 1: edited by V. Trenckner; vols. 2-3; edited by Robert Chalmers; vol. 4: Index of Words, edited by Mrs. Rhys Davids]. Pali Text Society [Publication], vols. 17, 39, 45, 47, 51, 99. 6 vols. in 4. (1888-1925); reprint (4 vols.), London: Luzac & Co., 1960-64.

Abhidhamma Piṭaka

Dhammasaṅgaṇipāḷi. [Pali Text in Burmese script]. Rangoon, Burma: Buddhasāsana Samiti, 1961.

Dhātukathā Puggalapaññattipāḷi. [Pali Text in Burmese script]. Rangoon, Burma: Buddhasāsana Samiti, 1961.

Vibhaṅgapāḷi. [Pali Text in Burmese script]. Rangoon, Burma: Buddhasāsana Samiti, 1961.

2. *Commentaries on Pali Texts of the Tipiṭaka*

Vinaya Piṭaka

Buddhaghosa. [*Vinaya Aṭṭhakathā* (*Samanta Pāsādikā*)]. [vols. 1-2:] *Pārājikākaṇḍa Aṭṭhakathā*; [vol. 3:] *Pācityādi Aṭṭhakathā*; [vol. 4:] *Cūḷavaggādi Aṭṭhakathā.* [Pali Text in Burmese script]. 4 vols. Rangoon, Burma: Buddhasāsana Samiti, 1963-67.

Sutta Piṭaka

Buddhaghosa. [*Dīgha Nikāya Aṭṭhakathā* (*Sumangalavilāsinī*)]. [vol. 1:] *Sīlakkhandhavaggaṭṭhakathā*; [vol. 2:] *Mahāvaggaṭṭhakathā*; [vol. 3;] *Pāthikavaggaṭṭhakathā.* [Pali Text in Burmese script]. 3 vols. Rangoon, Burma: Buddhasāsana Samiti, 1961-68.

———. [*Majjhima Nikāya Aṭṭhakathā.* (Papañcasūdanī)]. [Vols. 1-2:] *Mūlapaṇṇāsaṭṭhakathā*; [vol. 3:] *Majjhima-*

paṇṇāsaṭṭhakathā; [vol. 4:] *Uparipaṇṇāsaṭṭhakathā*. [Pali Text in Burmese script]. 4 vols. Rangoon, Burma: Buddhasāsana Samiti, 1957.

———. [*Saṁyutta Nikāya Aṭṭhakathā*] *Sāratthappakāsinī Nāma Saṁyuttaṭṭhakathā*. [Pali Text in Burmese script]. 3 vols. Rangoon, Burma: Buddhasāsana Samiti, 1957.

———. [*Aṅguttara Nikāya Aṭṭhakathā*] *Manorathapūraṇī Nāma Aṅguttaraṭṭhakathā*. [Pali Text in Burmese script]. 3 vols. Rangoon, Burma: Buddhasāsana Samiti, 1958-68.

Mahānāma. [*Paṭisambhidāmagga Aṭṭhakathā*] *Saddhammappakāsinī Nāma Paṭisambhidāmaggaṭṭhakathā*. [Pali Text in Burmese script]. 2 vols. Rangoon, Burma: Buddhasāsana Samiti, 1958.

Abhidhamma Piṭaka

Buddhaghosa. [*Dhammasaṅgaṇi Aṭṭhakathā* (*Aṭṭhasālinī*)]. *Aṭṭhasālinī Aṭṭhakathā*. [Pali Text in Burmese script]. Rangoon, Burma: Buddhasāsana Samiti, 1961.

3. *Subcommentaries on Pali Texts of the Tipiṭaka*

Vinaya Piṭaka

Kassapa Thera, Coliya. [*Samantapāsādikā Vinayaṭṭhakathā Ṭīkā*] *Vimativinodanīṭikā*. [Pali Text in Burmese script]. 2 vols. Rangoon, Burma: Buddhasāsana Samiti, 1960.

Sariputta Thera. [*Samantapāsādikā Vinayaṭṭhakathā Ṭīkā*] *Sāratthadīpanīṭikā*, [Pali Text in Burmese script]. 3 vols. Rangoon, Burma: Buddhasāsana Samiti, 1960.

Sutta Piṭaka

Dhammapāla. [*Dīgha Nikāya Ṭīkā*]. [vol. 1:] *Sīlakkhandhavaggaṭikā*; [vol. 2:] *Mahāvaggaṭikā*; [vol. 3:] *Pāthikavaggaṭikā*. [Pali Text in Burmese script]. 3 vols. Rangoon, Burma; Buddhasāsana Samiti, 1960-61.

———. [*Majjhima Nikāya Ṭīkā*] [vols. 1-2:] *Mūlapaṇṇāsaṭikā*; [vol. 3:] *Majjhimapaṇṇāsaṭikā Uparipaṇṇāsaṭikā*. [Pali Text in Burmese script]. 3 vols. Rangoon, Burma: Buddhasāsana Samiti, 1960-61.

———. [*Saṁyutta Nikāya Ṭīkā*] *Saṁyuttaṭikā*. [Pali Text in Burmese script] 2 vols. Rangoon, Burma: Buddhasāsana Samiti, 1961.

Sāriputta. [*Aṅguttara Nikāya Ṭikā*] *Sāratthamañjūsā Nāma Aṅguttara Ṭikā.* [Pali Text in Burmese script]. 3 vols. Rangoon, Burma: Buddhasāsana Samiti, 1960-61.

4. *New Subcommentaries on Pali Texts of the Tipiṭaka*

Sutta Piṭaka

Ñāṇābhivaṁsa. [*Dīgha Nikāya Abhinava Ṭikā*] *Sādhuvilāsinī Nāma Sīlakkhandhavagga Abhinavaṭikā.* [Pali Text in Burmese script]. 2 vols. Rangoon, Burma: Buddhasāsana Samiti, 1961.

5. *Treatises on Pali Texts of the Tipiṭaka*

Anuruddha, *Abhidhammattha Saṅgaha.* Edited by Ariyaratna Rerukana. [Pali Text in Sinhalese script]. Colombo, Ceylon: P.K. W. Siriwardhane, Granthadarsa Press, 1942.

Buddhaghosa. *Visuddhimagga of Buddhaghosācariya.* Edited by Henry Clarke Warren. Revised by Dhammānanda Kosambi. Cambridge, Massachusetts: Harvard University Press, 1950.

Trenckner, V. *Milindapañho, Being Dialogues Between King Milinda and the Buddhist Sage Nāgasena.* [Pali Text Society Publication Series no. 69]. London: Luzac & Co., 1880-1962.

6. *Commentaries on Treatises on Pali Texts of the Tipiṭaka*

Dhammapāla. [*Visuddhimagga Mahā Ṭikā*] *Paramatthamañjūsā Nāma Visuddhimagga Mahāṭikā.* [Pali Text in Burmese script]. 2 vols. Rangoon, Burma: Buddhasāsana Samiti, 1960.

Sumangala. [*Vibhāvanī Ṭikā*] *Anuruddhācariya's Abhidhammattha Saṅgaha with Abhidhammattha Vibhāvanīṭīkā.* Revised and edited by Bhadanta Revatadhammatthera. [Pali Text in Devanagari script]. Vārāṇasi, India: Bauddha Svādhyāya Sātra, 1965.

7. *Translations of Pali Texts of the Tipiṭaka*

Vinaya Piṭaka

Horner, I. B. trans. *The Book of the Discipline* (*Vinaya-Piṭaka*). vols. 1-3: (*Suttavibhaṅga*), vol. 4: (*Mahāvagga*), vol. 5:

(*Cullavagga*), vol. 6: (*Parivāra*), [Sacred Books of the Buddhists Series, vols. 10-11, 13-14, 20, 25] 6 vols. London: Luzac & Co., 1951-72.

Sutta Piṭaka

Buddhadatta Mahāthera, Ambalangoda Polvatte, trans. and ed., *Dhammapadaṁ: An Anthology of Sayings of the Buddha*. Colombo, Sri Lanka: Apothecaries Co., n.d.

Hare, E.M., trans. *Woven Cadences of Early Buddhists* (*Sutta-Nipāta*). The Sacred Books of the Buddhists, vol. 15. London: Geoffrey Cumberlege, Oxford University Press, 1945-47.

Horner, I. B., trans. and ed., *The Collection of the Middle Length Sayings* (*Majjhima-Nikāya*). [vol. 1: *The First Fifty Discourses* (*mūlapaṇṇāsa*); vol. 2: *The Middle Fifty Discourses* (*majjhimapaṇṇāsa*); vol. 3: *The Final Fifty Discourses* (*uparipaṇṇāsa*)]. Pāli Text Society [Translation Series nos. 29-31]. 3 vols. 1954-59. Reprint. London: Luzac & Co., 1970.

Rhys Davids, T. W. and Rhys Davids, C. A. F., trans. *Dialogues of the Buddha* (*Dīgha-Nikāya*). [vol. 1: translated by T. W. Rhys Davids; vols. 2-3; translated by T. W. Rhys Davids and C. A. F. Rhys Davids. Sacred Books of the Buddhists, vols. 2-4]. 3 vols. 1889-1921. Reprint. London: Luzac & Co., 1956-77.

Rhys Davids, C. A. F., and Woodward, F. L., trans. *The Book of the Kindred Sayings* (*Saṁyutta-Nikāya*) *or Grouped Suttas*. [Pt. 1: *Kindred Sayings with verses* (*Sagātha-Vagga*), translated by Mrs. Rhys Davids assisted by Suriyagoda Sumangala Thera; pt. 2: *The Nidana Book* (*Nidāna-Vagga*), translated by Mrs. Rhys Davids assisted by F. L. Woodward; pt. 3: translated by F. L. Woodward and edited by Mrs. Rhys Davids; pt. 4: translated by F. L. Woodward with an Introduction by Mrs. Rhys Davids; pt. 5: (*Mahā-Vagga*), translated by F. L. Woodward with an Introduction by Mrs. Rhys Davids. Pali Text Society Translation Series, vols. 7, 10, 13-15]. 5 vols. 1927-30. Reprint. London: Luzac & Co., 1956-71.

Woodward, F. L. and Hare, E. M., trans. *The Book of the Gradual Sayings* (*Aṅguttara-Nikāya*) or *More-Numbered Suttas*. [vol.

1: (*Ones, Twos, Threes*), translated by F. L. Woodward with an Introduction by Mrs. Rhys Davids; vol. 2: (*The Book of the Fours*), translated by F. L. Woodward with an Introduction by Mrs. Rhys Davids; vol. 3: (*The Books of the Fives and Sixes*), translated by E. M. Hare with an Introduction by Mrs. Rhys Davids; vol. 4: (*The Books of the Sevens, Eights and Nines*), translated by E. M. Hare with an Introduction by Mrs. Rhys Davids; vol. 5: (*The Book of the Tens and Elevens*), translated by F. L. Woodward with an Introduction by Mrs. Rhys Davids. Pali Text Society Translation Series nos. 22, 24, 25-27]. 5 vols. 1932-36. Reprint. London: Luzac & Co., 1936-72.

Abhidhamma Piṭaka

Rhys Davids, Caroline A. F., trans. *A Buddhist Manual of Psychological Ethics: A Buddhist Manual of the Fourth Century B.C., Being a Translation, Now Made for the First Time, from the Original Pali of the First Book in the Abhidhamma Piṭaka Entitled Dhamma-Saṅgaṇi (Compendium of States of Phenomena)* with Introductory Essay and Notes, Oriental Translation Fund, New Series, vol. 12. London: Royal Asiatic Society, 1900.

8. *Translations of Pali Commentaries*

Abhidhamma Piṭaka

Buddhaghosa. *The Expositor (Aṭṭhasālinī), Buddhaghosa's Commentary on the Dhammasaṅgaṇi, the First Book of the Abhidhamma Piṭaka.* Translated by Pe Maung Tin. Revised and edited by C. A. F. Rhys Davids. Pali Text Society Translation Series, nos. 8, 9. 2 vols. London: Luzac & Co., 1920-58.

9. *Translations of Treatises on Pali Texts of the Tipiṭaka*

Anuruddha. *Compendium of Philosophy, Being a Translation Now Made for the First Time from the Original Pali of the Abhidhammattha Saṅgaha.* Translated with Introductory Notes and Essay by Shwe Zan Aung. Revised and edited by Mrs. Rhys Davids. Pali Text Society Translation Series, vol. 2. London: H. Frowde, 1960.

———. *A Manual of Abhidhamma, Being Abhidhammattha Saṅgaha of Bhadanta Anuruddhācariya,* edited in the Original Pali Text with English Translation and Explanatory Notes. Translated by Nārada Mahāthera, Colombo, Ceylon: Vajirārāma, 1956. Rev. 3rd. ed. Kandy, Sri Lanka (Ceylon): Buddhist Publication Society, 1975.

———. *Abhidharmartha Saṅgrahaya.* Translated [into Sinhalese] by Śāriputra Sangharāja Mahāthera. Revised and edited by the Very Rev. Paññāmoli Tissa Thera. 2d ed. Randombe, Ceylon: W. E. De Silva, Hetumuni Semaneris De Silva and R. C. P. Weerasuriya Waidyaratna, 1916.

Buddhaghosa. *The Path of Purification* (*Visuddhimagga*). Translated from the Pali by Bhikkhu Ñāṇamoli. Colombo, Ceylon: R. Semage, 1956.

Rhys Davids, T.W., trans. and ed., *The Questions of King Milinda.* The Sacred Books of the East, vol. 25. Oxford: At the Clarendon Press, 1890. (Rept. 1965 Delhi, Motilal Banarsidass).

10. *Selections from Pali Texts of the Tipiṭaka*

Nyanaponika Thera, trans. and ed. *The Five Mental Hindrances and Their Conquest, Selected Texts from the Pali Canon and the Commentaries.* Kandy, Ceylon: Buddhist Publication Society, 1961.

Nyanatiloka, Comp. and trans. *The Word of the Buddha : An Outline of the Teaching of the Buddha in the Words of the Pali Canon.* Kandy, Ceylon: Buddhist Publication Society, 1959.

———. Comp., trans. and ed. *The Buddha's Path to Deliverance in Its Threefold Division and Seven Stages of Purity, Being A Systematic Exposition in the Words of the Sutta-Piṭaka.* Colombo, Ceylon: The Bauddha Sahitya Sabha, 1952. Rev. 3d ed. Colombo, Ceylon: The Bauddha Sahitya Sabha, 1969.

Soma Thera. Comp., trans. and ed. *The Removal of Distracting Thoughts, Vitakka-Saṇṭhāna Sutta, A Discourse of the Buddha* (*Majjhima-Nikāya No.* 20). Kandy, Ceylon: Buddhist Publication Society, 1960.

———. *The Way of Mindfulness, Being a Translation of the Satipaṭṭhāna Sutta of the Majjhima Nikāya; Its Commentary, the*

Satipaṭṭhāna Sutta Vaṇṇanā of the Papañcasūdani of Buddhaghosa Thera; and Excerpts from the Līnatthappakāsana Ṭīkā, Marginal Notes of Dhammapāla Thera on the Commentary. Kandy, Ceylon: Buddhist Publication Society, 1967.

SECONDARY SOURCES

Mahasi Sayadaw (U Sobhana Mahāthera of Burma), *The Progress of Insight Through the Stages of Purification, A Modern Pali Treatise on Buddhist Satipaṭṭhāna Meditation.* Translated by Nyanaponika Thera with notes and the Original Pali Text. Kandy, Ceylon: The Forest Hermitage, 1965. Reprint. Kandy, Sri Lanka: Buddhist Publication Society, 1973.

Vajirañāṇa, Paravahera. *Buddhist Meditation In Theory and Practice, A General Exposition According to the Pali Canon of the Theravāda School.* Colombo, Ceylon: M. D. Gunasena & Co., 1962.

INDEX

I

ENGLISH

suffering, the second Noble truth, 2, 29
Cutting off impediments, 19

Defilements: greed, hatred, delusion, 15
Delusion as source of suffering, 1, 2, 51
Dhamma: mind-objects, 147, 148
Dhammasaṅgani, the first book of the Abhidhamma, one of the three "baskets" (tipiṭaka) comprising the Pali Canon devoted to psycho-philosophical treatises, xii
Dīgha Nikāya (long discourses), one of the five sections of the Suttapiṭaka (Buddha's discourses comprising one of the three "baskets" of the Pali Canon), xii
Discernment, equivalent of wisdom, 92
Discipline, of restraint according to Pātimokkha, 17;—concerning the use of the requisites, 18;—purified livelihood, 17;—of sense restraint, 17
Discursive thought and excessive speculative thinking overcome by meditation upon breathing, 26
Disruption of concentration by hindrances, 30, 31
Divine abidings, 24
DN: see Dīgha Nikāya
Doctrinal context of jhāna, 1
Doubt, 4, 37
"Dry" insight: momentary concentration connected with mindful observation of phenomena, 136 path to obtain wisdom without having developed concentration, 6

Egoism: as overcome by meditation on impermanence, 41
Eight Attainments: four jhānas and four immaterial states, 5
Elimination of the hindrances, 38
Entirety, 23
Equanimity about insight: indifference towards further investigating characteristics of phenomena after having been perceived with insight knowledge, 89; defined from root *ikh* "to see" 88; divine abiding: socially directed meditative state transcending approval and resentment toward living beings equally without preference or discrimination, 89; only fouud at fourth jhāna since cannot coexist with pleasant feelings, 24; six factored: unbiased responses, free of attachment and aversion towards pleasant and unpleasant forms, sounds, smells, tastes, tangibles, and mental data coming through the six sensory channels, 88; specific neutrality, mental factor responsible for maintaining balance among component factors in state of consciousness, 89; treating all things equally rather than apprehension through 'signs' which cling to pleasant and reject unpleasant, 17, 70, 87; ten kinds of—, 88-89
Eradication of the hindrances, 45
Etymology of jhāna, 7
Extension of sign, 76

Factors of abandonment, 28; possession, 28
Faculty, 14
Faith: defined as internal confidence, 82
Feeling, 62; six kinds of, 63
Fifth abhiññā: divine eye, knowledge of passing away and rebirth of beings, 133
Fine material jhānas, 5
First Āruppa: The base of boundless space, 109
First jhāna and its factors, 49; Absorption: exerting the mind when slack, restraining it when agitated, 76; after access concentration, growth beyond merely holding hindrances at bay, 35; Applied and sustained thought differences, applied thought focuses mind on object, whereas sustained thought inspects and examines what is focused on, bringing deepening of concentration, 59; applied thought, most responsible for bringing about mind's absorption in counterpart sign, 56; as state of consciousness inclusive of additional factors of contact, feeling, perception, volition, consciousness, desire, decision, energy, mindfulness, equanimity, and attention, 69; Attainment: cessation of pain faculty, 96; comprised only of sustaining mental factors necessary to counteract hindrances, 51; difference of applied and sustained thought, 59; difference of joy and happiness, 65; factors of abandonment, factors eliminating five hindrances obstructing first jhāna's attainment, 28; factors of possession, acquisition of states composing first jhāna, 28; following counterpart sign, ten kinds of skill in absorption, 75; joy, 59; one-pointedness stabilization reinforced by applied

of equanimity about formation, 163; conformity knowledge, 165; change of lineage, 166; knowledge of the path, 166
Ten kinds of skill in absorption: making the base clean, balancing the spiritual faculties, producing and developing sign of concentration, exerting the mind, restraining it, encouraging it, looking with equanimity, avoiding distracting persons, approaching experienced people, be firm in resolution, 75-76
Ten Recollections, 23
Theravāda Buddhism, xi
Third Abhiññā: The Knowledge of others' mind 130
Third Āruppa (base of nothingness) removing attachment to by excluding consciousness filling boundless space, 115
Third jhāna attainment: cessation of faculty of pleasure (physical happiness and body contact), 86, 96; co-presence of both happiness and equanimity as simultaneous presence of two different feelings, 90;—factors: equanimity, mindfulness, and clear comprehension or discernment, happiness, 87; mindfulness and discernment are needed to check return of rapture which would bring about loss of Third Jhāna factor, 92; only with elimination of discursive thought and intensive rapture, does the mind become subtle enough to reveal mindfulness and discernment, 92; rapture or joy, embodying interest in varying degrees of intensity is not as subtle as happiness and is thereby eliminated through indifference, leaving happiness and one-pointedness, 86
Third path and fruit, 173
Thirty seven bodhipakkhiyā dhammā, 11
Thought of sensuality,—ill-will., 51; —harming, 52;—renunciation;—benevolence;—harmlessness, 53
The Three baskets: Tipiṭaka, the Pali canon, xii
Three gateways to liberation: signless liberation, desireless—,void liberation, 163
Three Jewels: Buddha, Dhamma, Saṅgha, 23
Three spheres: sense sphere, fine material—, immaterial—, 140
Three Trainings: the groups of wisdom, concentration, and morality comprising training of the Noble Eightfold Path in the goal of liberation, 13-14
Three wonders, 128; wonder of supernormal powers,—manifestation, —education, 128
Ṭīkās, third layer of Pali literature, comprising the subcommentaries, including Mahāṭīkā and *Paramatthamañjūsā* to the Path of Purification, xiii
Time: occurrence of arising of counterpart sign, suppression of hindrances, and access concentration entrance within same moment, 34
Tipiṭaka: the three "baskets", collection of scripture, xii-xiii
Training dwellings, 26-27
Tranquility, 63-64
Two vehicles: vehicle of serenity, —of insight, 146

Unbounded space, 113
Unification of mind, 83, 85
Unwholesome applied thought, 57; —intention, 52
Unwholesome roots: greed, hatred, and delusion, 51; hatred associated with aversion, 52
Unwholesome states of mind, see five hindrances, 32
Unwholesome thoughts: elimination leading to firm, settled, unified concentration of mind, 53; lustful thoughts overcome by reflection on unlovely objects, 40; overcoming by ignoring them, 53; overcome by reflection on their disadvantage, 53; removal by reflection on source of thought, 53; sensual happiness associated with greed,and directed toward pleasurable forms, sounds, smells, tastes, and tangibles, 87; sensuality, ill-will harming, 52; to overcome aversion of inanimate objects, reflection on the primary elements, 54; to ovescome aversion towards people, loving kindness, 54; to overcome clinging to material objects, reflection on impermanence, 54
Unwise consideration, failure to control mind, 36; reflection apprehending object through four perversions of considering impermanent as permanent, pain as pleasure, notself as self, and foul as fair, 51; the result of wrong reflection (through the four perversions) is to cause un-

II

PALI